OTTAWA RIVER CANALS

ROBERT LEGGET

Ottawa River Canals

AND THE DEFENCE OF
BRITISH NORTH AMERICA

UNIVERSITY OF TORONTO PRESS
Toronto Buffalo London

© University of Toronto Press 1988
Toronto Buffalo London
Printed in Canada

ISBN 0-8020-5794-2

Canadian Cataloguing in Publication Data

Legget, Robert F., 1904-
Ottawa River canals and the defence of British North America

Bibliography: p. Includes index.
ISBN 0-8020-5794-2

1. Canals – Ottawa River (Quebec and Ont.) –
History. 2. Canada – Defences – History.
3. Canada. Canadian Army. Royal Staff Corps.
I. Title.

HE401.088L43 1988   386'.3'097142   C88-094434-X

PICTURE CREDITS

Public Archives of Canada pages 26 (C12648), 56 (C479), 57 (C12633), 64 (C608), 75 (C88523), 101 (PA85718), 116 (C63582), 176 (C22576), 185 (PA85730), 189 (Grenville Canal 1904, PA85598; Carillon Canal 1909, PA85679), 193 (Carillon Canal 1914, PA85722), 196 (the tug *Gaëtan*, PA85815; M.V. *Ottawalite*, PA85840)
National Air Photo Library, Department of Energy, Mines and Resources, Ottawa pages 106, 107, and 123
Historical Society of Argenteuil County page 193 (barge transport)
Hydro-Québec pages 199 and 204
Robert Legget pages 133, 138, 198, 207, 208, and 212

Publication of this book has been assisted by the Canada Council and the Ontario Arts Council under their block grant programs.

In tribute to
the officers and men of
the Royal Staff Corps,
builders of the
OTTAWA RIVER CANALS,
and in particular to their commanding officer,
Lieutenant-Colonel Henry A. Du Vernet
1819–33

Contents

Maps and diagram

OTTAWA RIVER CANALS

The Ottawa River canals

One of the grandest natural sights in eastern Canada, until 1962, was the Long Sault of the Ottawa River, a long stretch of turbulent rapids, about midway between Montreal and Ottawa, Canada's capital city. For six miles the water of the great river, with an average flow greater than that of all the rivers of England and Wales combined, tumbled down a series of island-studded falls. In dropping almost fifty feet in these six miles, the Ottawa was 'white water,' indeed, a truly majestic spectacle.

Beautiful as was the Long Sault, it was also the most serious impediment to all early travellers up and down the Ottawa River. And for 200 years, the Ottawa Waterway was the gateway to the Great Lakes and all the mid-west, used also by all early explorers of the far west and of the western Arctic. Many travellers' tales, starting with the journals of the Sieur Samuel de Champlain, founder of Canada, recount the difficulties experienced by early expeditions in getting past the rough waters of the Long Sault.

Only with the advent of steamships and then railways, in the middle of the nineteenth century, was the canoe finally displaced from the Ottawa River. But early in the century, vessels larger than canoes came to be used for moving settlers and freight – first bateaux, then York boats, then Durham boats, and finally simple steamboats. Some way of getting these larger vessels around the Long Sault and the associated rapids became essential. Three simple canals, with locks, provided the solution, but, strangely, they were constructed in response to a military requirement.

One of the results of the War of 1812 between Great Britain and the United States of America, fought on Canadian soil and in Canadian waters as well as on the Atlantic, was the decision of the British government to provide an alternative military route by water between Montreal and Kingston. This was regarded as essential, since it was known that, should hostilities break out again (as they were expected to do), the military and naval supply line up the rapids of the River St Lawrence could be ambushed by U.S. forces.

The alternative route to Kingston from Montreal followed the Ottawa River as far as the Chaudière Falls, then the Rideau River into the Rideau Lakes, and finally the Cataraqui River down to Kingston. This vital military waterway was provided from what is now Ottawa to Kingston by the Rideau Canal. The Ottawa River fortunately was navigable from the Lake of Two Mountains to the Chaudière Falls, apart from only the Long Sault and two small rapids immediately downstream. These obstructions had to be circumvented, therefore, and so were built the Ottawa River canals.

The six-mile-long Grenville Canal bypassed the Long Sault, the smaller rapids being avoided by use of the short Chute à Blondeau Canal and the two-mile-long Carillon Canal. The Grenville Canal was started in 1819, but all three canals were not fully operational until 1834. Their construction was entrusted to the Royal Staff Corps, a little-known regiment of the British army, not to the Corps of Royal Engineers, as is still popularly imagined. Since the Staff Corps had already constructed the Royal Military Canal from Shorncliffe to Cliff End along the south coast of England, as one of Britain's defences against the anticipated invasion of England by Napoleon, it was not inexperienced in canal building.

Wars and rumours of wars provided the explanation for the building of the Ottawa River canals which, with rebuilding, served eastern Canada faithfully from 1834 until 1962, when the Carillon Dam and power station across the Ottawa at the foot of the Carillon Canal approached completion. Once the flood gates on the great dam were closed, all three Ottawa River Canals were submerged as the water level rose. Today, all that can be seen are remains of the lower locks at Carillon and the upper guard lock of the Grenville Canal. This lock is located close to what may be called the village green of the small Quebec town of Grenville, directly opposite the larger town of Hawkesbury in Ontario, the Sir George Perley Bridge linking the two. To stand on a quiet summer day by the side of the Grenville guard lock in its peaceful rural setting is a pleasing experience. It is difficult now to appreciate that the original lock was a matter of concern to the great Duke of Wellington until his dying day, since it was the narrowest lock and thus the bottleneck of the entire alternative route. The little canals were then part of a vital military waterway built for the defence of British North America, their conception was directly related to the bitter conflict between Great

Britain and France in the opening years of the nineteenth century, Napoleon himself thus being indirectly implicated.

But so it was. The full story of the Ottawa River canals has never yet been told.* If the interesting record of their construction and use is to be fully appreciated, it is necessary to place this in its proper historical perspective. Accordingly, the opening chapter of this volume presents a summary of the conflict between Britian and France, dominated by the figures of Napoleon and Wellington. The only canal that will then be mentioned will be the Royal Military Canal in southern England. It was built also as a military defence work but happily was never called upon to serve in this way. Today, it is a quiet, peaceful waterway used only by pleasure craft. So also were the Ottawa River canals until their disappearance. Some distance from main roads in both Quebec and Ontario, they were little known in recent years by Canadians, even by those accustomed to journey frequently between Montreal and Ottawa. All sailors who used them, in journeys up and down the Ottawa River, as well as travellers by land who did visit them, were enchanted by their quiet beauty. Those who lived nearby were much attached to them, older residents still referring to them as the 'military canals.' As part of a vital military waterway, they played a modest role in the early defence of the Canadas.

Small though they were, by standards of today, they had the further distinction of being Canada's first major public work. A few very small shallow locks – in the Soulanges section of the St Lawrence River, at Sault Ste Marie and at Yarmouth, Nova Scotia – had been constructed before the Royal Staff Corps started work at Grenville in 1819. But the better-known Lachine Canal was started only in 1821, the first Welland Canal only in 1824. There were simple roads in the early settlements but nothing requiring the knowledge of engineering design and construction practices that was called for in the building of the Ottawa River canals. Some splendid military fortifications had been built by French and British military engineers, but these were not civil works, and the term 'public works' is applied only to engineering works designed for civilian use. From the standpoint of the present time, therefore, the three canals on the Ottawa have a double significance, but at the time of their construction they were thought of strictly as an essential military waterway, necessary for defence purposes.

* After these words were written, Parks Canada published *The Ottawa River Canal System* by N. Lafrenière (details in bibliography).

As a prelude, therefore, to the story of the Ottawa River canals – how they were built and how they served for well over a century – the reader is invited to consider first a summary account of major conflicts in Europe which led to the War of 1812 in North America, yet another part of Canadian history that is today almost forgotten except by historians. And it was because of the War of 1812 that the Royal Staff Corps was called upon to build the Ottawa River canals.

1

Prologue: Wars and rumours of wars

The state of Europe at the turn from the eighteenth into the nineteenth century is a good starting point for the story of the defence of British North America, by British and Canadian arms, against the fledgling United States of America. In February 1793 France declared war against Great Britain, initiating a period of open conflict which, with two slight intervals, was to last until the Battle of Waterloo in 1815. In one of the first actions of the war, in 1794 the British were routed from Toulon by French forces under the command of a young artillery officer from Corsica named Napoleon Bonaparte.[1] William Pitt was the peace-loving prime minister of the British government. He attempted negotiations for peace with France but was not successful, and so fighting continued, on land and sea.[2] Although successful in his Irish negotiations, Pitt had to resign in February 1801 after a disagreement with King George III; he was succeeded by Mr Speaker Addington.

Under Addington's leadership, negotiations with France were resumed, and eventually the Treaty of Amiens was signed in March 1802. By this time, Napoleon was commander-in-chief and first consul of France, his ambition now almost without bounds. The Peace of Amiens gave him the breathing spell that he needed before making further conquests. He was soon assembling a fleet of flat-bottomed boats for the invasion of England, preparations that hastened the formal redeclaration of war in May 1803. Defeat of England was Napoleon's prime objective and England stood alone. At this critical juncture (1804), Addington resigned and William Pitt returned as prime minister. Although his health was broken (he was to die in office in 1806), he faced the danger of invasion with indomitable courage. Napoleon had now proclaimed himself emperor. He visited his invasion troops at Boulogne. Over 100,000 men and more than 3,000 small boats had been assembled. 'Let us be masters of the Channel for six hours,' Napoleon is reported to have said, 'and we are masters of the world.'[3] But it was not to be, just as another planned invasion a century and a half later would fail – and for many of the same reasons.

Three hundred thousand volunteers had been mustered in Essex and on the south coast of England to meet the planned attack. Pitt himself inspected the stretch of coast where Kent and Sussex meet, deemed by the experts to be the only possible landing place for French invaders. The implications of flooding Romney Marsh were explained. Through his ministers, he received a proposal from Lieutenant-Colonel John Brown for the construction of the Royal Military Canal as a protective channel between Shorncliffe and Cliff End.[4] So well conceived was this plan that the proposal was approved in less than a month, and construction began, under contract, with the famous John Rennie as engineer. The canal was to be sixty feet wide at the top and nine feet deep, so as always to contain seven to eight feet of water, providing the equivalent of a moat against invaders from the sea.

Discouraging progress with the building of the canal was made during the winter of 1804–5, with the result that in June 1805 the contractors were removed from the works which were then placed under the direct control of Lieutenant-Colonel Brown for construction directly by the Royal Staff Corps.[5] John Rennie continued as a consultant but ceased to have direct control of the work. Brown soon had 1,500 men engaged on the canal construction, a remarkably large work force for those days, and probably a reflection of the alarm being experienced in England about the imminence of invasion.[6] In August 1805 Napoleon was again at Boulogne, ready to launch the invasion, but naval set-backs led to a change in his plans, and finally he ordered the Grande Armée to strike camp and march on Austria. The threat of invasion remained, however, although it was not of such alarming immediacy.

Construction of the canal continued. In July 1807 the government passed an act for the maintenance and operation of the Royal Military Canal, when complete, under commissioners.[7] Never has any canal history had so distinguished a governing body – the prime minister was to be a member as was the speaker of the House of Commons. Despite other claims on the time of these leaders of the nation, they did meet, as canal commissioners, and supervised the canal until 1837, when control passed to the Board of Ordnance. It was under the commissioners, therefore, that Lieutenant-Colonel Brown brought the works to a successful completion in April 1809 at a total cost of about £235,000.[8] There was a brief flurry of excitement in 1811, when it was found that Napoleon was again considering invasion, but the threat passed. After the disastrous retreat from Moscow, later in that year, the possibility of invasion disappeared. The Royal Military Canal, however, remained and was soon serving usefully as a minor commercial waterway, a pattern that was later to be repeated with the Ottawa River canals.

While the Royal Military Canal was under construction in England, momentous events were taking place elsewhere, starting with Nelson's victory at Trafalgar on 21 October 1805. William Pitt died on 23 June 1806, just after the battle of Austerlitz, being succeeded by Lord Grenville as prime minister and head of a coalition government.[9] The new government made a serious error in declaring the whole coast of Europe, as now occupied by the French and their allies, to be in a state of blockade. No such blockade could be fully enforced, but Napoleon used the opportunity to exclude all British commerce from the continent, issuing his now famous Berlin (and Milan) Decrees.[10] Since these decrees could well ruin the trade of Great Britain, the Grenville government then passed orders in council in January 1807, by which neutral vessels voyaging to coasts subject to the British blockade were compelled to touch first at some British port. These warlike measures may seem far removed from the small colonies that constituted British North America, but they were to have a profound effect upon the early development of Canada. The decrees proved to be the first in a series of events that led, eventually, to the building of the Ottawa River canals.

The Grenville ministry was dismissed by the king later in 1807, to be replaced by a Tory government under the Duke of Portland with the redoubtable George Canning as foreign secretary. Opposition to Napoleon, who now controlled almost all Europe, must have seemed to be almost hopeless, despite British successes at sea. In May 1808 Napoleon treacherously attacked Spain. Canning decided to oppose this action and sent out two small British armies under Sir John Moore and Sir Arthur Wellesley to aid in the Peninsular War. Three days before Napoleon crossed the Nieman on his fateful march on Moscow, Wellesley – now the Duke of Wellington – crossed the Agueda on his march on Salamanca; it was one of the turning points in the Peninsular War, which was brought to a climax in 1813 by Wellington's great victory at Vitoria.

On the other side of the Atlantic, James Madison had been inaugurated on 4 March 1809 as the third president of the United States of America and was hailed as a peacemaker. Despite the provocation that the British orders in council were causing to American shipping, Madison was anxious at first to develop a treaty with Great Britain; he arranged the details of such a settlement with the British minister in Washington. Unfortunately, this draft was rejected out of hand by Canning, the British foreign secretary, another of the series of steps that led to the War of 1812.

Despite the fact that Napoleon continued to harass U.S. shipping, Madison stubbornly maintained his support of France. Feelings were running high on both sides of the Atlantic, but in England the public was now demanding the withdrawal of the orders in council that had initiated the troubles. With a change in the composition of the British government, Castlereagh took over the Foreign Office. The prime minister, Spencer Perceval, had just decided to repeal the orders in May 1812, when he was assassinated in the House of Commons by a maniac named Bellingham.[11] The Earl of Liverpool was called upon to head the new government. On 16 June Castlereagh announced in the House of Commons that the orders in council would be suspended, but it was too late. Under the urging of President Madison, the U.S. Congress declared war on Great Britain two days later. As the historian Admiral Samuel E. Morison has pointed out, Britain's action would not have been too late had there been a trans-Atlantic cable, but such a development in communications was yet to come.[12]

Wellington had now moved his army into southern France. Despite a valiant struggle by Napoleon and his small surviving force, his end was at hand. Paris surrendered on 31 March 1814; Napoleon abdicated and was exiled to Elba; the Bourbons were restored. Wellington was appointed ambassador to France in an attempt to support the Bourbon régime. In November he was asked by the British government (in a context described below) to leave his post in Paris in order to take charge of the British forces in British North America. He refused. How fortunate his decision was became clear when, on 1 March 1815, Napoleon escaped from Elba, landed at Cannes, marched over the mountains to Grenoble and Lyons, gathering men as he progressed, and entered Paris only twenty days after his landing. By an amazing effort he raised an army of 250,000 men. Wellington was recalled to military service and quickly gathered a mixed force of 80,000. And on 18 June 1815 the battle of Waterloo was fought; the Napoleonic era was finished, and Europe was freed from major wars for virtually a century.

With these turbulent events taking place in Europe, it is small wonder that the War of 1812 in North America began on such a restricted scale that, even today, it is but little known except by those who have had occasion to study its strange story.

The War of 1812 is one of those episodes in history that make everybody happy, because everybody interprets it in his own way. The Americans think of it primarily as a naval war in which the Pride of the Mistress of the Seas was humbled by what an imprudent Englishman has called 'a few fir-built frigates, manned by a handful of bastards and outlaws.' Canadians think of it equally pridefully as a war of defence in which their brave fathers, side by side, turned back the massed might of the United States and saved the country from conquest. And the English are happiest of all, because they don't even know it happened.[13]

This is the judgment of a modern Canadian historian, as witty as it is accurate as an assessment of current popular ideas about this 'incredible war' as it has been called by another Canadian writer.[14] But at the time, the conflict was certainly well known to the British government and people. After Napoleon's abdication in 1814, it became a matter of national concern, since so many British troops had been sent across the Atlantic to assist in the war that Wellington had to rely on levies from Belgium and Hanover to make up his small army prior to Waterloo.

It is strange now to find that the main reasons given by President Madison to the Congress for declaring war were: the impressment of American seaman; violation of American neutral rights and territorial waters by the British Navy in order to harass commerce; employment of 'pretended blockades' the real aim of which was to interfere with U.S. commerce; and the British refusal to revoke the system of orders in council. It is, therefore, not at all surprising to find that the House of Representatives voted only seventy-nine to forty-nine in support of the war, and that the Senate (even after some further consideration) voted only nineteen to thirteen in favour. The British minister in Washington urged a suspension of hostilities until word could get to England by fast sailing ship, but to no avail. And on the very day that the minister took leave of the United States, 23 June 1812, the British government provisionally repealed the orders in council. It appears that, at one time, there was a majority in the Senate against the war but the waverers were persuaded to change their votes. Some parts of the United States, such as Massachusetts and Connecticut, never did take an active part in the war. But once the declaration had been made, fighting began and continued until early in 1815. Variously known as 'Mr Madison's War' (which, in a way, it was) and the Second War of Independence (which it certainly was not), the war was terminated by the Treaty of Ghent, signed on Christmas Eve 1814. Fighting continued into the new year, however, lack of communications again adding yet another strange twist to the war, but hostilities terminated in February 1815. The U.S. Senate confirmed the treaty unanimously on the sixteenth day of that month.

John Quincy Adams described the Treaty of Ghent as 'a truce rather than a peace,' since 'nothing was adjusted, nothing was settled,' clear indication of the strong feelings that this strange war had aroused.[15] Stalemate is another word that has been applied to the unusual peace settlement, since it left all major questions and boundaries just as they were before the war started. It did have the satisfactory result of leading to the establishment of the commissions that finally determined the exact Canada-United States boundary. All the high hopes that the British commissioners had entertained from their instructions from Lord Castlereagh gradually evaporated in the months of protracted negotiations in the pleasant Belgian City of Ghent – and John Quincy Adams was one of the commissioners for the United States! Progress of the war in its final phases was responsible, in part, for this unsatisfactory ending. Before looking at the main features of the fighting, it may be useful to record the opinion of a modern U.S. leader. Thomas E. Dewey has said: 'If the British had not been spread out all over the world fighting France and the Netherlands, while she was also fighting the War of 1812 with the fledgling American Republic, we might well have lost. Even so, the War of 1812 was a stalemate but because of British commitments elsewhere in the world, including the Dutch East Indies, we negotiated a successful settlement, winning most of our objectives through the Treaty of Ghent in 1814.'[16]

At the outbreak of the war, the population of the United States was about 7.25 million, primarily settled along the Atlantic coast. The total population of British North America was about 500,000; about one-quarter of these British subjects were in the maritime provinces of Nova Scotia, New Brunswick, and Prince Edward Island, which were not involved in the war. All the fighting took place in Upper and Lower Canada (the two provinces partitioned from what had been Quebec by the Constitutional Act of 1791) and on the Atlantic, with final raids upon American coastal cities. In Lower Canada, about 80 per cent of the population were French-speaking Canadians. Upper Canada, with a population of only two-fifths that of Quebec, was almost entirely English speaking, most of the settlers being United Empire Loyalists who had immigrated from the United States after the Revolutionary War. Sir George Prevost was the governor of Lower Canada throughout the war and the commander-in-chief of both provinces, since the lieutenant-governor of Upper Canada (Francis Gore) was in England from 1811 to 1815. Prevost had a total force under his command in 1812 of about 5,600 British regulars, of whom only about 1,200 were in Upper Canada, where the fighting might be expected to start. The commander of the four companies of the Royal Artillery reported directly to the Board of Ordnance in London, as did the small detachment of the Corps of Royal Engineers. The problems created by such divided control can well be imagined. When to these complications the absence of any means of communication other than by hand is added, the wonder is that Sir George Prevost was able to achieve as much as he did.

The first engagement of the war in mid-July 1812 was the entirely unexpected capture by the British of Fort Michilimackinac, on a small island of the same name at the entrance to Lake Michigan. Long a famous fur-trading depot, in 1796 it had reluctantly been surrendered to the United States. The British fort had been re-established on St Joseph Island, whence the raiding party of Indians and French-speaking voyageurs under Captain Charles Roberts had set sail in their schooner and canoes. This somewhat romantic episode was not duplicated in the fighting on land which started in July with an American invasion across the Detroit River. Battles were won by both sides, one of the most crucial, since it prevented an attack on Montreal, taking place on 11 November 1813 at Crysler's Farm on the St Lawrence River. There was also some fighting in Lower Canada, the most dangerous threat being the advance of a second small United States army up the Chateauguay River which intended to join the army defeated at Crysler's Farm. A smaller force than the invaders, composed entirely of French- and English-speaking native Canadians under the command of Lieutenant-Colonel Charles-Michel de Salaberry, defeated the Americans roundly near Chateauguay on 26 October 1813. The danger to Montreal was thus averted.

These actions, important as they were to the future of British North America, were minor indeed when compared with the great events taking place at the same time in Europe. It was not until after the defeat of Napoleon and his exile to Elba that Sir George Prevost could expect any substantial reinforcements. Late in July 1814 Sir George was able to report to Lord Bathurst that over 10,000 British troops had landed, from Bordeaux, so that he was able personally to lead a substantial force across the U.S. border on 1 September for an attack on Plattsburgh, New York, which was captured five days later. The supporting British naval force on Lake Champlain (on which Plattsburgh is situated) was defeated. As a result, Prevost gave the order to his troops to retire after destroying surplus stores and munitions, a decision that led to immediate controversy but certainly turned the Plattsburgh campaign into a British defeat. As a result, Sir George Prevost was recalled to England and given the promise of a court martial to defend himself against the charges made against him, but he died before the court could be assembled. No formal decision was made, and the matter is still debated by military historians.

This naval action on Lake Champlain was insignificant compared with the Royal Navy's activities on the Atlantic coast. Vice-Admiral Sir Alexander Cochrane was appointed to the North American Command and soon displayed a more offensive attitude than his predecessor. Major-General Ross reached Bermuda on 24 July from France and soon had prepared a force of 4,000 men for invasion activities. Attacks on U.S. coastal cities followed: that on Washington was successful (even though it unfortunately included the burning of the White House); that on Baltimore was less so; that on New Orleans, early in 1815, was a disaster.

These few indications of what the fighting in the War of 1812 was like will at least indicate how widespread were the operations. The limitation of communications to messages that could be carried by hand – over water, through forests and along simple trails (there being no roads as known today anywhere in British North America), or over the snow and ice of winter – compounds the wonder that so much was achieved. There was yet another problem, which was the real key to the conduct of the war: the matter of transport of supplies for the forces in Upper Canada. All had to be conveyed by water, in the absence of roads, or in cases of extreme urgency over the simple frozen trails in winter along the bank of the River St Lawrence. Ships could sail up from the sea to Quebec City; smaller vessels could sail without trouble as far as Montreal. But from Kingston at the eastern end of Lake Ontario to Montreal, the St Lawrence River dropped about 240 feet in a series of majestic rapids spaced along the 180-mile journey. Today, this fall is harnessed in two great powerhouses at Cornwall-Massena and Beauharnois. In 1812 the rapids were hazards indeed, necessitating at least partial unloading of all craft, which were then hauled up the rapids by their crews. Only at the Soulanges Rapids (near Montreal) were there any aids to navigation, a series of small locks that had been constructed here by the Royal Engineers to provide a bypass for bateaux around three small rapids.

So difficult was this river journey up from Montreal into Lake Ontario and thence, after the great portage round Niagara Falls, into Lake Erie and then the other Great Lakes, that the westward journey up the Ottawa River was still the favoured route. The hazards of negotiating the rapids of the Ottawa were preferred to the dangers of sailing canoes in the open waters of the lakes. The St Lawrence route had indeed been discovered by early French explorers, who had paddled up the Ottawa River and been shown the St Lawrence route, after inquiry, by Indians on Lake Huron. But it was Lake Ontario that held the key to the fighting between 1812–14; and so Kingston became a crucial fortress and naval dockyard. From its beginnings as Fort Cataraqui in 1673, Kingston had been developed first by the French, then after 1758 by the British as a strongly fortified post with an associated

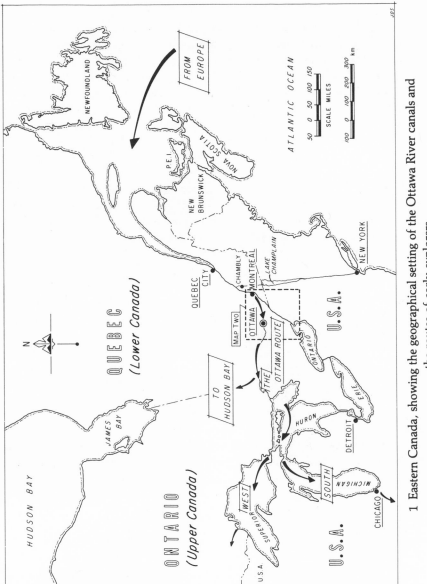

1 Eastern Canada, showing the geographical setting of the Ottawa River canals and the routes of early explorers

dockyard for the construction and repair of vessels of the small British fleet on the lake. All reinforcements, naval and military, all supplies (other than those available in the nearby forests), all munitions – everything that Kingston needed – had to be brought up laboriously in canoes or bateaux, despite all the unavoidable unloading and reloading as successive rapids were passed. First came the great Lachine Rapids at Montreal (which can be seen today almost the same as they were in 1812); then, after a sail across Lake St Louis, an enlargement of the River St Lawrence, came three rapids in what is still known as the Soulanges section of the St Lawrence; after another short sail across another enlargement called Lake St Francis came the Long Sault, a half-mile of turbulent water, one of the most impressive rapids in Canada, splendid to behold but the greatest of all the impediments to navigation; finally, there were a series of minor rapids, most of which could be sailed through safely coming downstream but where the inevitable tracking or unloading was necessary on upstream journeys. Thereafter, it was smooth sailing through what is now known as the Thousand Islands section of the St Lawrence into the harbour of Kingston.

Not only was this upstream journey one of great rigour, but the south bank of the St Lawrence, from the western end of Lake St Francis to Kingston, was United States territory, the international boundary (after 1784) going roughly up the centre of the great river as far as Lake Ontario. These was, however, very little settlement on either bank in this 'international section' (as it is still known). There were only two very small groups of settlers' houses, facing one another just to the west of the last rapid, at what are now the towns of Prescott, Ontario, and Ogdensburg, New York. There were trails through the woods on both banks but no established roads. All traffic up and down the river was by water during the seven or eight months when the river was 'open.' During winter months, although the turbulent waters of the rapids remained open, the main parts of the river were frozen over, facilitating cross-river visiting and aiding the limited traffic on sleighs, or snowshoes, near the banks. Lieutenant-Colonel Macdonell actually travelled over the ice to make a surprise attack on Ogdensburg from Prescott in February 1813.

Fraternization between the settlers on the two banks continued throughout the war. Several neutral-minded residents of Ogdensburg, for example, regularly crossed the river to dine with Lieutenant-Colonel Macdonell. On 8 August 1813 Lieutenant-Colonel Thomas Paterson sent an emissary across the river to Ogdensburg with a flag of truce to ask the local storekeeper, David Parish, what news he might have brought back from Washington! Even more surprising was the advice that General Drummond sent to Lord Bathurst on 12 April 1814 to the effect that he had authorized the purchase of an old printing press at Ogdensburg to replace one that had been destroyed at the village of York (now Toronto).

These peaceable sidelights should not give a misleading impression of the fighting that did take place. There were several devastating battles on land and many a murderous attack on the water, notably on Lake Ontario. The lifeline from Montreal was therefore a vital part of the war scene. A so-called 'Provincial Marine' had been established on the lake prior to the war by the Quartermaster-General's Department of the British Army in Canada. Its purpose was to ensure the safe delivery of personnel and supplies to the several inland forts that had been established. The schooners of the marine also transported supplies to the fur-trading posts of the North West Company, then in its hey-day. (It merged with the Hudson's Bay Company in 1821.) The possibility of real fighting on the lake, should hostilities with the United States commence, had been foreseen even in the days of Lieutenant-Governor Simcoe, the first governor of Upper Canada (1792–6). The crucial importance of Kingston had therefore long been appreciated when, at the outbreak of war in 1812, it was called upon to be the bastion of British forces in Upper Canada.

A regular courier service along the St Lawrence River was established as one of the first steps in organizing the transport link between Montreal and Kingston. Men were stationed in pairs along the river-bank trail for carrying the messages between Upper Canada, the military establishment in Montreal, and the governor at Quebec City. Efforts were made in 1813 to improve the river road, but they failed, since all the militia assigned to the work had to be busy garnering the harvest. Reliance therefore continued to be placed upon water transport. Boats were sent up river in convoy from Montreal, under the direction of the men of a Corps of Voyageurs which had been formed of men who were voyageurs in the service of the North West Company. Overnight stopping points along the route provided small detachments of troops to guard the weary travellers before they resumed their upstream journeys. The system worked well. In the fall of 1814, the complete frame of a fifty-five-gun frigate for the Royal Naval fleet on Lake Ontario was shipped in pieces across the Atlantic and then transshipped by this hazardous route up the St Lawrence to Kingston. The resulting vessel, H.M.S. *Psyche*, was launched on Christmas day 1814.

Sir George Prevost had earlier requested that the Admiralty should take over the responsibility for the fighting on Lake Ontario. This request was granted, and Captain Sir James Lucas Yeo, RN, was appointed commodore and naval commander-in-chief on 19 March 1813. He made his headquarters at Kingston and served in this post until the end of the war. Gradually, and as naval personnel could be released from other stations, he built up his establishment and carried out some quite remarkable ship-building. In 1813 he launched two frigates mounting, respectively, thirty and twenty-four thirty-two-pounder guns and thirty-two-pounder cannon-ades. And in 1814 his fleet was completed by a three-decker, built at Kingston, which was more powerful than Lord Nelson's flagship at Trafal-gar, mounting 112 guns and having a crew of 837 men – this on Lake Ontario! Yeo had not only the lakes to control but also the navigable part of the St Lawrence down to Prescott. He used small gunboats for this purpose, so successfully that only one convoy (of fifteen bateaux) with its escort was ever captured by American gunboats, a remarkable record considering all the circumstances.

The importance of naval supremacy on Lake Ontario was widely recognized, not least by the Duke of Wellington. When he was asked by the British government to leave his ambassadorial post in Paris in November 1813 to assume command in British North America, his reply contained these words:

I have already told you and Lord Bathurst that I feel no objection to going to America, though I don't promise myself much success there. I believe there are troops enough for the defence of Canada for ever ... That which appears to be want-ing in America is not a General, or General Officers and troops, but a naval super-iority on the Lakes. Till that superiority is acquired, it is impossible, according to my notion, to maintain an army in such a situation as to keep the enemy out of the whole frontier ... The question is, whether we can acquire this naval superiority on the Lakes. If we can't, I shall do you but little good in America; and I shall go there only to prove the truth of Prevost's defence, and to sign a peace which might as well be signed now.[17]

This percipient assessment of the Canadian situation was an early indica-tion of the Duke of Wellington's concern for the defence of British North America which he was to feel for the rest of his long life, even though he would never cross the Atlantic.

Sir James Yeo's fellow commander of land forces at Kingston was Lieu-tenant-General Gordon Drummond; they worked well in harness and must have sent back good dispatches on the basis of which those in supreme com-mand were able to make their judgments. Both men were fully appreciative of the danger presented by the supply line from Montreal. Even before they knew that the war was over, the quartermaster-general had asked General

Drummond to have a study made of an alternative route between Montreal and Kingston. Drummond was able to say in reply (on 7 January 1815) that 'Lt. Col. McDonell and Capt. Sherwood have personally examined the route.' Again, in writing to Sir George Prevost on 17 January 1815, Drummond reported that 'under the presumption that the enemy will endeavour to interrupt the present line of communication from the Lower Province, in the ensuing spring, I have directed Col. Myers ... [to have a new survey made of the alternative route] ... [concluding that] ... I am of opinion that the difficulties will be immense and the expense enormous.'[18]

This marked the start of a series of surveys and studies of the alternative route, using the Ottawa River as far as the Rideau River, then the Rideau River into the Rideau Lakes, and finally one of the smaller rivers emptying into the St Lawrence. The route would be longer than the direct route up the St Lawrence and would involve an ascent to the elevation of Rideau Lake followed by the descent of this extra 162 feet to Kingston. A military waterway capable of conveying small war vessels would require the canalization of all the rapids. It was no wonder that General Drummond was so appalled by the magnitude of the proposed alternative route. His fears of U.S. intentions, however, were well founded. Colonel C.P. Stacey, the Canadian military historian, discovered in a confidential letter book a letter from the U.S. secretary of war, James Munroe, dated 10 February 1815, addressed to Major-General Brown (U.S. Army), giving a complete plan of campaign for renewed war against the British, including a full attack on the St Lawrence route.[19] Once the Treaty of Ghent had been signed, warlike feelings abated somewhat, to such an extent that in November 1815 Major-General Brown told Major-General Frederick Robinson, the new British commander in Upper Canada, about the proposed attack on the St Lawrence route. This information was duly relayed to Lord Bathurst, who early in 1816 directed the lieutenant-governor of Upper Canada to take preparatory measures for the development of the alternative route. Surveys were started, but the discussions continued.

Following the signing of Treaty of Ghent, the British government indicated that it had no intention of allowing the Canadian border to suffer again from neglect. The wartime naval commander on the lakes, Commodore Sir James Yeo, was consulted. His first reaction was that 'the preservation of the province of Canada by means of a Naval force on the Lakes will, in my opinion, be an endless, if not futile undertaking.'[20] Bowing to 'superior judgement' at the Admiralty, he did concede that, if a naval force were to be of any use, the opening up of the Ottawa and Rideau rivers was essential. Captain W.F. Owen, RN, was ordered to Canada in March 1815 to make a survey of the naval defence of British North America. His reports were rendered between June and November of the same year but apparently were not seriously considered until the following year. Rear-Admiral Sir David Milne, RN (soon to be in command at Halifax), was consulted. His final judgment on Canada was that 'From what I have seen it would be lucky for this country (Britain) to be well rid of it. It is certainly a fine country but too distant for us to defend against so powerful a neighbour.'[21] Fortunately, this opinion was not generally shared, but it is not too surprising to find that the Admiralty began a slow retreat from its initial post-war ideas. In this, it was soon to be aided by the lords of his majesty's Treasury with their natural emphasis on economy.

On the diplomatic front, Lord Castlereagh, as foreign secretary, was determined to do what he could to restore cordial relations with the United States. He initiated discussions with the American minister in London (John Adams) about the possibility of limiting armaments on the Great Lakes. Knowing that he had the support of the cabinet, he transferred the talks to Washington, and so it was with his full support that the British minister, Sir Charles Bagot, worked out a firm agreement with the U.S. acting secretary of state, Richard Rush. This was formalized by an exchange of notes between these two men on 28 and 29 April 1817 and was later approved by the U.S. Senate and the British government, although not as a formal treaty. This was the Rush-Bagot agreement which is still in force today, having been amended only in minor degree to cover changes in armament types, one of the best of all tributes to continuing understanding between Britain, Canada, and the United States.

The issue of inadequate communications is raised again as one realizes that while this agreement was being negotiated, the British Admiralty was still considering the policies to be followed in developing naval operations on the lakes. Cancellation of the construction of all land defence works in the Canadas in 1815 had shown clearly that reliance was then being placed on naval operations on the lakes for the defence of the Canadas, until such time as an overall defence policy had been decided upon. But the officers of the Royal Navy in command in Canada were not kept advised of the Rush-Bagot discussions until their completion and so were naturally surprised when ordered by the Admiralty in the early summer of 1817 'to pay off the whole of H.M.'s vessels on the Lakes, and place them in a state of ordinary.'[22] This command was going further than was required by the international agreement but was said to be the result of the continuing pressure for economy. Arrangements were made for the maintenance of naval vessels, which were deteriorating quite rapidly. A new naval station was established at Penetanguishene on Lake Huron, in place of one at the shallow mouth of the Grand River on Lake Erie, as a station for British naval vessels on the upper lakes.[23]

In the spring of 1819 Captain Robert Hall, RN, then in command on the lakes, died, and his command was assumed by Captain Robert Barrie, previously the commissioner at Kingston. He was soon involved in discussions with the Admiralty on the place of the British Navy on the lakes, the 'dilapidated state' of his vessels raising awkward questions about the future.[24] The drive for economy continued. The annual cost of the establishment was £47,000 (for 1820), salaries alone absorbing £28,000. A decision was reached in 1822 for a much-reduced establishment but one still responsible for maintaining some of the fleet. The total annual expenditure was to be reduced to about £12,000. Relations between Britain and the United States became strained again in 1827-8, but the crisis passed with the death of Canning in 1827 and the defeat of John Quincy Adams in the presidential election of 1828. The need for economy continued to be pressed, and with the change in the British government in November 1830, when Earl Grey became prime minister, in place of the Duke of Wellington, the 'enormous' annual expenditure on the Great Lakes naval station of £18,000 to £20,000, and the value of naval stores amounting to £180,000, were looked upon askance. In 1831 the vote for annual repairs was discontinued, and most of the vessels in storage were disposed of in 1832. Finally, with the consent of the Colonial Office and with firm statements that defence of British North America would continue, the British naval establishment on the lakes was practically completely closed down. Two clerks were left to look after the stores until 1837-8. A final vote of £200 for 'contingent expenses in breaking up the establishment' was passed in 1837-8, and with that action the Royal Navy disappeared from the Great Lakes of North America.

During this same period, however, the long-planned alternative route from Montreal to Kingston had been completed, having been opened throughout in April 1834. Despite the threat of war that still remained and would still be considered for many years to come, the original purpose of the new waterway had disappeared. The route did, however, provide the first navigable link between the Atlantic and all the Great Lakes (the Welland Canal having been opened in 1829) as well as the planned military link between Montreal and Kingston. The waterway was therefore welcomed as a route for settlement and commerce and was immediately used for these purposes, as well as for the conveyance of military personnel and stores. The details of the alternative route it provided must now be considered.

2

Montreal to Kingston:
The alternative route

The Ottawa River is the greatest of the tributaries of the St Lawrence River and itself is a mighty river. This size is well attested to by its old name – the Grand River – by which it was universally known in the days when the explorers and fur-traders used it as their route to the mid-west, the west, and the north of the continent. The Ottawa River also provided the key to the alternative military route which was so urgently required as the War of 1812 came to its strange close. Its valley was that down which flowed the discharge from the great glacial lakes when the last ice-front gradually receded to the north across Canada, about 11,000 years ago. Practically all Canada was covered by the continental ice sheet during this last glaciation of North America. The profound effects that the movement of the ice had on the underlying bedrock, and the deposition of glacial soils, have given to Canada its unique network of inland waterways and lakes. By walking over short portages across the upper ends of some of the glacial outwash channels and portaging around rapids, it is possible to travel by canoe along the corresponding rivers from the Atlantic to the Pacific coast of Canada, and from either coast up to the shores of the Arctic Ocean, journeys measured in several thousands of miles. Alexander Mackenzie was the first white man to make these stupendous journeys – in 1789 from Montreal to the Arctic coast; and in 1793 from Montreal to the Pacific coast in the first such crossing of the North American continent.

The Indians knew all the main waterways and had used them for their own journeys for thousands of years. They shared knowledge of the routes with white men who won their friendship; Alexander Mackenzie was a fine example of the intrepid explorer who appreciated his Indian guides. The Indians regularly used the Ottawa River before the coming of the white man. They shared their knowledge with the first explorers of the Ottawa from Europe, notably with Samuel de Champlain whose young aides were the first white men to canoe up the Ottawa, Champlain following them on his first journey, as far as Pembroke, in 1613; and on his second journey in 1615 for the full length of the 'Ottawa Waterway' over into Lake Huron. Fortunately, Champlain left written records of his journeys, so that the Ottawa gradually came to be widely known. Its use steadily increased, first by heroic Jesuit missionaries, then by young French explorers who, bringing back furs to Quebec City, laid the foundations of the great fur trade of the eighteenth and early nineteenth centuries. The fur-traders also used the Ottawa River route, until the amalgamation of the North West Company and the Hudson's Bay Company in 1821, after which the Hudson Bay route took most of this traffic. Only towards the middle of the nineteenth century did the St Lawrence route begin its steady progress towards its modern role as a great international waterway of commerce.

Despite the unique place that the Ottawa occupied for more than 200 years as the 'gateway to the continent,' no permanent settlement along its banks took place except close to Montreal until after the transfer of power from France to Britain in 1763. One or two French residents, from among those who chose not to return to France appear to have remained on the banks of Ottawa, one certainly near Montebello (about seventy-five miles from Montreal), and one or two around the shores of the Lake of Two Mountains. The first settler to penetrate further upstream than the present site of the city of Ottawa was Joseph Mondion, in 1786. He established himself near Chats Falls but sold his little property around the turn of the century and 'returned to the city.' The first man to settle in the vicinity of the modern city of Ottawa was a Yankee from Woburn, Massachusetts (now Winchester, a suburb of Boston), Philemon Wright by name, who came north with his family and a group of other immigrants over the ice of the frozen river in March 1800, after two earlier reconnaissance visits. By the early 1800s the virgin forests were still almost continuous along the banks of the Ottawa, broken by only a few small clearings.

Some names of localities along the Ottawa have been mentioned. Before more detailed attention is directed to its lower reaches, the overall character of the river should be outlined. The Ottawa rises in a group of lakes, typical of those found everywhere in Canada on the Precambrian Shield, about 155 miles due north of the modern capital city. It flows at first almost due west, for about 160 miles. Forming the border between Quebec and Ontario, it enters the head of Lake Temiskaming, flowing south through this lake for about ninety miles. From its source it has now dropped in elevation over 600 feet; it still has to fall more than 400 feet before it reaches the St

Lawrence at Montreal. At the small town of Mattawa, the Ottawa makes another turn, this time to the east. It then flows along a generally easterly course, down what is today known as the Ottawa Valley, until it reaches the enlargement known as the Lake of Two Mountains, immediately to the west of the Island of Montreal. Here the Ottawa splits into four channels, two of which join the St Lawrence around Île Perrot. The part of the Ottawa water that joins the St Lawrence remains distinctive in colour (as can be clearly seen today from the air) until the combined river tumbles down the Lachine Rapids, from the foot of which is clear sailing to the sea. The other two channels encircle Île Jésus which lies immediately to the north of the island on which the city of Montreal is located. These channels, which flow to the north, as the Rivière des Mille-Îles and the Rivière des Prairies, flow down numerous rapids with the same total drop as at Lachine, until they unite to form the one St Lawrence River at Bout de l'Île. In each of these channels dams now control the flow for power generation.

The distances mentioned will show clearly that the Ottawa is a large river by any standard, even though it is only a tributary of the St Lawrence. It drains an area of 57,000 square miles, considerably more than the combined area of England and Wales. Its average flow, of about 70,000 cubic feet per second, is therefore greater than the average flow of all the rivers of England and Wales. When this great volume of water is considered in relation to the total drop in level of the Ottawa, 1,100 feet from its source, it is not surprising to find that, today, over 4 million horse power are generated in the water power plants, great and small, that have been built on the main river and its tributaries. These power stations have been constructed in the twentieth century, close to the sites of rapids that once constituted formidable impediments to travel by canoe, most of which had to be circumvented by arduous portages along trails parallel to the rapids, all vividly described in the records of early travellers. At only a few of the rapids, in addition to the Lachine Rapids, can the Ottawa be seen today just as it was prior to this century, but these few glimpses show what stamina the journeys required of their crews, in portaging canoes and their loads when going upstream and in shooting the rapids (when this was possible) on downstream journeys.

Travel on the waterways of Canada was an adventurous business, aided by the superb qualities of the birchbark canoes which derived from Indian travel. On the Ottawa River *canots de maître* were used, splendid craft usually thirty-six feet long, which would carry a crew of eight or ten and a payload of up to three tons, four tons in all. Such a canoe would weigh about 600 pounds. If damaged, it could be repaired along the way with bark from birch trees, spruce roots (*wattape*) for sewing bark together, and spruce or pine gum for caulking. Hardwood strips were used for ribbing and thin cedar for flooring. 'Spare parts' were often carried in the form of a roll of birchbark. When it was necessary to travel up small rapids, the cargoes might be left in the canoes with a steersman, while the crew went ashore to tow the loaded canoe, usually using one long line. If towing (or 'tracking') were not possible, then poling was resorted to, an activity that called for the greatest balancing skill. In rapids that could not be navigated in these ways, the cargo might have to be unloaded and carried up on men's backs (usually two packs at a time, each weighing seventy-four pounds) to the head of the rapid, while the empty canoe was hauled up by tracking; this was known as a *décharge*. In the worst rapids of all, not only the cargo would have to be carried, but the canoe itself would be hauled out of the water and carried up the portage trail on the padded shoulders of (usually) four members of the crew – a true *portage*, even though this word is commonly used to describe all three operations.

Practically all travel for the fur trade was by canoe, smaller ones (*canots du nord*) generally being used west of Lake Superior. As settlement began, however, something larger was necessary, and so the flat-bottomed bateau was developed and first used by the French on the St Lawrence. These boats were built of timber and had sharp ends and low, almost vertical sides. Their flat bottoms permitted heavier loads to be handled than could safely be accommodated in canoes. They were equipped with poles, oars, and simple masts with square sails for taking advantage of any wind on open water. Earlier types carried up to three tons, but for later versions capacities of up to four and a half tons are recorded. Durham boats were a logical development, although they seem to have been introduced on the St Lawrence from the United States in the early years of the nineteenth century. They were shallow vessels, with flat bottoms but having keel or centre boards and a rounded bow; they were longer than bateaux and had up to ten times the capacity of a bateau. Both types of vessel were handled somewhat like a canoe, except that they could not be carried along portage trails and always had to be poled or tracked up rapids. They were, however, readily handled by expert crews when descending rapids. Only on the St Lawrence below Montreal and on Lake Ontario were keeled and decked sailing vessels found until the final transition to steamboats.

To provide an alternative to portaging around the greatest of all the rapids on the Ottawa the Grenville Canal, one of the three Ottawa River canals, was constructed. The other two, at Carillon and Chute à Blondeau just downstream of the Grenville Canal, performed the same function around smaller rapids. The three canals are located about half-way between

Montreal and the Chaudière Falls, now close to the centre of the city of Ottawa. It was this stretch of the Ottawa that came to be of such critical military importance as a result of the War of 1812. With the aid of the accompanying maps, it must be considered in some detail so that the logistics of the canal-building may be better appreciated.

Starting in the harbour of Montreal, one is in water connecting directly with the sea. Today, as a result of river improvements, mainly great dredging programs, large ocean vessels sail right up to the great port of Montreal, many now sailing into the St Lawrence Seaway to continue their journeys up into the Great Lakes. Before any river improvements had been made, however, although it was possible for small vessels to sail from the Atlantic into the then primitive harbour of Montreal, the Lachine Rapids prevented further travel up river. Almost the full flow of the St Lawrence here falls nearly forty feet in a spectacular stretch of white water, still to be seen in all its natural beauty, although the day is bound to come when the power it represents will be harnessed in a modern power station which, with its associated dam, will then completely block the river. An attempt had been made as early as 1700 to construct a small canal from the harbour of Montreal around these rapids in a direct line to Lake St Louis, but it was not completed. Travellers to the west therefore went by land to avoid the rapids along what would one day be the route of the Lachine Canal. The departure point for all canoe journeys was the small settlement that grew up on Lake St Louis at this point of embarkation, derisively given the name of La Chine. This was a true reflection of the hopes and dreams of the early French explorers – that up the Grand River they would come to the Orient, one of them (Jean Nicollet) even taking with him on his journey of 1633 a robe of Chinese damask to wear when he met the first Chinese.

Lachine is located at the head of the great rapids, at the east end of the expansion of the St Lawrence known as Lake St Louis. Canoes could be easily paddled thence, except in storms, for twelve miles as far as the western end of the lake. Here the St Lawrence enters the lake down the group of Soulanges Rapids, the lowest being clearly visible from the lake, while the Ottawa joins it through the two channels on either side of Île Perrot from the Lake of Two Mountains. There is always a small drop in water level here, giving small rapids in both channels, known today as those of Vaudreuil (to the south) and Ste Anne-de-Bellevue (adjacent to the Island of Montreal). With the growth of the fur trade up and down the Ottawa, a rough road was constructed in the late eighteenth century all the way from Montreal past Lachine to Ste Anne. The canoes had still to be loaded at Lachine and paddled by their crews up to Ste Anne, but passengers often took the rough road out to the end of the island. Ste Anne-de-Bellevue therefore was a significant landmark, its small church welcoming devout voyageurs, who would say their vows before departing for unknown adventures up the Ottawa. The name is descriptive, since the site is a lovely one, the view up the Lake of Two Mountains being one of great beauty which has attracted the attention of many artists on canvas and in words. The 'Canadian Boat Song' of Thomas Moore was almost certainly written here, those lines that begin: 'Faintly as tolls the evening chime / Our voices keep tune.'

The fall in water level through the Ste Anne rapids varies throughout the year with changing flows in the river and consequent differing levels of the two lakes. This difference can be as high as five feet at times of high flow, as in the late spring, but can be as low as little more than one foot. Loaded canoes could, therefore, be hauled up with ropes, and lightly loaded canoes could readily shoot the rapids when coming downstream. Then came another smooth sail across the Lake of Two Mountains, an enlargement of the Ottawa River. The two mountains of Rigaud and Oka would be visible on the respective banks, rising from the level plains around (now valuable agricultural land, but in the early 1800s still untouched forest), the lake gradually narrowing as the western end was approached. A roar would then be heard, twenty-five miles upstream from Ste Anne, and the Carillon Rapids would come into view just after the sluggish-looking North River enters the lake from the north. It was on this river that settlement started in a very modest way, just before the close of the eighteenth century. As the lake became the river again, the banks steepened appreciably, a reflection of changing geology. Although the Carillon Rapids were concentrated in a relatively short stretch of the river, now about a half-mile wide, the drop in level varied up to almost ten feet, so they presented a fine show of 'white water.' Four miles upstream, the river gradually narrowing to about a quarter of a mile in width, another small rapid was encountered, known as Chute à Blondeau. Here the drop in water level was about five feet, easy to run downstream but necessitating the inevitable hauling to get loaded canoes up into the still water above.

There was little respite for the crews, however, since the roar of the greatest rapid on the Ottawa could be heard shortly after Chute à Blondeau was passed. The river narrowed still further, a short section resembling a gorge, the water correspondingly swift and flecked with foam from the great rapid that became visible after a slight swing to port. In the next six miles, the Ottawa roared and tumbled down a rocky island-studded course, dropping forty-five feet in what was so rightly known as the Long Sault. It

The Long Sault on the Ottawa River, with an early raft of timber, as sketched by Colonel J.P. Cockburn in 1827

was a truly magnificent sight, admired as one of the great natural spectacles of eastern Canada until it was forever flooded by the construction of the dam and power house at Carillon, in which the once untamed power of the rapids is now harnessed. This great change in the river occurred only in 1962, so that many older Canadians can remember vividly what the Long Sault looked like. One had to walk along the banks, however, to appreciate to the full the majesty of this stretch of the Ottawa.

Despite the singular name, the Long Sault was not one continuous rapid but rather a series of turbulent small falls with swift water and minor rapids between. At the head of the Long Sault on the north shore now stands the quiet village of Grenville. Here used to be the most violent of all the rapids, the combination of rock formations and swift current throwing the water upward and backward with such effect that it was known as 'The Cellar.' One of the three portage trails (990 yards long) bypassed this upper section, since no canoe could possibly navigate it, even though it could be 'shot' by expert canoists going downstream at most stages of the river. These levels varied between high water in the spring flood and low water in the fall, there being sometimes as much as a fifteen-foot difference between the two. After the first rapid, the most remarkable feature of the next section was the number of large boulders resting on the shallow bed of the river, sure

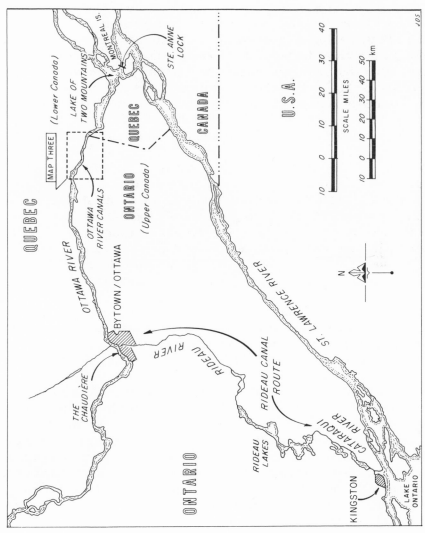

2 The Montreal-Ottawa-Kingston 'triangle,' showing the two water routes to Kingston – up the St Lawrence, or by way of the Ottawa River and Rideau Canal

evidence of the last glaciation, interesting geologically but hazardous to all river men. The swift water was constricted in its passage by the group of small islands centred around Stevens Island (or Île Verte) which itself blocked almost half the width of the stream. Here, too, was violent turbulent water, but since canoes could be tracked up, there was no well-recognized portage trail around it. Another mile of swift water followed before relatively quiet water was reached, but even here the river flow was fast by all normal standards until Chute à Blondeau. Here was the second portage trail, 140 yards long, around another concentrated rapid adjacent to Ordnance Island.

All who saw the Long Sault must have marvelled at the manpower that had to be exerted by all travellers going upstream for over 200 years, and correspondingly at the skill of those guiding the canoes that shot the rapids going downriver. The idea of taking cribs of large timbers down these waters seems almost beyond belief, but this was done for about 100 years, always under the skilled guidance of local river pilots starting along the south shore but then moving to mid-stream. It is small wonder that the most renowned river men of all in Canada came from the small towns that grew up in the vicinity of the Long Sault.

Once past the Long Sault, however, there was plain sailing upstream for the next fifty-six miles, the river widening again to its usual half-mile width, flowing smoothly between generally low-lying banks. The only breaks in the continuous forest along both banks were the openings where tributary streams and rivers joined the Ottawa, the South Nation River (as it is now known) on the south roughly halfway to the Chaudière, and the Rouge, the Petite Nation, and the Lièvre entering from the north. The prominent escarpment marking the southern limit of the Precambrian Shield comes close to the north bank in several locations but then recedes again, although still visible as the great Chaudière Falls are approached. Here indeed is a meeting of the waters, the Gatineau River (largest of the tributaries) joining from the north almost directly opposite a spectacular waterfall down which the Rideau River enters the Ottawa from the south, about two miles from the Chaudière. The French names are truly descriptive, the falls of the Rideau River looking indeed like a curtain and the Chaudière showing its waters as in a boiling cauldron, the English translation of the Indian name (*Asticou*) which Champlain translated as Chaudière.

The Chaudière was a real barrier to travel up the Ottawa and required a portage route around the main fall of about forty-two feet and a second portage to circumvent the swift rapids above the main fall. Fortunately, the second portage has been preserved in a small park and can be seen today by

interested visitors just as it was used in the great days of river travel by
canoe. It was because of this barrier, almost certainly, that Philemon
Wright established his small settlement of Hull on the north shore of the
Ottawa. The Wright family were active in clearing land around the mouth
of the Gatineau River, which flows almost due south from its source in lakes
close to the source of both the Ottawa River (flowing west) and the St
Maurice River (flowing east, to join the St Lawrence at Trois-Rivières). The
Gatineau, a swift-flowing river with many rapids in its course, was therefore another of the waterways used by the Indians and shown by them to
early white travellers as an alternative route to the Ottawa River. When the
lower Ottawa was controlled by hostile Indians, in the mid-1600s, the Gatineau and its connection to the St Maurice provided a safe route regularly
used from up-river points to Quebec City. Its main rapids have now also
been tamed in modern water power plants, some of the energy thus generated supplying the city of Ottawa just a few miles away.

The Rideau River has quite a different character and is considerably
smaller than the Gatineau. It rises in a group of lakes, collectively known as
the Rideau Lakes, formed in depressions within an extension of the Precambrian Shield that crosses the Ottawa and St Lawrence rivers, known to geol-
ogists as the Frontenac Axis. The Rideau is a quiet-flowing stream with few
rapids once it leaves the lakes. The more important sudden drops in level
are at Long Island, Hog's Back, and the entry into the Ottawa River, all
relatively close to or even within the modern city of Ottawa. The lakes in
which the Rideau River rises are often interconnected. Short portages make
it easy to go from one to another. There are two routes available, once the
lakes are reached, for gaining access to the St Lawrence and so to Lake
Ontario and Kingston. One is down the Cataraqui River, which joins the
lake very close to Kingston; the other is down the Gananoque River, a
somewhat shorter route to the St Lawrence but entering it about eighteen
miles downstream of Kingston. These routes, well travelled by the Indians,
were probably known to fur-traders and early voyageurs, even though the
first written records about them date from the late 1700s.

When, therefore, the British military commanders discussed the desirability of an alternative route between Montreal and Kingston, they knew
that such a route did exist, although nobody knew just what engineering
works would be necessary to convert it into a military waterway. Starting
at Lachine – where active consideration of a canal before the War of 1812
seemed to assure its early construction – the first impediment met was the
small rapid at Ste Anne-de-Bellevue, or the corresponding one at Vaudreuil,
both of which could easily be surmounted by a single lock. After the Lake of

Two Mountains the three sets of rapids at Carillon, Chute à Blondeau, and Grenville (the Long Sault) were encountered. Then followed the clear sail up to the mouth of the Rideau River just below the Chaudière. The route would then follow the Rideau River, traverse the Rideau Lakes, and take either the Gananoque or Cataraqui rivers to the St Lawrence.

Canalization of the Rideau and Catarqui rivers (the latter being finally chosen) was clearly a major undertaking, the distance from the Ottawa River to Kingston harbour being 123 miles, with a rise in elevation from the Ottawa River of 277 feet to the summit level in what is now Upper Rideau Lake, and then a fall of 162 feet to Lake Ontario in Kingston harbour. Achieving these changes in elevation required the construction of forty-seven masonry locks and fifty-two dams, one of which was a masonry arched dam more than sixty feet high. The construction of this military canal was entrusted in 1826 to the Corps of Royal Engineers. Lieutenant-Colonel John By was selected to be the superintending engineer. Although surrounded by virgin forest, he was able to complete the entire project in five full working seasons, and the opening took place in May 1832. The canal as built remains in use today and has been well maintained down the years. It now carries more traffic than at any time in its long history, the annual 'invasion' comprising tourists from the United States who join with Canadians in their varied pleasure craft in exploring the beauties of the country through which the old canal passes. Colonel By established his construction headquarters in a forest clearing on the banks of the Ottawa, today the centre of Canada's capital city of Ottawa, through which the Rideau Canal runs between colourful and well-kept gardens.

The story of the building of the Rideau Canal, as the major part of the alternative route from Montreal to Kingston, has been told in the writer's *Rideau Waterway*. This canal will naturally call for incidental mention as the building of the smaller Ottawa River canals is described. The contrast between the two canalization projects is marked. Not only are the Ottawa River canals much smaller than either of the two sections of the Rideau Canal, but their construction started in 1819 and was not finished until 1834, thus delaying the opening of the entire through route by two sailing seasons. Located on the northern shore of the Ottawa River and not visible from the older main roads in Ontario between Ottawa and Montreal, the little canals were some distance also from the main road in Quebec between the two cities. They were therefore but little known by the Canadian public, and now they have almost completely disappeared from sight because of the construction of the Carillon water power plant. They were built by the Royal Staff Corps, a British regiment that is today little known in any circles, to such an extent that the official plaques that now mark the two ends of the old canal system, erected by the Historic Sites and Monuments Board of Canada in 1933, still indicate incorrectly that the canals were constructed by the Royal Engineers. Even an official publication of the government of Canada, replete with references, repeats the error. The plaques are to be corrected.

It is to the building of the Ottawa River canals and the lock at Ste Anne, that attention will now be exclusively directed. The small rapids at Ste Anne and those at Carillon and Chute à Blondeau were relatively minor, by Canadian standards, and were little different from the innumerable rapids on Canadian rivers that had to be passed by all early travellers. They receive scant, if any, notice, therefore, in the written records left by many of these early travellers. Canal construction around them had its own problems, as will be seen, but there is little need to say more about the rapids themselves – short sections of swift water, tumbling down as small but turbulent waterfalls at the rock ridges which, in almost all cases, were the cause of the rapid. The magnitude of the Ottawa River, and the volume of water flowing, alone make these smaller rapids distinctive. These features also made the Long Sault a magnificent sight, especially at high water. This was so dangerous a stretch of the river, however, that something more must be said about it before early studies of the alternative route are reviewed.

Even the best of photographs or the most vivid of paintings fail to give any real indication of what these six miles of white water were like. As one approached the Long Sault from any direction the continuous roar of the churning water could be heard from far away. The Ottawa being relatively straight throughout the six miles, one could generally see most of the Long Sault from any of the convenient vantage points. The presence of the few small islands and the extremely rocky nature of the northern shore added to the beauty of the scene but also to the hazards of navigation. The Long Sault was regularly navigated, in more recent years only by adventurous and skilled canoeists. One friend of the writer who spent his boyhood in his family home adjacent to the great rapid, came down the Long Sault many times, always in safety, although he expended several canoes in his journeys. Up to about the beginning of this century, there lived near the rapids a number of skilled pilots, who used to be charged with the difficult task of guiding down the Long Sault cribs of big timbers, broken out from the great multi-crib rafts that floated down the smooth waters above and below the rapids. One of these intrepid men piloted down the Sault on a well-known occasion one of the steamers of the 'upper river fleet' which was needed downriver – the S.S. *Queen Victoria*, a side-wheeler, 169 feet long. The transfer was safely made, high water in the river assisting the hazardous shooting of the rapids.

The written records left by travellers up and down the Ottawa, up to the time of the canal-building, almost without exception, have derogatory comments on the passage past the Long Sault, starting quite naturally with Champlain. In his record of the 1613 journey up the Ottawa in a frequently quoted passage he says that

On Saturday, 1 June, we passed two more rapids ... here [at the Long Sault] we had much labour; for so great is the swiftness of the current that is makes a dreadful noise, and, falling from level to level, produced everywhere such a white foam that no water at all is seen. This rapid is strewn with rocks and in it here and there are some islands covered with pines and white cedar. It was here we had such difficulty, for being unable to portage our canoes on account of the thickness of the woods, we had to track them, and in pulling mine, nearly lost my life, because the canoe turned broadside into a whirlpool and had I not luckily fallen between two rocks, the canoe would have dragged me in, since I could not quickly enough loosen the rope which was twisted around my hand, which hurt me very much, and nearly cut it off. In this danger, I cried aloud to God and began to pull my canoe towards me, which was sent back to me by an eddy such as occurs in these rapids. Having escaped, I gave praise to God, beseeching Him to preserve us. Later on, our Indian came to my help, but I was out of danger.[1]

Similar dangers were faced by all who had to track their canoes up this rough water. Two short portage trails were eventually developed so that canoes as well as their loads could be portaged, but even then there were still dangers to be faced. The words of another traveller bear vivid witness. John Jeremiah Bigsby was a colourful character who came to Canada in 1818 as the medical officer of a regiment of German mercenary troops. Later he was appointed to serve with one of the first of the international boundary commissions and so travelled up the Ottawa in 1822 to join his party. He records that, at the Long Sault,

the river being this season eight feet above its usual level, the rapids were unusually vehement, and, in places, the woods around were flooded. We walked the nine miles to the head of the Long Sault Rapids, through swamps and woods. To avoid wading, Mr Robinson and myself struck deep into the forest, lost ourselves, and wandered about uneasily, until we came upon a decent loghouse in a small clearance (township of Grenville). After some rapping, the door was opened by a very handsome tall young woman, with auburn hair, tidily dressed. I inquired our way. She shook her head without a smile. In great surprise for she looked British all over – I addressed her in French; but I only got another shake of the head, when her brother appeared, and told us that they were Highlanders, and that his sister could only speak the Gaelic. He put us in the right way for the head of the rapids.[2]

It is not surprising that settlement started around the shores of the Lake of Two Mountains and in the vicinity of the mouth of the North River. Small fur-trading posts had existed on the lake from the earliest days. It has been suggested that the name Carillon is actually a derivative of the second name of Philippe Carrion du Fresnay, who maintained one such post on Carillon Island as early as 1681. Permanent settlement came later, but by the late 1700s there were a few homesteads around the shores of the lake. Carillon itself was an early settlement but it was not until 1785 that the first houses were established at what was to become the town of St Andrews on the North River. The beginnings of the town of Lachute, located further up this small river, date from 1796. The possibilities of settlement along the Ottawa River had received official attention shortly after the transfer of power to the British. In 1783 two officers of the British Army, Lieutenants French and Jones, were sent up the Ottawa and the Rideau to survey the river banks for land suitable for settlement. Lieutenant Jones was responsible for studying the Ottawa River as far as the Chaudière; Lieutenant French had the more difficult job of examining the Rideau River and following it into the Rideau Lakes, then into the 'Gananoncoui River' and down to the St Lawrence. Both officers found extensive tracts of fertile land which they deemed suitable for agriculture. The possibilities of the Ottawa-Rideau route were, therefore, officially known from the date of this first military survey.

From the early days of the French regime, large parcels of land along all the main rivers of New France, including the Ottawa, had been given as seigniories to leading citizens. Those on the Ottawa changed hands several times without being occupied until the end of the eighteenth century. That closest to the site of the Ottawa River canals was the seigniory of Argenteuil. First granted in 1682, it was finally bought in 1796 by a Major Murray, who intended to bring settlers to live on his land. He made great efforts, to no avail, and eventually sold it to Sir John Johnson in 1814. The land beyond the seigniories was surveyed, so far as was possible from the limited river bank access, and subdivided into regular lots so that these could be given to men of the British Army upon their discharge after service in Canada. The first map of land subdivision, dated 1788, is in the Public Archives of Canada; Rankin was the surveyor. Subdivision is shown from the western limit of the seigniory as far as the islands at the head of the Long

Sault. Grants of these lots were made, such as those to Captain McDougal (2,000 acres), Captain Daniel Robertson (3,000 acres), Captain Malcolm Fraser and his son (5,000 acres), and Brigadier McLean (5,000 acres) – names that will be encountered later, when land problems in the building of the Grenville Canal are considered. Because of the large areas involved, very little was done in the way of land clearing until the early years of the nineteenth century.

In 1799 the area to the west of the Argenteuil Seigniory was designated as the township of Chatham, in honour of William Pitt, prime minister of Great Britain. Since only the lots fronting on the river were accessible, the area they occupied was soon known as 'The Front of Chatham,' a local name that persisted and could still be heard, used by older local residents, until recent years. The village of Grenville was surveyed in the year 1811, but one settler had cleared some land in Grenville in the preceding year – Archibald McMillan, who soon became a notable figure in the district. Across the Ottawa, on the south shore, the first small water-mills near the head of the Long Sault had been built in 1810; this was the start of what is today the town of Hawkesbury. Below the foot of the Long Sault, opposite Carillon, an area of 1,000 acres had been surveyed for a townsite in 1788, but little clearing had been done, except close to the river. Here William Fortune and others started the establishment that would eventually become the village of Pointe Fortune. In these same years (the first decade and a half of the nineteenth century), a few more settlers had preceded Philemon Wright and had travelled up the Ottawa after passing the Long Sault; the most important was Nicholas Treadwell, an American citizen who had purchased L'Orignal, the only seigniory in what was, after 1791, Upper Canada. A small mill had been built and a modest settlement was developing.

When, therefore, the first serious studies of the alternative route between Montreal and Kingston were initiated by the senior British military commanders, the Ottawa River from Ste Anne-de-Bellevue to the Chaudière Falls was still almost in its virgin state, forests coming to the water's edge on both shores, except where the few individual settlers had started clearing their land. Legal land subdivision had been carried out as far upstream as the head of the Long Sault, but the few survey markers in the forest were usually the only indication of ownership. Despite this wilderness state, Sir George Prevost had made some preliminary plans of what the alternative route could be. He sent them to General Drummond at Kingston with a letter, dated 29 December 1814, asking for his opinion on the development of this waterway.[3] General Drummond had the proposal examined by Quartermaster General Nichol, Lieutenant-Colonel Myers (his deputy), and Captain Sherwood, captain of guides. In his reply to Sir George, General Drummond said in a letter of 17 January 1815 that 'I differ with this latter officer [Nichol] as to the total impracticality of the scheme, but I am of the opinion that the difficulties will be immense and the expense enormous.'[4] Despite this lukewarm opinion, steps had been taken to study the route more carefully, Lieutenant-Colonel Myers having written two days previously to Captain Sherwood, saying that, on the orders of General Drummond, he wished him to 'prepare an ample sketch with explanatory notes of the same, made out from the recent observations you have made and information you have collected.'[5]

Confirming what has been said about the widespread fear that hostilities would again break out with the United States, despite the Treaty of Ghent, it is interesting to find General Drummond prefacing his letter (of 17 January 1815) to Sir George Prevost with these words: 'under the presumption that the enemy will endeavour to interrupt the present line of communication from the Lower Province, in the ensuing Spring, I directed Colonel Myers ...' That the fears did not disappear is shown by a letter sent directly to General Drummond by Lord Bathurst, secretary for war and the colonies, from Downing Street on 10 October 1815, which starts:

His Majesty's Government being deeply impressed with the importance of carrying into execution the works necessary for the improvement of the Water Communication between the Upper and the Lower Province I am to direct that you will take the necessary measures for procuring an estimate of the expense which will be incurred by rendering the Ottawa and Rideau Rivers navigable and completing that line of communication; and also of the sum which will be required for constructing the Canal proposed between Montreal and La Chine in order that His Majesty's Government may decide as to the propriety of undertaking these works either separately or simultaneously.[6]

The studies necessary for the preparation of the estimates requested must have been thoroughly discussed during the remainder of the winter of 1815–16, when no work in the field could be done, with the result that surveys were initiated in the early spring of 1816.

Instructions were issued on 27 April 1816 by the commanding officer of the Royal Engineers, after approval by General Drummond, to Lieutenant J. Jebb to start immediately on a survey of the Rideau route, from the Ottawa River to Kingston. Lieutenant Jebb carried out his task with expedition, reporting to Lieutenant-Colonel Nichols on 8 June. This report was the basis upon which further studies of the Rideau Canal were later made. The survey of the Ottawa River part of the route was entrusted to Lieutenant Baron, also of the Royal Engineers, in a letter dated 9 May 1816, also from Lieutenant-Colonel Nichols, and also approved by General Drummond.[7] The heading to this letter refers to 'navigation by batteaux from Montreal to the River Rideau by the Ottawa or Grand River.' Lieutenant Baron was stationed at Île aux Noix on the Richelieu River. After completing arrangements there, he was to report to Montreal, where he would be furnished with 'a batteau and crew of Canadians ... and with two intelligent men of the Nova Scotia Fencibles.' He was first to make a survey of the Rivière des Prairies (the 'Back River' at Montreal) and is then 'to proceed up the River Ottawa as far as where the Rideau falls into it, in like manner reporting on each obstacle to Navigating by Batteaux.' He was not to bother with those parts of the river already navigable by bateaux but he was asked to 'lay down and report upon such places on the Ottawa as appear to you best adapted for Posts and Depots with a view to the forwarding and protecting the communication between Montreal and Kingston, by the Ottawa.'

The establishment of the Royal Engineers in British North America at this time was so limited that these extra duties must have caused concern among the senior officers, as shown by the request that General Drummond had addressed to His Royal Highness the Duke of York, commander-in-chief of British forces, asking approval of his action in ordering the transfer of the two companies of the Royal Staff Corps which had landed on 28 April 1815 in Halifax, Nova Scotia, for service on the Montreal to Kingston 'communication.' This request was acknowledged for HRH the Duke of York from the Horse Guards on 24 July 1815, with further specific reference to the Lachine Canal and 'on the improvements in the Lower and Upper Province,' with the addendum that the prince regent would be asked to permit the detachment to remain in Canada for the present.'[8] The men of the Royal Staff Corps were therefore transferred, leaving Halifax on 20 May by ship and arriving at Quebec on 15 June 1816. Then they moved up to the small locks on the St Lawrence at Coteau du Lac and the Cascades. They had relieved the Royal Engineers of their former duties at these two locations by the summer of 1816, as recorded in a letter dated 3 July 1816 from the governor's military secretary.

There appears to be a possibility that the Staff Corps also took over the survey assigned to Lieutenant Baron. His report, corresponding to that of Lieutenant Jebb, has not been found in the records, but the Public Archives of Canada does possess a plan of the Ottawa River from the Long Sault to Chute à Blondeau 'showing the situations of the proposed works for their improvement of the Navigation.' It is dated 1816 and is signed by Lieuten-

ant Kingston D. Lloyd and Ensign Edward J. Cleather of the Royal Staff
Corps. This marked the start of the long association of the Staff Corps with
the Ottawa River canals and, correspondingly, the end of the links between
the Royal Engineers and the Ottawa, except for two somewhat unusual
assignments given to Lieutenant-Colonel John By while he was building the
Rideau Canal. It would be interesting to know the nature of the relations
between the two regiments, but direct evidence is lacking. Indirectly it is
possible to detect somewhat less than cordial views, as would be expected
when the origin of the Royal Staff Corps is considered (the founding and
history of the Royal Staff Corps are summarized in appendix A). When, for
example, Major Andrew Long, commanding the two companies of the Staff
Corps at work on the St Lawrence canal locks, sent on 25 October 1816 an
estimate of the cost of proposed work at Coteau du Lac to the governor's
military secretary at Quebec, it was acknowledged by Colonel Durnford
(who was now the commanding Royal Engineer in Canada), naturally pre-
senting his compliments but adding that he did not know why there was not
an officer of the Royal Engineers present. The officers of both regiments,
however, shared frustrations at the demands of the headquarters staffs at
Quebec, seemingly made with little appreciation of the difficulties attending
work in the field. Major Long, for example, on 23 June 1817 appealed for a
continuation of 'field rations' for his men, because 'vegetables are so expensive' (at Coteau du Lac) and 'the Men are in the habit of working extremely
hard (and so) require more nourishment than the common rations, under
the above circumstances, will afford.'[9] There is a more familiar ring to the
request of Lieutenant Thomas Harris, RSC on 29 June 1816 asking if it is
really necessary for him to send seven copies of the monthly estimates (all of
which had to be copied by hand) in order that two certified copies might be
returned to him.[10]

These were very minor problems, however, compared with the changes
in command at Quebec. When Sir George Prevost returned to England on 3
April 1815, General Sir Gordon Drummond was appointed administrator
and so served for just over a year, sailing in turn for England on 21 May
1816. John Wilson then served as administrator of Lower Canada for two
months, until the arrival of Sir John Sherbrooke, who was transferred from
his post in Nova Scotia to be governor and commander-in-chief, arriving in
Quebec on 12 July 1816. He remained for only a few days more than two
years. When to these changes in the highest command is added the real
problem of communication, one of special significance in view of the
distances involved even in the governing of Upper and Lower Canada, the
wonder is that so much was accomplished. The absence of the lieutenant-

governor of Upper Canada, Francis Gore, between 1811 and 1815 has already been noted. He did not return to Canada until 21 September 1815 and served only until 11 June 1817. It was from his office that there was issued one of the strangest of all communications regarding the alternative route between Montreal and Kingston.

Dated in York on 19 February 1817, it appeared as a public notice in the *Quebec Mercury* of 24 June 1817, stating in both French and English: 'Tenders will be received at this Office from such Person or Persons as may be desirous of Contracting to render the whole or any part of the Water Communication between Lachine and Kingston, by the course of the River Rideau navigation ... The Tenders are to specify the number of Locks and the places at which it is proposed to build them: also the number of Flood Gates in each Lock, and the period for completing the work by the Irish Creek.'[11] In view of the entirely undeveloped state of the country through which the route would pass, this request for 'Design-Construct' tenders (as they would be called today) is so ludicrous as to be almost incredible – and yet such a notice was published. It must have had the approval of Sir John Sherbrooke, but neither he nor Francis Gore knew anything of the route to be canalized. One must take the notice as an indication of the somewhat desperate wish to 'do something' about this much-discussed military waterway. Somewhat naturally, nothing further can be found about this strange suggestion, and nothing more appears to have been done until 1818. In that year yet another governor arrived in Quebec to take office; it was not long before he saw what the situation was and proceeded to do something about it.

The changes in command in the Canadas and the lack of action on the military waterway reflected the concurrent difficulties of the British government of Lord Liverpool. The Treaty of Ghent had brought no satisfaction, and strong feelings remained that the War of 1812 had been a stab in the back. After the victory of Wellington at Waterloo on 18 June 1815, national gloom was changed temporarily to rejoicing. The threat from Napoleon was averted, but the difficult problems of resettlement and the redeployment of troops and naval forces had to be faced. The first rumblings caused by the Industrial Revolution were heard (the Luddite riots had taken place in 1811), and talk of reform was in the air. Emigration was encouraged, a public notice appearing in Edinburgh as early as 1815 with offers of free land in Canada and assistance in settlement. This was also the time of 'the clearances,' when highlanders were displaced from their crofts and their homes destroyed in the interests of sheep-raising. The first shiploads (and that expression must be used) of Scots settlers were soon on their way across the Atlantic, to provide more problems for the distant colonial administration, while starting that inflow of new citizens upon which the development of Canada was so largely to depend. Many travelled up the St Lawrence to join United Empire Loyalists in new homes along its shores. Others followed the same route but then turned inland from the St Lawrence (generally from Prescott) to establish new villages in the forests of the Ottawa Valley, some almost completely military settlements to begin with that were regarded as a second frontier. By coincidence, the first large groups of settlers to leave Montreal by way of the Ottawa River made their difficult journey in the summer of 1818. It has been suggested, by the present writer and others, that the harrowing experience of transporting women and children up the Long Sault might have had some influence upon the early start of work on the Grenville Canal. The records leave little doubt, however, that the start was actually made because of the keen military sense of the new governor who landed in Quebec City on 30 July 1818, His Grace the fourth Duke of Richmond.

3

The Grenville Canal: The start

Charles Lennox, fourth Duke of Richmond, Lennox, and Aubigny, was one of the most remarkable men ever to be the senior royal representative in Canada. He was appointed governor of Lower Canada and commander-in-chief in May 1818, landing in Quebec to take up his office on 30 July of that year. One of the very few governors to die in office, he served only until 28 August 1819. His achievements in these thirteen months raise the natural question of what might he have done for Canada had he been able to serve for his complete term.

He was fifty-five years old when he took office, with a wealth of experience behind him. As a young captain in the Coldstream Guards in 1789 he had challenged His Royal Highness the Duke of York to a duel, which was fought on Wimbledon Common, the Duke of York firing into the air but Lennox grazing the Prince's curl. His fellow officers paid tribute to his courage but decried his judgment. Shortly thereafter he exchanged his Guards' captaincy for the colonelcy of the 35th Foot Regiment, but before joining his new regiment in Edinburgh, he fought another duel with a man named Swift who had published a pamphlet reflecting on Richmond's character. Edinburgh Castle was illuminated in his honour, on his arrival in the Scottish capital, and he was presented with the freedom of the city. He served with his regiment in the Leeward Islands, fortunately escaping the yellow fever that decimated the ranks of both officers and men. Upon his return to England, he made rapid progress in the army, serving as an aide-de-camp to the king and attaining the rank of general. He had been elected a member of Parliament for Sussex in 1790, as a supporter of Pitt, and continued to represent this constituency until he succeeded his father in the dukedom on 29 December 1806.

On the first day of April of the next year the Duke of Richmond was sworn as a privy councillor and appointed lord lieutenant of Ireland, serving in this office until 1813. Here began his association with Colonel Arthur Wellesley, later the first Duke of Wellington, who was then the chief secretary for Ireland. Upon leaving Ireland, the duke took up residence in Brussels with his large family (seven sons and seven daughters), and it was he, with his duchess, who gave the famous ball on the night before the battle of Waterloo. He was present at the battle, in the Duke of Wellington's suite. He was still resident in Brussels when he was given his Canadian posting, his dutiful acknowledgment to Lord Bathurst, dated 6 May 1818, asking the colonial secretary to 'assure His Royal Highness [the prince regent] that every Effort on my Part shall be exerted to fulfil the High Office His Royal Highness had done me the Honor to appoint me to.'[1]

Less than four months after his arrival at Quebec, Richmond was able to send to Lord Bathurst, as his thirteenth dispatch, a wide-ranging review of the measures he deemed necessary for the defence of British North America against possible attack from the United States. Dated 10 November, this report includes the following comments on the proposed waterway between Montreal and Kingston:

The next and perhaps most important point to be considered, is the Establishment of a Line of Communication between the Upper and Lower Provinces, independent of the St Lawrence, the possession of which River *above* Cornwall for the conveyance of Regiments or Stores, *ought* not to be ours for more than three Days after the Commencement of Hostilities. The line of the Ottawa and Rideau is the only resource. The former affords, with the single exception of the Carillon Rapids, one of the finest Navigations in the Country; to overcome these is therefore a most important object. I have directed an accurate survey which is just completed by Captain Mann of the Staff Corps, but the details of which not having reached me, I am unable to state them with precision. I understand, however, that the Expense is estimated at about £20,000 and from the great necessity of this Work I have little doubt that if Government would pay half, the Province might be easily prevailed upon to pay the other.[2]

Captain Frederick W. Mann's 'Report on the Navigation of the Ottawa or Grand River from Pointe Fortune to the Head of the Long Sault with observations on the means of Improving it and rendering it practicable for loaded Batteaux, Gunboats etc., surveyed in October 1818' was submitted also on 10 November. The Duke of Richmond sent a copy to Lord Bathurst, together with a companion report by Lieutenant-Colonel Francis Cockburn about military settlements along the Rideau, with his twenty-second dispatch on 14 January 1819.[3] In his covering letter the governor said that 'I propose employing the Staff Corps on the Ottawa as soon as the weather will admit next Spring and joining to them, the assistance of such labourers as may seem appropriate for this object and the Country itself will allow of our procuring.'

Before detailing Captain Mann's report, the further interest of the Duke of Richmond may be outlined. Having decided to see the territory of which he was governor, the Duke set out from Quebec City on 21 June 1819 by one of the first steamboats on the St Lawrence, the *Lady Sherbrooke*. He was accompanied by three of his daughters and two sons as well as members of his staff. On the way to Montreal they stopped at Sorel and here on 28 June the Duke was bitten by a tame fox that he was inspecting. Beyond Montreal, all travel had to be by canoe or bateau, but despite this restriction, the Duke travelled as far as Drummond Island at the head of Lake Huron, where there was a military outpost. On the return journey the Duke left the members of his family and staff at Kingston, where they had sailed from York in one of the first steamboats on Lake Ontario, the *Frontenac*. He was determined to examine personally the alternative route from Kingston to Montreal, even though it meant difficult travel through the bush. The country through which he would have to pass was still virgin forest with only a few rough trails. It is a measure of the man that he would attempt such a journey.

Accompanied by Lieutenant-Colonel Cockburn (the inspector of military settlements) and Major George Bowles (his military secretary), his faithful Swiss valet, and one other servant, the duke left Kingston on 20 August. A few miles were traversed in a wagon, but then saddle horses were used because the trail was so rough. After putting up for the night in humble quarters, they reached Perth on 21 August after what was described as a 'rough journey.' Here the duke was honoured by a grand dinner party on 22 August and was formally greeted by the new settlers. When the small group set out again on the morning of 24 August, the duke complained of a pain in his shoulder and was clearly not well, but he insisted on going on. They reached Sergeant Vaughan's shanty at Beckwith that night and Sergeant-Major Hill's small inn at Richmond the next day. Here a surgeon was consulted about the duke's condition, since he was now experiencing occasional muscle spasms. Despite the concern of his two companions, the duke dined with a group of retired officers on the evening of 26 August, and insisted on carrying on with his journey the next morning.

He then knew that he was suffering from rabies and that his chance of recovery was slim. He dictated to Major Bowles an affectionate message to members of his family. Together they prayed, the duke asking for strength to meet his misfortune like a soldier. The records left by his two soldier companions are moving documents, clearly demonstrating his strength of character even under the stress of this final illness.[4] But he insisted on proceeding. Richmond residents had thoughtfully arranged for him to travel down the Jock River to the Rideau by canoe, so he embarked early on the morning of the 27th. But the sight of water so distressed him (as is inevitable with rabies) that he had to leave the canoe after about a mile. His companions tried to persuade him to return to Richmond, but again, the water in the first brook he had to cross agitated him greatly, and they turned around and journeyed a short way to Twin Elm farm. Here he rested in a barn; the surgeon was sent for and the duke was bled again. Late in the afternoon he was moved into the farmhouse, where he spent a restless night. At exactly eight o'clock on the morning of 28 August, he died, supported in the arms of his valet and in the presence of his companions.[5]

A rough wooden box was made for his body and was then transported by cart to the Ottawa. Here it was transferred to a bateau at the 'Richmond Landing' and sailed down the Ottawa to Montreal. His sons had been advised of his death and had managed to reach St Andrews by coach, but, since this settlement was some distance away from the Ottawa, they missed the bateau and so had to return to Montreal. Here the governor's body lay in state from 2 to 4 September before being transferred to the steamer *Masham* for the final journey to Quebec City. The duke was buried there on 12 September in the chancel of the Anglican cathedral, Bishop Mountain preaching to the large congregation. The cathedral is the oldest Anglican cathedral in the world, outside the British Isles. It was built as a replica of St Martin's in the Fields, London, and Captains Hall and Robe of the Royal Artillery were in charge of the work, the gift of King George III; today it is still recognized as of 'royal foundation.' The Duke of Richmond was buried in the centre of the chancel, between the present-day choir stalls. The only other burial ever to take place within the cathedral was that of Jacob Mountain, the first bishop of Quebec. A small brass plate in the floor of the chancel is inscribed

BENEATH ARE DEPOSITED THE
MORTAL REMAINS OF
CHARLES
DUKE OF RICHMOND,
LENNOX AND AUBIGNY
THE MONUMENT TO WHOSE
MEMORY IS PLACED IN THE
NORTH GALLERY OF THIS
CHURCH

It is not difficult to imagine the regret with which Captain Mann and his small detachment of the Royal Staff Corps must have watched the bateau carrying the simple coffin as it approached the head of the Long Sault, where they were encamped according to the duke's instructions. Captain Mann was awaiting the visit of the governor so that he might receive specific instructions about the building of the Grenville Canal, even though he knew that his report of 1818 had been accepted and was to provide the basis for the works to be built. The two companies and their officers had come up to the Long Sault as soon as the ice in the river had broken up, and work at the site started early in June 1819. All they then had to guide them were the recommendations outlined by Captain Mann. The report that he had made after his visit to the site in October 1818 gives an admirably clear picture of this turbulent stretch of river, how the rivermen managed their small craft in its rapids and what should be done to improve the upstream passage in particular. His ten-page report, which was accompanied by a relatively accurate map of the Ottawa from the head of the Long Sault to downstream of the Carillon Rapids, may now be summarized.[6]

Travelling upstream, the first swift water of the Carillon Rapids was encountered at Pointe Fortune. For just over another mile up river, the water was swift and shallow. The channel used for passing through the rapids was on the south side, so that the unloading of parts of the cargoes of bateaux going upstream probably was first carried out on the north bank, and cargoes were then conveyed along a trail up to the head of the Long Sault. (It is known that prior to the construction of the canals, there were rough trails along both banks parelleling the rapids.) The channel was generally too far from the bank to permit tracking of upstream vessels; poling up must have been the means of getting boats through this swift water. Captain Mann was especially concerned about the difficulties encountered by the variation in the river water levels, as between high water in the spring and low water in the fall. This varying water level made it possible to use at times a simple channel and lock that had been built on the south bank by John Macdonnell. It must have been a very simple structure indeed, Captain Mann saying that the channel was formed only by 'banks of stones thrown up'; somewhat naturally these walls did not retain water well. He described the lock as an obstruction, not a help and suggested that it be removed. (Macdonnell made the mistake of charging tolls for the use of his lock by thirty-seven military bateaux; when this act was reported to the provincial authorities, orders were issued for the lock to be destroyed 'if this can be done without causing a riot.'[7])

Captain Mann's proposed improvements consisted of building catchwaters to guide the water into a simple dredged channel close to the shore, so that all vessels travelling upstream could be pulled from a towpath along the bank. His estimate of the cost was a modest £1,200. Downward-bound vessels had little difficulty in shooting the rapid, but he suggested that it would be better if two or three vessels came down his suggested channel together. Four miles upstream from the Carillon Rapids the small Chute à Blondeau Rapid, with a total fall of about four feet, could be ascended with difficulty, vessels using deep water that was found along the south shore. Since the full drop occurred suddenly in the North Channel between Ordnance Island and the bank, this channel was never used. Captain Mann considered the possibility of building a small dam equipped with a lock across this North Channel, but seeing that all excavation would have to be in rock, he recommended instead the deepening of the channel along the south shore at an estimated cost of only £200.

The description of the Long Sault in the report is vivid – the several individual rapids were detailed, as were the channels used by vessels, now on both sides of the narrowed waterway. Removal of boulders from the river bed is mentioned as one possible improvement. As the successive rapids are described, one can see how Captain Mann was still hoping to be able to recommend simple remedial measures such as have been described for the two lower rapids. But concerning the final stretch of three-quarters of a mile of continuous swift water, this able engineer saw clearly that the only possibility was to bypass the entire rapid with a canal. Having reached this conclusion, he appears to have re-examined the full length of the Long Sault, since his final recommendation is that 'the construction of a Canal on the North Side of the River, about five miles and a half in extent, by which the whole of the Long Sault would be avoided, appears the work most to be recommended; this side is preferred, the ground being less rocky than the opposite and there being a stream running nearly in a parallel direction to the River for about two miles.' His estimate of cost was £11,000 for the canal excavation and £4,340 for the locks, this figure being arrived at by allowing the sum of £47 for each foot of rise, clearly with extra allowance for guard locks. His total estimate for all the works was £16,740.

These recommendations were approved by the British government and formed the outline plan of all the work carried out until some basic changes were made in 1827. The Grenville Canal, as planned and built, was exactly as Captain Mann had suggested. His suggestions were based on passing loaded bateaux and small gunboats up and down this difficult stretch of river so that a depth of water of only four feet was contemplated, with a twenty-foot-wide channel provided with passing places so that two vessels could readily pass. This limited capacity must be stressed, since it explains the very low estimate of total cost, a figure exceeded by more than twenty times when all three canals were finished to dimensions that would enable steamboats to be passed through.

The first steamboat on the St Lawrence, the *Accommodation*, had been built by John Molson late in the summer of 1809. The final fitting-out was done at the Molson Brewery, already well established.[8] It began a regular service between Quebec and Montreal in 1810 and proved so successful that Molson built four more of these 'steam barges' (for they were little more than that) in 1812. This small fleet was much used for the transport of troops and supplies during the War of 1812. It would not be until 1822 that the Ottawa River would see its first steamboat, so that the concentration upon bateaux as the vessels to be accommodated by the Ottawa River canals during the first seven years of their construction, is understandable. Since the officers and men of the Royal Staff Corps went down to Montreal for the winter season, they must have known, and some would have seen, the 'new-fangled' steamships. The Ottawa River canals works, however, were well advanced by the time the first steamship appeared on the Ottawa River; it is not too surprising that attention was not given to revising the necessary size of locks and canal channels until the mid-1820s, as will later be seen.

During that first summer (of 1819) Captain Mann and his two companies started work at the head of the Long Sault. Clearing the ground for a camp was a priority. Simple workshop buildings were then erected and a start was made at clearing the forest along the line to be followed by the canal. This was a formidable task, as all early descriptions of the forests of the Ottawa Valley make clear, especially since only hand-axes were available for felling trees, and oxen and horses were the only means of hauling. The complications caused for Captain Mann and his associates by the death of the Duke of Richmond can well be imagined, waiting as they were for the governor's visit for their final instructions. The situation was further complicated by the fact that two new companies of the Royal Staff Corps had been ordered out from England to relieve those under Captain Mann, which had been in Canada since 1815. The new commanding officer was Captain Henry Du Vernet. At the end of the next (1820) working season some question must have been raised about the start of the works at Grenville, for Du Vernet wrote, from Montreal on 20 November of that year, a long, six-page report on the early developments 'as the circumstances may not be exactly known under which I received the direction of the Canal on the Ottawa River.'[9]

Du Vernet explains that the Duke of Richmond had applied to the commander-in-chief for permission to send Captain Mann and his two companies to work on the Ottawa River, instead of sending them home 'as directed' and without waiting for the arrival in Canada of his own two companies. They had reached Quebec on 29 July 1819 and 'were put on board the first steam boat for Montreal and I received a Route directly on my arrival at that place to march up to La Chine and from thence proceed in Bateaux to Grenville on the Ottawa River where we arrived on the 9th August.' The two officers met in Montreal and Captain Mann explained 'how the Detachment he commanded was employed.' Then follows this remarkably restrained account of what must have been a difficult period of transition:

As I [Du Vernet] had received no order with respect to the Works, he (Mann) continued in the direction as the Duke of Richmond was shortly expected from the Upper Province, who it was supposed would arrange everything concerning the Canal. His unfortunate death, however, left Captain Mann and myself awkwardly situated for I found that what had been commenced was either done at his own risk or from verbal orders which he had received from His Grace or were privately communicated to him by Major Bowles, the Military Secretary, particularly with regard to making the Canal larger than what appears to be the original intention. Having waited for instructions a month, on the 9th September, I wrote to Lieutenant Colonel Cockburn, Deputy Quarter Master General representing my situation, and I received an answer informing me that Captain Mann had been written to by the same post and directed to hand over to me the Plans and Papers relative to the Works of which I was to take the direction and I was shortly after furnished by Captain Mann with a copy of the letter which directed him to Survey and Report on the practicability of improving the navigation of the River, a copy of the Report he had made, a copy of a letter dated 30th May 1819 which directed him to commence the Canal after the manner he had proposed and containing an authority for such things as were required being purchased on his requisition without waiting for an approval from Head Quarters, accompanied by an official letter from himself stating that so far as he had proceeded with the Canal, it was calculated to admit the same description of vessels as the proposed La Chine Canal viz. sufficient width and depth for a small Steam Boat, 20 feet surface of water, 4 feet deep and where the ground was favourable, sufficient width to allow the next class of boats (Durham Boats) to pass each other (30 feet surface of water). This is the entire of the official correspondence I received relative to the Canal.

This transfer of duties is confirmed in a letter that Captain Mann addressed from Grenville on 20 September 1819 to Major Bowles, military secretary to Sir Peregrine Maitland, the lieutenant-governor of Upper Canada, who acted with James Monk as administrator of Lower Canada following the death of the Duke of Richmond. Captain Mann explains that he has passed over the charge of the works to Captain Du Vernet and sends copies of all his requisitions for stores as well as an abstract of the expenses for labour, amounting to £1,554, expressing the hope that 'this sum will not be thought very considerable.'[10] He repeats the understanding about the size of the canal given by Captain Du Vernet, and outlines the work of clearing the ground that had been done near the head of the Long Sault.

The only written instructions received by Captain Mann appear to be those contained in the letter to him from the governor's military secretary, dated 30 May 1819, just three weeks before the duke left on his long journey to Upper Canada. It states that

it being the intention of His Grace the Commander of the Forces to employ the Detachment of the Royal Staff Corps under your command to carry into execution the improvements to the navigation of the Ottawa River suggested in your Report of October last, I am directed to convey to you His Grace's direction for your proceeding without delay on such parts of this work as you may judge it most advisable to commence at this Present Season. His Grace leaves the choice of (?) on which you will encamp as well as all Minor arrangements to your discretion.[11]

The duke requested that expenditure on the works be kept distinct and separate from other costs and that copies of all requisitions be sent to his military secretary every two months, exclusive of the regular pay and allowances for the Royal Staff Corps. Orders had been given to the Commissary Department to furnish all materials that were requisitioned for the new project. These were very general instructions indeed for the start of a major construction project that would eventually last for fifteen years.

The official authority of the British government is contained in a letter sent from the Treasury Chambers in London on 25 May 1819 (a copy being forwarded by Lord Bathurst to the Duke of Richmond on the same day) addressed to Henry Goulburn and signed by S.R. Lushington, the member for Canterbury, parliamentary secretary at the Treasury.[12] It states that

having laid before the Lords Commissioners of His Majesty's treasury your letter of the 23rd of March last, enclosing one from the Duke of Richmond with Plans for improving the Communication between Upper and Lower Canada by the Line of the Ottawa or Grand River, I am commanded by their Lordships to acquaint you, for

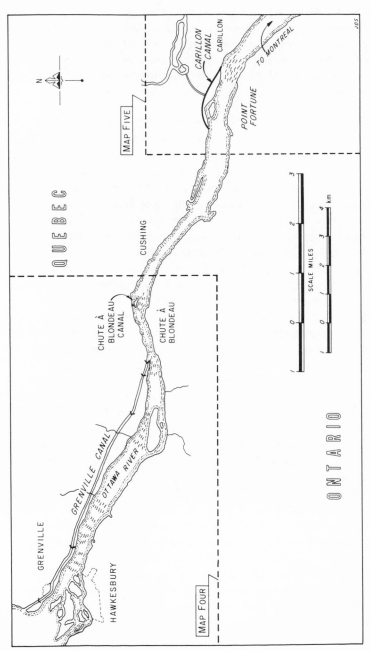

3 The Ottawa River canals

the information of Lord Bathurst, that my Lords will not object to sanctioning the execution of the several works proposed for the formation of a Communication between the Provinces of Upper and Lower Canada by the Line of the Ottawa, as detailed in Captain Mann's Report, provided the Colonial Legislature will take measures for the payment of a Moiety of the Expense, in which case, my Lords will authorize the payment of the Crown's Moiety out of Army Extraordinaries.

The use of the singular for legislature may be significant, since it could indicate some lack of understanding in London of the interprovincial character of the military waterway that was to connect Montreal with Kingston. The Rideau Canal was in Upper Canada, the Ottawa River canals in the lower province. Similarly, the expectation of the British government that the provincial legislature(s) would be willing to pay even a moiety of the cost of the waterway, although mentioned by the Duke of Richmond, indicated a lack of appreciation of the insecure financial positions of the two fledgling governments. Quite naturally they took the view that since the defence of British North America was still a responsibility of the British government, it was its responsibility also to pay the complete cost of what was then seen to be a purely military project. It would be some years before the commercial potential of the waterway would be generally evident.

That the British government had authorized a start of the work, however, in such a relatively remote part of the empire may well be an indication of the influence of the Duke of Wellington. Returning from his duties in Paris, he had been appointed master general of the ordnance on 26 December 1818 and took up his new duties in the following month. He saw the Duke of Richmond's dispatch of 10 November 1818 and endorsed it, in all but relatively minor details, in a strong memorandum to Lord Bathurst dated 1 March 1819.[13] This is a remarkable document, showing that the Duke of Wellington had very quickly developed an accurate appreciation of the main actions necessary for the defence of British North America. It was the beginning of an interest in Canada and its defence that would thereafter remain with the duke throughout the rest of his long life.

Wellington's interest in Canadian affairs has been little recognized, receiving no mention in any of the recent and well-known biographies of the 'Iron Duke.' His masterly memorandum of March 1819, however, leaves no doubt of the firm grasp he had of necessary Canadian defence measures. It was defence on which he concentrated, indicative of the mood of the time, dismissing all possibility of offensive measures, just as he had done when consulted in 1814. He was greatly attracted by the possibility of developing the alternative route between Montreal and Kingston, as a safe supply line for troops in Upper Canada and naval forces on the lakes. He even mentions the possibility of a railway or a canal to Lake Simcoe by the Black or Rideau rivers but this strange idea can be readily overlooked when it is remembered that the upper reaches of the Ottawa River were still known only to the voyageurs and first mapped accurately only in the 1840s. On the Ottawa River and Rideau canals, however, his judgment was firm and well founded. So it was that, under the influence of the recommendations of the two dukes, the British government did sanction the start of defence expenditures in Canada that would eventually amount to several million pounds. A new fort was begun on the Richelieu River at Île aux Noix (Fort Lennox). Construction of 'bomb-proof' storehouses on Île Ste Hélène at Montreal was inaugurated. A new citadel at Quebec was undertaken and fortifications at Kingston were improved. And a start on the building of the Ottawa River canals was approved.

Rarely can a major civil engineering work have been started with so little preparation. Du Vernet, in his long report of November 1820, states without any suspicion of complaint that he 'received no Plans either of the projection of the Canal or the ground through which it was intended to pass.' Nor did he 'find any new Estimate made,' because the dimensions of the canal had been increased from those Captain Mann had originally prepared. Captain Mann returned to Montreal immediately after he had turned over the works to his fellow officer and sailed for England in October 1819 with most of his detachment of two companies. Almost the only note of irritation that is allowed to creep into Du Vernet's ever-courteous letters is a complaint that Captain Mann took back with him to England twenty-eight good artificers whom Du Vernet had hoped to employ on the works when the project restarted in the spring of 1820. One can detect slight annoyance in another reference in the long report to the fact that he found that part of the stores that he inherited at Grenville 'had been brought up from Coteau du Lac where everything *good* and *bad* [and the emphasis is his] had been handed over from a Store belonging to the Engineer Department.' He found also that the work already completed consisted only of the removal of soil from the rock surface at the upper end of the canal but that no rock excavation had been started. The soil cover was so thin that 'it was with great difficulty a place could be found to fix a Tent upon.' But being the man he was, he got down to his job, studied the whole route of the canal, took levels of the river, and made arrangements for the winter.

Captain Du Vernet would have been told that the first frosts could be expected in October, the ground was usually frozen by early November, and snow arrived either just before or just after the onset of continuing cold weather. He had, therefore, little time for permanent construction work in what was left of the 1819 season between the departure of Captain Mann and the start of winter. After making sure that all was in good order for the five or six months' cessation of work, the whole detachment moved back to Montreal. Some would be garrisoned there; others travelled further to the military establishment at Chambly on the Richelieu River (where some of Du Vernet's winter reports were written). A few references in the old records show that officers and men were engaged in other engineering tasks during winter months. In future years, a small detachment would be left up the Ottawa at Grenville, but merely for caretaking, hauling wood, and similar tasks, the art of winter construction being yet something for the future.

In the spring, reports would be available in Montreal as to conditions on the Ottawa River, since the date of the spring break-up of the ice varied year by year. Once the ice went 'out,' travel up to Grenville by water was again possible although often fraught with danger if the spring flood (possibly as much as five times the average annual flow) came early. Throughout the winter, the river would have a surface of solid ice both above Grenville and below Carillon, but the Long Sault and the other swift water below would always remain 'open.' The water would at times be super-cooled as it came down the rapids, leading to the formation of *frazil* (needle ice). When there was a solid ice cover on the river in the gorge below the foot of the Long Sault, the *frazil* would be swept under this ice sheet. As it accumulated, it would force up the level of the ice cover, on occasion as much as forty feet, the jagged broken sheets of ice forming an awe-inspiring sight for the few travellers who witnessed this natural phenomenon between Grece's Point and Ordnance Island.[14]

Although the site of the Grenville Canal is only about forty-two miles from the centre of Montreal (an hour's drive by automobile today), it must be remembered that in 1818 the journey between the two involved some difficulty. All freight had to be carted from Montreal to Lachine and there loaded into bateaux. These craft would be sailed up Lake St Louis and then up through the rapids at Ste Anne de Bellevue into the Lake of Two Mountains, across which there was a twenty-five-mile sail to the landing at Carillon. The trail thence to Grenville was so rough that the use of oxen for hauling is not surprising. It would not be until the 1820s that the trail was improved sufficiently to be usable by a stage coach service which was then started from St Eustache. The coach usually took three days for the journey, clear indication of what the so-called roads of the time were like. Passenger traffic, therefore, was almost always by canoe, along the route just described but a good deal faster than was possible with laden bateaux. Simple ferries were operated across the Ottawa from Grenville to the mills that grew into the town of Hawkesbury, and from Carillon to Pointe Fortune. (The latter service still operates today, but with a diesel-propelled steel barge that carries automobiles.) Either one of these crossings would be used by the hardy men who walked down to Montreal, the trail on the south shore being shorter and easier than that around the north side of the lake. One well-known early settler (E. Pridham) was reported to have walked to Montreal from Pointe Fortune in two days, taking three for his return journey.

These were the transportation logistics that faced Henry Du Vernet in his challenging task of building the Grenville Canal. He first checked the drop in water level to be provided by the canal and found it slightly less than Captain Mann's report had suggested. He saw that the line of the canal could follow closely that of the river bank. Having no plans to guide him, he decided that he would 'Keep (the canal) on the same level as long as can be conveniently done and to bring the Locks as close together at the lower end as possible; it appears that this can be done nearly in a straight line and that two Locks can be brought together which will save a pair of Gates; in all eight Locks will be required.'[15]

Reference to the accompanying plan of the canal (map 3) will show how well Du Vernet achieved this general objective, developed (it must be recalled) before the line of the canal had been cleared of trees. In his general report of 1820, he explains with his usual caution that 'a good deal of the Ground through which the Canal has to pass is still un-cleared and the Wood very thick [so that] I may on a better knowledge of [it] be induced to alter the direction a little.[16] But his changes were relatively minor. As finally constructed, the Grenville Canal had seven locks and a total length of 5.78 miles, running in almost a straight line, as can be seen from map 3.

The only change that Captain Du Vernet made from the general overall plan Captain Mann had discussed with him was in the location of the entrance to the upper end of the canal from the Ottawa River. In his 1820 report[17] Du Vernet explains that

Captain Mann's first intention was to open the Canal into the River immediately at the Head of the Rapid and throw out a catchwater, but it proved in the autumn that opposite this place to a considerable distance the bed of the River would require to be deepened in order to allow the 4 feet of water when the River is at its lowest ...

[and] In the Spring boats are obliged to be towed entirely round into the Bay before they can with safety proceed up the River. I therefore think that the proper place for the Canal to open into the River will be at the mouth of the small river marked 'A'.

This revised location was, as the map shows, around the head of the rapids and in a small sheltered bay. Ever conscious of costs, Du Vernet says that this change will 'increase the length of the Canal but at the same time save the first level being carried so deep as it otherwise must be by 2 feet 6 inches ... in a very hard rock and when the Government goes to such an expense I think it will be better that the thing should be done properly at once and the Navigation be rendered undoubtedly safe.'[18] This is how the canal was built; when seen in use, prior to 1962, the location that Du Vernet chose for the upstream lock was clearly the correct one, providing an approach (or exit) outside the strong current in the main river.

After all three canals had been opened, the upstream lock was numbered eleven, the downstream lock at Carillon being number 1. Since this was the reverse of the order in which they were built, these early numbers will not be used in this account. The first lock constructed was the guard lock at the upstream end of the Grenville Canal, controlling its entrance for downward bound vessels. The rise and fall it provided varied with the water level in the Ottawa River, which varied as much as seventeen feet between extreme high and low water conditions. It was this lock, because of its narrow width, that was the bottleneck of the entire system until it was rebuilt in the 1870s. Once through the guard lock, vessels had a run of about a mile and a half before reaching the second lock, this stretch being designated in official reports as the 'First Line.' A fall of seven and a half feet in this second lock led to another long level run of about three miles to the third lock, which had a fall of six feet. Slightly less than another mile downstream (and so at the end of the 'Third Line') came the fourth and fifth combined locks with a total drop of sixteen feet. Combining these two locks into one structure, as also the sixth and seventh locks, was one of Du Vernet's brilliant design features. The two pairs of locks were separated by 1,500 feet, the lower pair giving exit to the Ottawa River with a combined fall of sixteen and a half feet. The width of the canal prism was generally about forty-four feet, varying between twenty-three and sixty-four feet; the maximum depth of cutting was twenty-five feet and the minimum eleven feet, depths that allowed a maximum permissible draft for vessels using the canal of about five feet.

This summary description of the finished canal will give an overall picture of the amount of work involved in its construction. All seven locks were built of cut masonry, stone having to be quarried on the south shore of the Ottawa, since that excavated along the canal was unsuitable for hand working. The quarry was located on the Little Rideau River in an area now home to the Hawkesbury Golf Club. This part of the work was not unusual for those days, but the entire excavation of the canal channel was in solid rock. This cut of almost six miles in length had to be excavated by drilling holes into the hard rock with hand-held drill steels, packing these holes with black powder (the only explosive then available), blasting with crude and dangerous blasting caps, and then man-handling the broken rock, hauling it away either in stone boats pulled by oxen or horses or in wheelbarrows for the more fragmented rock. Apart from wheelbarrows (most of which had to be made on the job) the only pieces of equipment available for use were simple hand-operated winches for lifting heavy objects, such as blocks of cut stone for the locks. The amount of arduous manual labour that went into this excavation is difficult to appreciate today, when efficient mechanized construction equipment is available for almost every kind of building operation. But that is the way in which these early canals had to be built.

It is somewhat ironic to find that, although the Grenville Canal was so little known by others than its users and the village of Grenville by others than its residents and their friends, the name Grenville is today well known throughout the world of geology. Not only is it applied to rocks similar to and of the same age as those first studied at Grenville by Logan in the 1840s, now known to cover an immense area in Quebec and to underlie the Adirondack Mountains, but the name has been used also to designate the major geological event of almost 1 billion years ago (the Grenville Event) by which the original sedimentary rocks were metamorphosed (i.e., transformed) to their present crystalline character.

William (later Sir William) Logan was the first director of the Geological Survey of Canada and was appointed as the provincial geologist for Upper and Lower Canada in 1842. Since his travelling was restricted to the waterways of eastern Canada, it was natural that some of his earliest field investigations should have been along the Ottawa River and its tributaries. In the late 1840s Logan studied the bedrock in the Grenville area, finding it to be a mixture of shales, sandstones, and limestones, now metamorphosed into very hard crystalline rocks, the limestone into marble. He gave the name *Grenville* to a 'single band of limestone ... varying in thickness from 60 to 1000 feet,' and the name was later used to delineate all the rocks of the area. Part of the Precambrian Shield, they are among the oldest rocks in the world and are extremely hard and tough. The geology of the sites of the three little Ottawa River canals could not be chosen; what was there had to

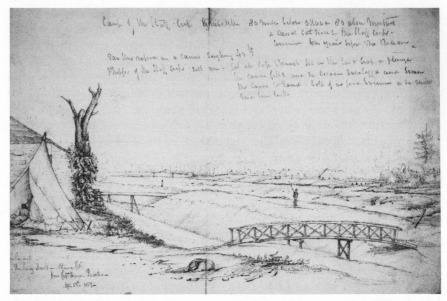

Sketch at the camp of the Royal Staff Corps at Grenville, Lower Canada, in 1827 by William Denny

be accepted. It was unfortunate for the Royal Staff Corps, however, that all the excavation for the canals had to be carried out in such recalcitrant rock. When thought be given to the fact that the volume excavated represented approximately one-sixth that of the Great Pyramid of Egypt (about 400,000 cubic yards) and that all excavation was done by hand, unaided by mechanical equipment, the achievement of the RSC is remarkable indeed.

The normal pattern of operations was to move up from Montreal by bateaux the two companies of the Royal Staff Corps as soon as the Ottawa River was 'open.' At Grenville, the camp would have to be re-established and a start made at engaging men to do most of the labouring. This work consisted of clearing the forest from along the route of the canal; then removing the two or three feet of soil cover over the rock with shovels and wheelbarrows; and finally the arduous, tedious and demanding work of hand-drilling the rock, blasting, and then removing the blasted rock from the slowly developing canal cutting. Only in 1824 was the excavation work at the site of the first lock sufficiently advanced for a start to be made on the masonry work of the lock. Throughout the summer working season, charcoal would have to be either made or purchased for use in the blacksmiths' shops, always busy in sharpening the drill steels. Later, attempts would be

The Ottawa River above Grenville, looking upstream with the head of the rapids on the far left, as sketched at the clearing and camp of the Royal Staff Corps, about 1825 by Colonel J.P. Cockburn.

made to burn the limestone in order to procure lime; eventually, extensive lime kilns were constructed, remains of which lasted into this century. The better trees would have to be felled, trimmed, and sawn to provide dimensioned timbers for the lock gates and other purposes. All ironwork for the locks had to be brought from Montreal, as did all stores, tools, and food, since there were only limited supplies available locally, other than some wild game that might have been hunted in the forests around and fish caught in the river. Essentially, almost all food for the full complement of men had to be brought from Montreal. One would not expect to find many problems in such simple operations other than logistics, but that is the view from today; Du Vernet had to deal with a great deal more.

4

The Grenville Canal: 1820–7

'The expense of transporting the Detachment backwards and forward being great, it would be desirable to get the work done as soon as possible but by the employment of many workmen the expense will be increased, as an additional number of tools must be provided.'[1] This was Du Vernet's first identified problem – that since the Staff Corps had no bateaux of its own, it had to rely on hiring them from rivermen for all movements of men and supplies, since there were yet no regular (or regulated) shipping services on the Ottawa. Far more serious was the fact that, in order to keep the actual expenditures on the canal to what had been authorized (apart from the pay and allowances to the men of the corps which came from the Army Extraordinaries) the annual cash outlay must not exceed £8,000. This severe limitation on annual outlays goes far to explain the relatively slow progress made on the works until after 1827. Du Vernet's success in controlling his expenditures will be seen when the cost of building the canal is considered, but the experience must have been a frustrating one, as he daily saw the amount of work still to be done before the canal would be usable.

His detachment consisted of about 100 officers and men of the Royal Staff Corps. These numbers he found

too small to be able to contribute much towards the excavation, supposing the whole of the 94 men (privates) to be in good health the utmost we could furnish would be 20 miners, 10 overseers of Civilians, 1 Sergeant and 6 [men] with the oxen to carry backwards and forward the tools to be repaired and powder for the miners and the rest being artificers employed at their several trades, principally in repairing and making tools. A Guard has also to be furnished which takes 8 men. There are 9 officers Servants [?] Waiter and Hospital orderly, 2 Cooks and a Sergeant and Private for issuing the Stores and Provision; out of the total there might be as many

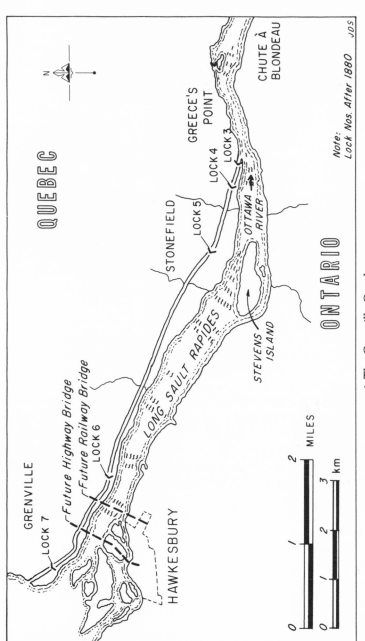

4 The Grenville Canal

as 8 deducted for Sick and Prisoners. When the Companies arrived in this Country they were complete but by casualties we now want 2 Sergeants and 26 Privates and having learnt that the Corps has been lately recruited to the full establishment it would be desirable that the Detachment should be completed again in the Spring (of 1821) for I am afraid we shall every summer lose a number by Desertion; amongst those who have gone have been some of our best workmen.

It was small wonder that he concluded his report for the governor by saying that 'I am particularly desirous of knowing if he approves of what I have proposed should be done, or at all events of receiving some positive Instructions for my guidance.'

There were problems even with materials. He had to report that 'Very little of the Stone we have found in the Canal is fit for building and that we have found capable of burning into Lime is but an indifferent quality after burning ... [adding that] I had only an opportunity of Trial a few days before I left Grenville (in late 1820); we perhaps may be ultimately more successful.' And again: 'In general the Trees are unsound, and are only fit for firewood but in clearing we found a few which answer for the repair of the Tools but no valuable Timber; indeed the soil is too shallow to admit of any.' Stores and records of materials in store were to be one of the Commanding Officer's most annoying problems. Even the start was inauspicious since the stores he took over on assuming command 'were in charge of Lieut. Daniel Frazer who, being on half pay, was appointed to act as Clerk of the Works and shortly after was put again on full pay of the Corps and returned to England with the Detachment he belonged to, which was ordered off in such haste that there was no opportunity of having the Stores inspected.'

Of all the problems, however, dealing with irate land owners was to prove the most difficult and time-consuming. When it is recalled that practically all the land occupied by the canal was virgin forest when construction started, and that (apart only from Archibald's MacMillan's small clearings at Grenville) no clearing had been done at all, even though some of the lots had been granted to retired officers of the army, the wonder is that land claims were a problem at all. For the first time, however, and certainly not for the last, as soon as it was found that 'The government' was using private land for construction purposes it immediately became, in the eyes of its owners, just about the most valuable land in the whole of Lower Canada. Captain Du Vernet was ready to meet this problem too.

In order to prevent any misunderstanding with the Proprietors of the Land through which the Canal passes, I think it would be advisable to have the quantity required valued before we go on any further. The 9th lot in the front range of Grenville belongs to Mr McMillan who cleared it last year [1819]; No. 8 is a Crown Reserve leased by him upon which we have set up our Buildings and No. 7 on which his House stands is but an indifferent pasture for which he expects *great* compensation; No. 6 also belongs to him, but what we have cut through is a Rocky Ridge and a Swamp in a Ravine, full of Trees and Granite Rocks and unfit for cultivation. The next 4 Lots belong to Colonel Harris who does not appear to have fulfilled the engagement under which the grants of Lands are given and for No. 1 there is a doubt if it is still a crown reserve or was by an after arrangement given to Colonel Harris. In the Front Range of Chatham there are no crown reserves and several lots are in a state of cultivation.

It may be recalled that the report from which the preceding extracts have been quoted was made at the end of the first full working season (1820). Clearing along the route of the canal had been completed by then as far as these cultivated lands in the Front of Chatham. Some drainage of swamps had been started and many of the granite boulders removed. Rock excavation had begun, Du Vernet's figures showing that this process was costing one shilling and six pence per cubic yard. The locations of the first lock and the second had been selected on the ground but excavation was not yet far enough advanced for masonry work to commence. Although he had to direct the work under severe limitations, a new appointment gave Du Vernet great encouragement in mid-summer. A new governor and commander-in-chief took up his office at Quebec in 19 June 1820: the ninth Earl of Dalhousie, a distinguished Scottish nobleman, who, despite later political difficulties in Canada, went on to become the commander-in-chief in India. Within two months of his arrival, he had visited the Grenville Canal works, even though doing so involved a canoe journey up from Ste Anne de Bellevue, if not from Lachine. This was the first of what were to be regular annual visits until the governor's return to England for about one year's leave, between June 1824 and September 1825. Thereafter he was helpful to Lieutenant-Colonel John By as well in regard to the Rideau Canal works. His participation with this officer in the critical selection of the site for the entrance to the canal from the Ottawa River made him one of the founders of the city of Ottawa.

The small number of men under Captain Du Vernet's command is surprising today. Companies of the Royal Staff Corps, however, as was the general practice at the time, consisted of fifty rank and file with two sergeants, one bugler, one captain, and two lieutenants.[2] Accordingly, in

September 1819 there were 192 men at Grenville, plus the officers of the four companies. After Captain Mann's departure, the total fell to 116 rank and file. This represented the men of two companies plus seven sergeants and two buglers, with five men off sick. This total slowly declined to eighty-five in August 1822 when reinforcements arrived from England, bringing the complement up to 144. Captain William Dumaresq, in command of the second company and junior to Captain Du Vernet, returned with twenty-five men to England very shortly thereafter, and the total strength became 119. By the end of 1826 this number had fallen to ninety-four, most of the losses being due to desertions, a few to discharges because of illness, and one or two to honorable discharges at the end of service.

The two senior officers were assisted by four lieutenants – Henry Piers, George Longmore, Edward Boyd, and Thomas Harris. The first two returned to England with Captain Du Vernet when he went on leave on 15 November 1824. Ill health forced Lieutenant Boyd to take a good deal of sick leave, but he did serve at Grenville, intermittently, until October 1826. Lieutenant Harris died while on duty on the Grenville works. Captain William Dumaresq does not appear in any of the canal records still available, but army records show that he resigned his commission in March 1829 and later settled in New South Wales, where he became a somewhat controversial figure, owing to the fact that his brother-in-law was the new governor. Lieutenant Piers was promoted to major in the Staff Corps, retiring on half-pay in 1831; Lieutenant Longmore also became a major, retiring on half-pay one year later. Lieutenant Boyd recovered from the illnesses that had plagued him in Canada and retired on half-pay in 1829; he rejoined the army in 1842, serving until 1850 in the 29th Foot Regiment, with a final rank, granted after final retirement, of Brevet Lieutenant-Colonel. This first small group of officers must have been a congenial group of companions, their arduous living conditions and isolated work site probably assisting in developing the esprit de corps that is so evident in references in letters from the commanding officer, Henry Du Vernet.

Captain Du Vernet was clearly an outstanding officer. As one reads his ever-courteous letters, gracious even when he was greatly provoked, one wishes that more was known about him as a man, in addition to what the official records tell of him as an officer and a gentleman. He was born on 4 April 1787, the son of Colonel Abraham Du Vernet, RA. The available records show that he was commissioned as an ensign in the Royal Staff Corps on 22 December 1803 directly from civil life; thus he did not attend the Royal Military College as a cadet. Until going on half-pay as a lieutenant-colonel on 1 July 1834, he had the longest record of service (thirty years) of any officer in the short history of the Royal Staff Corps. Captain Frederick Mann is the 'runner-up' with a record of over twenty-seven years in the corps. Du Vernet served in the Mediterranean and later in the Peninsular War, taking part in the retreat from Corunna with Sir John Moore. Apart from one long period of leave, he served as commanding officer of the Ottawa River canal works from the start in 1819 until their completion at the end of the 1833 working season, when he returned to England. Placed on half-pay on 1 July 1834, he was advanced to a full colonelcy on 23 November 1841, but his name does not appear in the army Lists for 1842. He had retired to Scotland and occupied the manor house of Bredisholm southeast of Glasgow, but at the same time he had changed his name to Henry Abraham Du Vernet Grosset Muirhead and so died, on 16 December 1843 at Bredisholm; it is believed that he was buried at Parson's Green, Fulham.[3]

His wife is referred to in the account left by one early traveller up the Ottawa as a 'Sicilian lady,' but she was actually Martha Maria Iqnalin, daughter of Admiral Van Kemper of the 'Dutch service.' She clearly spent some time in the camp at Grenville. There are several brief references in early records to the hospitality extended to travellers by the Du Vernets at Grenville, one even mentioning musical entertainment, but so briefly as to be tantalizing. Henry Du Vernet himself must have travelled up the Ottawa, at least as far as the Chaudière (the site of Ottawa today), since the Public Archives of Canada possesses one tempera painting of his signed 31 [?] June 1823. The title, engraved on a brass plate on the back of the frame, is 'A View of the Mill and Tavern of Philemon Wright at the Chaudière Falls, on the Ottawa River, Lower Canada' (the underlining is on the plate). One of the few printed references to this painting says that it is one of 'Scenes on the Ottawa River', the use of the plural suggesting that it is one of a series, but no others have yet been traced. This one view is a quite delightful rendering which has been useful in delineating buildings of what was to become the city of Hull, adjacent (on the north bank of the Ottawa) to what is now Canada's capital city of Ottawa (on the south bank), first named Bytown (about 1827) after its establishment around the construction camp of the Royal Engineers building the Rideau Canal.

Members of the Du Vernet family, although not direct descendants of the commanding officer, have continued to serve Canada with distinction until the present day in a variety of callings, including the professions, one having been an archbishop in the Anglican Church of Canada. The 'Canadian Du Vernets' are descendants of Major Frederick Du Vernet, a brother of Henry and also an officer in the Royal Staff Corps, who died in 1833 while

Mill and tavern of Philemon Wright at the Chaudière Falls, 1827, a reproduction of the only known painting by Henry Du Vernet, now in the Public Achives of Canada

returning from Ceylon. He had been stationed at Saint John, New Brunswick and while there had married Eliza Jane Parker, sister of the noted Judge Parker; when widowed, she continued to live in Saint John, where she raised her children. These family details are recorded in a history of the Du Vernet family, privately prepared by Miss Adela Du Vernet of Greenville, South Carolina, which was kindly made available to the writer by Mrs Gwen Du Vernet of Ottawa, her son, and daughter. It is a fascinating document which describes the distinguished background of Henry Abraham Du Vernet, the commanding officer for the building of the Ottawa River canals, his work at Grenville being one of the few gaps in this family record. A brief summary is all that can be given here, but the outstanding character of Henry A. Du Vernet appears to warrant this.[4]

The Du Vernet family originated in France, their roots having been traced as far back as the year 1150. One of the two branches into which the family divided at the time of the Reformation remained in France; the second (Protestant) branch moved to the Low Countries following the Edict of Nantes (1685), and some members were received at the court of William and Mary.

Some of them followed, or accompanied, William to England (1688) and continued to enjoy royal favour, since Colonel Abraham Du Vernet (Henry's father), who was born in 1760, received a gift from Queen Charlotte (wife of King George II) and entertained Prince William in 1788 while on duty with the Royal Artillery in Halifax, Nova Scotia. Prince William then agreed to be the godfather of Abraham's second child, William, who was born in Halifax. Henry was then just over one year old, and so one wonders if he, too, was in Halifax.

Abraham had ten children by his wife, originally a resident of Kent, Miss Miriam Groll. When she inherited the estate of Bredisholm, near Glasgow, in 1817, she assumed the title Lady Miriam Grosset Muirhead. Her distinguished Scottish family had had no male children born into it for many years; it had become a tradition in the family that the oldest daughter and her husband would assume the family name on inheriting (when Henry, in turn, fell heir to the estate after the death of his mother in 1842, he too changed his name). His father was accidentally killed on 23 October 1806 after a fall from a two-wheeled cart in which he was riding. His widow, left with ten children, the oldest (Henry) nineteen, the youngest (John) just over one year old, was helped by Prince William who arranged for the sons to get commissions in the army or navy. This patronage probably explains why Henry had been commissioned directly as an ensign. Three of the brothers became colonels, one (Frederick) a major, and one served briefly in the Royal Navy.

Henry Du Vernet had won his promotion to lieutenant before his father's premature death. It was as a captain of a company in the Royal Staff Corps that he came out to Grenville in 1819. His first child, Henry Robert, was then just over one year old; his second child, Gertrude, was born in 1821 while he was still at Grenville; and the third child, George Grenville, is known to have been born also in Canada, his name suggesting that his mother was then living at Grenville in the small camp of the Royal Staff Corps. In the family tradition, the elder son, Henry Robert, had two daughters, the elder assuming the family name even when she married a Stuart. Her daughter, in turn, did the same. Gertrude also married and had four daughters, but also one son (her second child). Henry's third child, George Grenville Du Vernet, went on duty to Australia, liked the country, and obtained permission to settle there, where his descendants today form the 'Australian Du Vernets.' Beyond this, the records are silent about Henry Abraham, both the family history and the official letters and reports still available in the Public Archives of Canada. We do not know, therefore, how long a period Mrs Du Vernet spent with her husband at Grenville, although there is no doubt that she spent some time there and bore at least one of her children while in Canada, if not two. The fact that his daughter Gertrude was appointed one of the executors of her father's will suggests that Mrs Du Vernet had died before her husband, but even this fact is not known with certainty. If only Henry's personal records and diary could be found, these questions would be answered, but in their absence, we must return to what the official records do tell about the building of the canals, starting with two letters he wrote in November 1818, shortly after Captain Mann had left for England with his detachment.

Du Vernet stayed at Grenville until the beginning of November; one naturally wonders how much he had been told about the severity of the Canadian winter. He indicates, in a letter of 6 November 1819,[5] that he has left the apothecary surgeon at Grenville with a small detachment in charge of Ensign Geddes, adding that it is necessary to have a medical man there and 'the Surgeon at the headquarters of the Corps has little or nothing to do.' On the 21 November he wrote again to the military secretary to the governor, from Montreal, asking that lodging allowance be granted for his officers and noting that the barrack master in Montreal refused to issue to him any stoves for their use, since his authority extended only to the issue of stores to the 37th Regiment.[6] This was a mild introduction to the difficulties with stores with which he had to deal throughout his stay in Canada.

Stores were awkward enough; horses and their forage presented a far more complex administrative problem. Another letter went to the military secretary (Major Bowles) on 8 December very courteously questioning the decision of the lords commissioners of His Majesty's Treasury not to grant a supply of forage for one horse for each officer and two for himself 'as Commanding and having direction of the works on the Ottawa River.'[7] Du Vernet patiently explains that 'The Canal which was begun in late summer independent of the other projected works will take a long time to complete and is situated in a remote and uncleared part of the Country where the Detachment is encamped in the woods and exposed to many privations and inconveniences'; he proceeds to outline the vital need for the officers to be mobile so as to be able to visit all parts of the works.

This very reasonable request must have been reconsidered, since no reminder appears in the records. The referral of so detailed a matter for approval from Canada to the Treasury Board in London was typical of the centralized control still exercised over many such minor matters, control that must have been frustrating to commanders in the field. Even getting rid of horses was a problem. Captain Francis Read (temporarily in command in 1825 when Du Vernet had gone on leave) had to ask the military secretary for permission to sell one of the horses at Grenville, since it was useless 'and would not draw an empty cart,' but the sale would have to be in Montreal, because nobody could be found in Grenville who would purchase the animal. Another of the horses was injured in the winter of 1827. The military secretary had appointed a board of review to report on the situation, but Captain William King (now the commanding officer in 1825) had to advise that the horse had died before the board was able to meet, so might he please have authority to purchase another in its place?

These details might be thought to have no place in a record such as this but, whereas on a modern construction project they would be dealt with and settled in a few minutes, on the Grenville Canal works, three days' distance even from Montreal, they loomed large. This is the more understandable when the strict budget under which Du Vernet had to work is considered, limiting the number of men he could employ and so the rate at which work could proceed. At the end of the first full working season (1820), for example, he had to report that 'the ground is opened up for about 2,700 yards but has only partially been carried to the depth intended in consequence of the great difficulty there is of excavating the Rock, which is in general found at two or three feet from the surface consisting of a sort of Slate mixed with Limestone.'[8] On the basis of the experience of this first season, he prepared a revised estimate of cost for the completed canal. This amounted to £26,538-10-0. Hauling of granite boulders and tree stumps with oxen is one of the unusual items. Oxen were available for clearing land, and Du Vernet's estimated cost was £3 per acre.

That modest statement about the difficulty of excavating the hard rock concealed a long summer of arduous physical labour on the part of the men drilling, holding drill steels, hauling and sharpening them, and removing the blasted rock from the canal. Accidents inevitably took place, the two main causes throughout the works being improper blasting procedures and falls from scaffolds when the masonry work at the locks was under way. A small hospital was established at Grenville; a list of stores requirements for it included items such as pewter chamber pots, flannel gowns and night caps, as well as normal bedding and kitchen equipment, with three spitting cups as another unusual item.[9] David Jearrard was the assistant surgeon to the Royal Staff Corps in Canada from 1815 to 1819 and again from 1823 to 1828; he himself was in ill health and had to take sick leave, finally returning to England in 1828 only to die in January 1829. His work was taken over by Hospital Assistant Primrose, Jearrard himself having been promoted to his surgeon's rank from that of hospital mate. The sum of sixpence per man per month was collected from the men on the job to pay for medicines, an interesting example of early health insurance. But the facilities must have been simple in the extreme, since serious cases were sent to main hospitals in Montreal or Quebec.

One of the first serious cases to be reported was that of James Cardy, a civilian miner who blew himself up on the work

and is still in Hospital here having lost both Eyes and got his scule (sic) fractured, the particulars of which I have mentioned to His Excellencey when here and that he is sufficiently recovered to be removed. This unfortunate young man is only 21 years of age, is a native of Ballantay County of Antrim Ireland, came to this country about two years ago (with his brother who is now in the United States) ... and he has no other relation in this country; he therefore wishes in his present helpless state to be sent home to his Parents. I think his Excellency said something about his being placed in one of the Public Hospitals at Montreal but the circumstance of his being a Protestant may probably be an objection to his being received at a Catholic Institution and I believe there are none other. He has received nothing since he met with the accident but a Ration per day which has been given to the Hospital to defray the Expenses of his nourishment.[10]

Cardy was moved to the hospital of the 37th Regiment in Quebec, where he died on 7 March 1822; a statement of his belongings was sent to Captain Du Vernet by Sergeant D. Chisholm of the 37th. It is a pathetic little list including merely the clothes in which he had come to Quebec with two extra shirts, one extra pair of stockings, and one black handkerchief. His mother in the village of Macra in Cashel County, Ireland, was advised. As the work progressed, Du Vernet took it upon himself to supply all injured men with rations and appealed for permission for all injured men 'to receive pay while they remain under the Surgeon's hand and are unable to work.'[11] Crude though these arrangements may now seem, they indicate the continuing concern that the commanding officer had for all the men working under him, whether in the Staff Corps or not. He had even persuaded the governor to apply for a pension for James Cardy, even though he was a civilian. On 7 February 1822 the Treasury advised Lord Dalhousie that it would be pleased to grant a pension to Cardy of 1s 6d per day – but it was too late.[12]

Slowly and painstakingly the work proceeded. On 17 October 1821 Captain Du Vernet reported directly to Lord Dalhousie on the progress during the 1821 season, advising him that all civilian workmen had by that date been discharged. He was still at Grenville, 'cleaning up details,' having also taken the first steps to survey the site for a village, the beginnings of the Grenville of today.[13] After he left, a few 'wheelers' (wheelwrights) of the detachment remained to complete their work, but they reached Montreal on 20 January 1822, leaving behind just one sergeant and four privates at Grenville 'to take care of the Stores and 2 Public Horses. The Horses are at present employed in bringing home forage for the ensuing summer and it can now be procured with less difficulty and at less than half the price it could in the Spring.'[14]

There was an unusually high spring flood on the Ottawa River in the spring of 1822, but by 12 June the water level had fallen, so that work could begin. This still consisted of the laborious excavation, working downstream from the Grenville end. Du Vernet had 200 men already at work this early in June 'and more were arriving every day.'[15] This comment might suggest that there was some movement of settlers up the Ottawa but such activity was as yet very limited. The little camp still had to be generally self-sufficient for supplies other than the simplest of building materials. Food was plain but presumably adequate, since there are few references in the records to any complaints. Some was obtained locally, but a typical list of provisions sent up from Montreal during 1822 included items such as bread (surprisingly), flour, biscuits, beef, pork, salt beef, and rum (1,534 gallons of which were sent up as the season's supply at a price of one shilling sixpence per gallon).[16]

Du Vernet's progress report for the 1823 working season was written at Chambly, not Montreal, on 16 November. He had to record a 'very wet working season.'[17] Indicative of the scope of the work was the employment of eight yoke of oxen for eighty-nine days, engaged in clearing the land and hauling; sixty-seven miners for 102 days; and no less than 412 labourers also for 102 days, the number of days worked showing how short the working season had been. A great quantity of charcoal had been used, but this, with a supply of lime, had been made on crown lands. His men had made 200 new wheelbarrows. Captain Du Vernet reports also that he had sent specimens of local stone, such as a white-specked marble which he had found three miles up the Ottawa from Grenville. Presumably he had been searching for suitable stone for the masonry of the locks, since the rock being excavated was too hard for working. He had made an agreement with the landowners along the lower section of the canal, in the Front of Chatham, to fell the trees on their property, clear the site of stumps, and erect a log fence on both sides of the canal route, all for $12 an acre. All had agreed, with the exception of a Mr Grece, but his neighbours had undertaken to clear his property for him. Despite the increased activity, total expenditure had been kept to just over £7,000.

Captain Du Vernet spent the winter of 1822-3 at Chambly whence he wrote to the military secretary on 21 April to say that he was getting ready to go up again to Grenville and would travel to Montreal, with his baggage, 'by the Chambly Steamboat.'[18] This is an indication of the rapidity with which steamboat travel had started in Lower Canada. Chambly is located on the Richelieu River which joins the St Lawrence at Sorel, the journey from Chambly to Montreal being about 100 miles by this route. Examination of map 1 will show that the land route between the two points is much shorter. It is not, surprising, therefore, to find that Canada's first railroad was built to effect this 'portage'; the little line from La Prairie (opposite Montreal) to St John's (now St Jean, twelve miles upriver from Chambly) was opened in July 1836. Du Vernet, however, must have been glad to avail himself of even a simple steamboat for his journey to Montreal. The first steamboat on the Ottawa above Grenville had been launched in 1822, a very simple craft indeed, but it marked the beginning of continuous steamship service on the lower Ottawa for the next century. Records are unclear as to when the corresponding first steam-powered vessel appeared on the Lake of Two Mountains, but it is almost certain that it was in either 1822 or 1823. The service it provided would slightly reduce the time required to come up from Montreal to Carillon, but for passenger travel the canoe continued to dominate for several years more. By either the new steamboat, bateau, or canoe, Captain Du Vernet continued his journey from Montreal up to his camp at Grenville, where he was well settled again by 14 June, when he was forced to send one of his regular complaints about stores to the military secretary.

During the 1823 season, land problems were to be an even more difficult problem. We have already seen the steps that Du Vernet took in his first working season to have valued the lands to be affected by the canal. Archibald McMillan, the original settler at Grenville, had written to the governor as early as 16 April 1821 claiming damages done to his land. He had forgotten, however, that in an exchange of letters in August 1819 he had agreed with Captain Mann that the canal works could proceed through his land with his permission. In September 1821 Du Vernet was able to advise the military secretary that McMillan wanted full value for swampy land and, a little later, that McMillan was farming a large area on which the proposed village was to be started to which he had no legal right. The issue was resolved the next spring when, before the Court of King's Bench in Montreal, McMillan's claims were dismissed with costs against him, since the land for which he was claiming damages was a crown reserve. In some of the grants of land along the Front of Chatham, specific allowance was made for a reservation of land needed for the canal, such as the grant made to

Colonel Taylor. There was, therefore, no trouble with most of the settlers, one of them (Donald Cameron) even writing to say that he is 'perfectly willing to take what His Excellency has so liberally offered.'[19] But Mr McMillan and Mr Grece more than outweighed their more reasonable neighbours.

This dissension can, perhaps, best be shown by the record we have of the governor's regular visit to the canal works in September 1823, when the woods around the little camp clearing would be at their most beautiful. When 'Camped at the Head of the Canal' on 17 September, Lord Dalhousie set down in his own hand simple instructions for the guidance of whoever might be appointed by him to assess the claims that had been made. According to the governor:

Mr Donald Cameron and others who have petitioned for compensation for damages done by the works of the Canal are informed that I am entirely disposed to grant that compensation which is justly due to them all individually when that shall be properly ascertained. But while I am ready to do them justice, it is also my duty to take care that the interest and the rights of the King and the public are not neglected. It is my intention to send up a person properly qualified to receive about 1st October all the claims that individuals have to present on the matter and who will judge upon the spot the fairness and propriety of each claim separately.[20]

The governor was in Montreal five days later, having arranged for Mr Findlay, JP, of Lachine to proceed up to Grenville for the claim evaluation. He records in more detail his experiences at Grenville and has this to say:

Mr McMillan and Mr Grece have both conducted themselves with so much violence, and the latter particularly with such outrageous insolence, that I should feel myself justified in refusing them the smallest compensation or relief without an Award at Law but there are others who have acted with that respect and moderation in their application to H.M. Government, that entitle them to my better opinion and to that liberality with which H.M. Government always acts, and to these I am anxious to listen accordingly ... Although I think McMillan and Grece unreasonable yet I will not follow their example in conduct. I will do to them as I do to others there, if they present their claims; if they do not, they must proceed at Law for I will not renew to them any such opportunity as this.[21]

These are events of long ago so that further detail would be out of place. The governor's feelings give an indication of what Du Vernet had to put up with from these men. The following extract from Mr Findlay's report dated 20 October 1824 will similarly demonstrate the unreasonableness of some of the claims. With specific reference to Grece's land, he says 'for the rocks are so numerous as merely to admit of interstices, for the trees to grow up between them. As a proof that the Proprietors are well paid at £2 per acre for clearing and fencing, there are now Canadians clearing the land near Alexander Cameron's for the sake of remuneration of the Potash they make from the burning of the Timber on it.'[22] But even such an expert view did nothing to change the minds of Mr McMillan and Mr Grece, as later events were to prove. In view of the attitude he took, it is somewhat surprising to find that Mr Grece had settled along the line of the canal only in 1820, the year after work had started. Du Vernet was forced to complain again about his behaviour (to the governor's military secretary) in July 1824, having found him 'drunk and abrasive,' but he was determined to 'bring him to his senses.'[23]

More pleasant diversions from the continuing supervision of the work seem to have been available. When the Earl of Dalhousie visited the works in September 1823, he mentioned to Du Vernet his intention of sending an officer of the detachment 'to New York for the purpose of copying certain plans which are in the possession of the American Government,' when the work at Grenville was suspended for the winter. In November Du Vernet wrote to say that Lieutenant Piers was 'desirous of the employment' and as a good draftsman he was suitable for the duty, but his services were needed for making up the financial accounts for the year. Captain Read would carry out the assignment, if so ordered, but beyond this, the records fail us and nothing more has been found about this interesting suggestion.[24] As an indication of the fine type of young man whom Du Vernet had under his command, a letter that Ensign Frederick H. Robe sent directly to the governor, from 'Grenville Camp' on 13 May 1824 is worth mentioning.[25] Elegantly written and well composed, it asks the governor to use his influence with the authorities to obtain for the writer a position on the expedition of Captain John Franklin which was planned for 1825. This was the second expedition made by way of the Ottawa waterway and the water route to the Arctic, but Robe was not included in the complement; he was promoted to the rank of lieutenant in April 1825, transferring to the 84th Foot Regiment in 1827.

Progress on the works proceeded at a slow, steady pace. By the start of the 1824 working season, Du Vernet was able to report that 4,500 square feet of good quality stone was already 'worked' and so was ready for setting in the first lock.[26] In preparation for this major step forward, he asked for one 'barrel of Parker's Roman Cement, advertised for sale in Quebec by James White; that for the Lachine Canal cost 20/5d for a 5-bushel barrel.'[27]

At the end of the season artificers were fabricating cranes and lock gates, presumably from timber cut from the forests around, and 12,000 square feet of finished stone were ready for use.[28] Low water in the river had slowed the work, but clearly good progress had been made, when he had to dismiss all civilian workmen 'perceiving that I had somewhat exceeded the annual sum of £8,000 allowed to be expended.'[29] This was the only year in which he 'overspent,' total cost for the year being £8,770-2-8¾.

If a true picture of the progress of the work is to be given, it is necessary to refer again to the problem of stores and the necessary accounting for them, an issue that used up more paper in exchanges of letters than any other feature of the project. In June 1823, for example, Du Vernet had to write a four-page letter in answer to a request from the deputy commissary general of accounts at Quebec.[30] In response, the commanding officer had set up a board of survey, but he had to add that 'it is impossible for me to account for everything that has been expended, in the manner directed, as sufficient memorandums have not been kept for that purpose ... [adding plaintively that] ... Every possible care has been taken of the Public property I have charge of.'[31] His frustrations are indicated by the fact that he had talked privately to the governor at his summer residence at Sorel about the stores problem. He informed the commanding Royal Engineer about this, adding that he could not 'take an oath on it,' as he thought parliament required.[32] He even had to sign receipts for the cost of laundry, there being one statement in the surviving records for the washing of 100 bed cases at fourpence each and seventy-two bolster cases at one penny each by Ann Bird. The Board of Survey completed its report on 27 October 1823, the report bearing the signatures of the four members headed by Captain Read (who was 'President of the Board'); it listed a considerable number of items that were unserviceable and unfit for use. Typical were some of the tents that had been supplied and had deteriorated in storage.[33] Du Vernet's concern for the welfare of his men is clearly shown by the forceful complaint that he lodged about this poor supply service. Eventually, permission was granted for unfit stores to be sold, which was done at a public auction held in Grenville on 18 June 1824.

It would be interesting to continue the 'stores story'; when examining the old records, one can sympathize so readily with the superintending engineer in his repeated requests for release from responsibility for stores. In March 1824, for example, he wrote to Colonel Durnford (the commanding Royal Engineer in Canada) that 'I wish to have nothing further to do with the Stores in the Shape of a Public Accountant,' but as commanding officer he could not escape from this administrative worry.[34] As the working season of 1824 ended, he had another source of concern. It had been arranged that, with his two companies, he would return to England at the close of the summer's work. He wrote to the military secretary on 15 October 1824 expressing his keen disappointment at not having heard of the arrival of the vessel that was to transport them to England but asking that the necessary bateaux be sent up to Grenville to convey the two companies down to Montreal.[35] The vessel did arrive and sailed from Quebec City in November. Stores bothered Du Vernet right to the end of his stay; he wrote to the military secretary on 12 November, on the point of embarking for the voyage home, expressing his concern about the stores but assuming that Captain Read would be appointed superintendent of the works and that, accordingly, the stores problem would henceforth be his.[36] In this assumption he was correct, but apparently Captain Read shared his views, since he wrote, also to the military secretary, only ten days later to say that he did not wish to be a 'Public Accountant' and that the clerk of works should be responsible for all stores matters.[37]

Captain Read had arrived from England with one company of men in August 1822, having sailed from Deptford on 10 June aboard the transport *Brunswick*. Some of the detachment came on the *Fanny*. It was upon his arrival that Captain Dumaresq and his company left to return to England, so that from August 1822 until Du Vernet's departure in November 1824 the strength of the Royal Staff Corps on the works was about 100. It then dropped to about fifty and remained around this figure until the arrival in June 1825 of Captain King with a new company which had crossed in the transport *Numa* and landed as usual at Quebec.[38] Captain Read was clearly determined to do the best he could with his limited manpower. Early in January 1825 he wrote to the military secretary asking if the requisition for timber could be filled as soon as possible, so that the wood would be well seasoned when required for use, suggesting also that the coal on order should be sent up 'during the sleighing season' and asking permission to purchase two horses, since the works were now so extended in area.[39] He also had to ask for authority to have a small office at Grenville for a 'Drawing Room' since he had had to use his 'private dwelling' for the preparation of drawings and the storage of public papers.[40] A useful reminder of the primitive conditions in which the men of the Royal Staff Corps were working was a further request for a spirit level and theodolite which could be obtained only in England.[41] These instruments were ordered but arrived only late in the 1825 season, with consequent delays to the work.[42] And in February Read asked, very politely, if he could have the same latitude as Du Vernet in making decisions on the spot, in the public interest.[43]

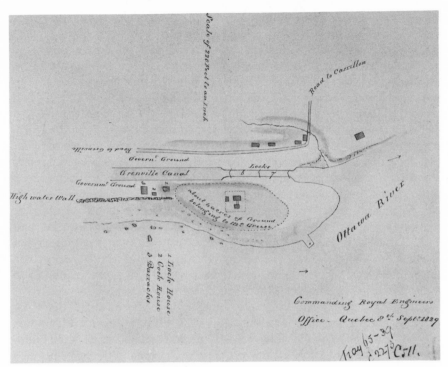

Lay-out of the works at the lower entrance to the original Grenville Canal, typical of the excellent drafting of the Royal Staff Corps, 8 September 1829

In his letters Captain Read makes the first mention of the problem of bootlegged liquor, writing as early as 25 November (as usual to the military secretary) about Daniel De Hertel, who, although a magistrate, had been convicted and fined for retailing wine on Crown Reserve No. 8 at Grenville.[44] De Hertel had opened a store adjacent to the works, and Read had heard that he had applied for a liquor licence which he trusts will not be granted. Read was later called upon to answer a request that De Hertel had sent to the governor and in the course of his reply observes that 'when our Canteen has been short (during working hours) men have been detected quitting their work and purchasing spirits at Mr De Hertel's, as also men from the Hospital.[45] Upon his arrival at Grenville, however, Captain Read found that the De Hertel store had been taken over by a Mr Morris, who wrote very politely, advising that he proposed to sell 'dry goods, Crockery, Hardware, Groceries, Spirits and Wines, the latter to be sold without allowing any to be drunk in the said House.'[46] The problem was to prove a recurrent one even on this very early construction project.

Captain Read had reported that the ice was still on the Lake of Two Mountains in mid-April 1825 but that he hoped to start his journey up to the works on Monday 2 May.[47] Later, he advised that he was not able to start until 7 May, arriving at Grenville on the evening of the 10th.[48] He had set to work some good masons whom he had brought up so as to avoid losing them, but he did not know what to do about stores, since the storekeeper and clerk of works appointed by the governor had not yet arrived. Even before leaving Montreal, he had written complaining very politely about the letter books issued by the Ordnance Department, asking if he could return those 'of very inconvenient size' and purchase some 'such as will meet my purpose.'[49] On the job, he had to appeal for some biscuits to be sent up, since the bread supplied under contract could not be eaten, and 'flour is useless to those who have not the means to bake it,' a comment that probably indicated their shortage of manpower.[50] On 31 May he was driven to complain that 'as yet not one article has arrived which was contained in the approved requisition of 19th April last.[51] Lest it be thought that complaints about the Commissary Department were not justified, let it be recorded that during this month of May 1825, Deputy Assistant Commissary General Green was in residence at Grenville and had some small buildings. Read asked if he could use some of them to expedite the work but was told that Green had no authority to permit this.[52] Read accordingly had to write an official request to the governor's military secretary to Quebec City. He arranged for a board of survey, headed by Lieutenant Boyd, appointed to report on the stores he had taken over. Its report, in itself a fascinating list, was completed by the end of May, but 'these papers were only received by the Military Secretary on 22nd September 1825 having, it would appear, been missent to England and returned via Halifax by the August Packet.'[53]

The arrival of Captain King and his company in mid-July must have been a welcome event, especially to Captain Read. He knew that Captain King was his senior in the corps, so there was no problem about the transfer of authority. Read served on the works until June 1828, although he had to take some weeks of sick leave in 1827; he died about a year after his return to England. Captain King had been commissioned as an ensign in the corps in May 1805; he served on the works until they were well advanced. Returning then to England, he was placed on half-pay as a major in 1830, finishing his army career as a major-general. He was clearly an active and thoughtful man. Within a month of his arrival at Grenville, he wrote to the military secretary asking that the governor consider the possibility of carrying on the work in the winter:

It has hitherto been customary to leave a Non-Com'd Officer and 4 or 5 rank and File, chiefly with a view to taking charge of the Establishment here, as the services of so few could avail but little, but I can not help thinking that much of the work might be forwarded during that season, were an Officer and a proportion of the Detachmt. stationed at Grenville, allowing each Officer to take his turn during the winter. Many of the Civilians might be employed with advantage to Government at that season of the year, as I understand their wages are lower ... should they obtain the approval of the Governor, no time must be lost on improving the present Quarters for an Officer and the men, those they now occupy being of a temporary nature and not habitable as Winter Quarters.[54]

He lists the types of work that in his opinion could be carried out during the winter – one being quarrying – but since he had yet to experience his first Canadian winter, it is not too surprising to find no further reference to this imaginative proposal. The limitation on expenditure each year to £8,000, in itself, would have rendered Captain King's suggestion impracticable, but it is yet another tribute to the skill of these men of the Royal Staff Corps that such a suggestion should have been so seriously advanced. It was an interesting and very early foreshadowing of what is today known as 'winter construction,' for which Canadian contractors of recent years have become internationally famous.

All Captain King's letters were businesslike in tone and written in a strong, firm hand. In September he noted that although it had been usual to hire bullocks for hauling, he did not 'think their performance equals the cost of their Hire' and so requests permission to 'purchase six horses of the common Canadian breed.'[55] He further asked if he could purchase a boat complete with oars, since the attendance of officers on the south side of the river was frequently necessary, because it was on the Upper Canadian bank that a quarry had been successfully opened up with the intention of hauling the cut stone across the ice in winter: 'A similar indulgence I understand has been granted at other stations, and here in particular would prove of exceptional service.'[56] Naturally, it was not long before he too had to complain about stores, his first worry being about the deterioration of bedding, to such an extent that he thought that it should be destroyed. But he did have Lieutenant Hopper (an infantry officer) as storekeeper and clerk of works and so was spared from some of the irritations of his predecessors. Hopper's services must have proved satisfactory, since in February 1827 Captain King obtained the governor's approval for an increase in his pay from five shillings to seven shillings sixpence per day.[57] Even with an official storekeeper, however, King had still to appeal to the governor over a detailed matter such as obtaining stoves for the use of the troops in the small camp hospital, the barracks master in Montreal having no authority to issue such stores.[58]

Upon his return to Montreal for the winter, Captain King reported on the progress made during the 1824 season.[59] Low water in the Ottawa River had led him to suggest extra excavation at the upstream entrance to the canal, where he had built 'formidable retaining walls' on either side of the approach channel in Nelson's Bay. The lack of an accurate level had made it impossible to set the sill for Lock No. 2 until 14 September, by which time the new instrument had arrived. He arranged for Lieutenant Hopper to stay up at Grenville for the winter and (as usual) had to seek the governor's approval for the necessary extra charges for rents and fuel.[60] But contrary to Captain King's hopes, no major construction was carried on.

Lines of communication were not always clear, as was evidenced by a complaint that King had to lodge with the military secretary, late in 1825, about more trouble with the Commissary Department due to regulations of which he had no knowledge.[61] The governor's military secretary through these years was Colonel (later Major-General) Darling, and his letters show how helpful he was to the successive commanding officers at Grenville. Some of the reports on construction progress and allied matters were submitted by the commanding officers to Colonel Durnford, the commanding Royal Engineer in British North America, stationed at Quebec. Surprisingly, the War Office in London wrote directly to Captain King on 28 September 1825 with regard to the size of the detachment under his command.[62] If it exceeded 125 men, he was given authority by the secretary for war to employ on acting paymaster at a wage of 3 shillings per day, this sum to be charged to the accounts of the detachment. (The need for this extra man did not arise, since the complement soon fell below 100, owing to deaths and desertions). But Captain King, in duty bound, had to send a copy of the War Office letter to the governor through the military secretary. Almost all the official letters and copies of letters that are today found in the safe keeping of the Public Archives of Canada were written on good quality, legal-sized parchment paper, much of which carried a distinctive watermark, the scripts used being, in almost all cases, clear and legible. Sheets were folded in four and sealed with wafers for transmission.

Captain King was not only in command of the works at Grenville but was also responsible for regular inspections of the king's locks on the St Lawrence River at Coteau du Lac, upon the construction of which the men of the Royal Staff Corps were engaged when they were first diverted to work on the Ottawa River canals in 1819. He informed the governor that the snow was too deep for him to visit Coteau in the early spring of 1826, but he visited the St Lawrence during the summer and so was able to report in the fall upon the repairs that had been made to the small locks at Coteau.[63] Since this activity was outside his normal duties at Grenville, he had to submit expense accounts for his cross-country journeys to Coteau for approval by the governor.

An early start was made in the 1826 working season, when a small detachment (a sergeant and twenty men) travelled over the ice and snow in early April to carry out repairs to the wharf at Lachine and to stores buildings at Grenville. They also had the job of getting cattle and horses across the frozen Ottawa River near Grenville before the spring break-up. Captain King personally had made an earlier winter journey in March from Montreal to Grenville and back, and upon his return he duly reported to the governor. This must have been an interesting experience for him, since it was the end of only his first winter in Canada. Once the river was open again, work was resumed on the excavation and on the building of the first lock, still under the rigid limitation of annual expenditure. Quarrying of good building stone was also proceeding but naturally on the south shore of the river; a suitable supply of stone had been found on the property of Thomas Mears, one of the earliest settlers on this part of the Ottawa.

This activity led to another confrontation with a group of the new settlers before the 1827 season started, arising from a petition submitted to the governor on 10 April of that year.[64] It is a two-page, very polite request, written in 'copperplate' script, about the danger to a local bridge that would be caused by transport of the heavy blocks of quarried stone to the water's edge, for transfer by scow to the works on the north bank. Of special interest is the fact that it was signed on behalf of the petitioners by George Hamilton. In 1807 he had bought from Thomas Mears, the first small watermill erected near the head of the great rapids and went on to develop a large milling establishment and to found one of the famous Ottawa Valley lumber companies, despite severe personal tribulations.[65]

Once on the job at Grenville, Captain King advised the military secretary that he quite agreed with Mr Hamilton's complaint and that he was arranging to reinforce the bridge. Indicative of the good relations he had established was his report that Thomas Mears and other settlers were going to assist with his work on the south bank by providing oxen for hauling timbers and by supplying other materials.[66] How different were the relations with Mr Grece! Before this season was over, he was complaining again to the governor, this time about the state of the fences on his newly cleared land, submitting an inspection certificate signed by 'John Bowron, Fence Viewer and Inspector of Drains,' further indication of the start of real settlement in the vicinity of the canal works.[67] But this problem had to be dealt with by Du Vernet, who had recently returned from England, now as a major in the Royal Staff Corps, to resume command of the Ottawa River canals works, arriving in Quebec on 30 May 1827 on the transport *Southworth*.

Throughout these years, from 1819 to 1827, traffic up and down the great river continued by canoe. Indians would be the most familiar travellers, along with fur-traders of the North West Company in the spring and fall, until after the union of their company with the Hudson's Bay Company in 1821. All travellers bound upstream would face the struggle of getting their frail craft and their heavy loads up the swift waters of the Long Sault, harassed by the numerous large boulders on the north shore, which was the one upon which the short portages had been developed. Observing these arduous labours, the officers of the Royal Staff Corps, being the resourceful men they were, must have felt bound to try to improve this difficult passage. There are indirect references in the records to the use of oxen, employed by the Staff Corps, for moving boulders. This work led to the clearing of narrow channels, flanked by the boulders that had been moved (some of which weighed more than a ton), which were known in later years as 'Treadwell Trenches,' after another early settler, Nathaniel Treadwell, who had chosen a site above the Long Sault for his small village prior to 1800. One can only speculate that he may have suggested this assistance to the commanding officers, and as a result had his name associated with the trenches. They were studied by local historians before the Long Sault was flooded when the river was impounded behind the Carillon hydroelectric dam in 1960. At that time some large boulders were found which had been split by drilling, a fairly clear indication that men of the Royal Staff Corps were responsible for this very minor but significant improvement to navigation up the Ottawa River.[68]

The regular travellers knew what to expect at the Long Sault and somewhat naturally left us no records of their impressions. Travellers going up the Ottawa for the first time, who kept journals of their journeys, did, however, leave written accounts of what they saw at the Long Sault. One of the earliest of these personal documents was kept by Nicholas Garry, a director and deputy governor of the Hudson's Bay Company, who came to Canada in May 1821 to inspect the posts of the two great companies which had just combined forces. With an expert crew of voyageurs, accompanied by William and Simon McGillivray, Garry left Ste Anne de Bellevue on 9 June and records that, after coming up the Lake of Two Mountains:

At 11 o'clock we approached the Long Sault and landed at a small village [Pointe Fortune] where Mr Miles Macdonald is living in a deranged state of mind. Here our Canoe was towed up by ropes about one mile. During a distance of 15 miles there are several Décharges and Portages which are called the Rapids of the Long Sault. At last we landed on the Upper [?Lower] Canada side and walked about 5 miles and on Travelling through Woods were dreadfully attacked by Mosquitoes. Here Government is making a Canal to avoid the Rapids of the Sault, in the same manner as the Canal intended to be made at Montreal is to avoid the Rapids of St Louis at La Chine ... At the Top of the Canal we found an encampment of the Staff Corps commanded by Captain Duvernet and Le Merrick [Dumaresq?] who received us most hospitably. Mrs Duvernet, an Italian Lady, appeared to be a very amiable Woman. At seven o'Clock we embarked.[69]

Another traveller at about the same time was Dr John Jeremiah Bigsby, a medical doctor and amateur geologist, who, after military service, had been appointed secretary of the International Boundary Commission and had to go up the Ottawa Waterway to join up with other members of the commission. He published his recollections of his years in Canada many years later in England; it is, in consequence, a little difficult to say exactly in which year he recorded in a footnote in his book that

A summer or two after this [?] I spent a fortnight at a charming encampment, a few hundred yards below Major McMillan's, of two companies of the Staff Corps, then constructing the Grenville Canal, to avoid the Long Sault Rapids. I passed the day in geologising, and the evening listening to the guitars of two accomplished sisters, Sicilians, who had married officers of this corps. I was the happy guest of Col. Robe, then a studious and zealous lieutenant in this useful regiment. I wish I had time to describe the primitive kraal-like huts of the officers, and other droll makeshifts of the wilderness.[70]

Mention has already been made of the regular annual visits of the governor-in-chief, the Earl of Dalhousie, until he also returned to Great Britain for a long leave (from June 1824 to September 1825). He made another journey up the Ottawa in September 1826, just after Lieutenant-Colonel John By had gone up to the Falls of the Chaudière (now Ottawa) in order to lay out the start of work on the Rideau Canal, which was a turning point in the history of the Ottawa Valley. One year before, the works were visited officially by another military party, headed by Major-General Sir James Carmichael Smyth. We have no record of the details of their visit, but, in the report of the commission headed by his distinguished soldier, we have this brief account of what they saw: 'Here the Staff Corps are occupied in cutting a Canal to turn the Rapids of the "Long Sault" of the Ottawa. The Canal will be about 6 miles long. Five sixths of the excavation may be said to be finished, and one lock will be completed this year. There are to be 9 locks in all. The whole work will be finished in 1827.'[71]

This over-optimistic estimate of the progress that could be made on the Grenville Canal is one of the few points in this document that can be criticized. The report was a complete survey of the works necessary for the defence of British North America. Its main findings, when transmitted to London, would set the work on the Ottawa River canals on a much accelerated course and be the instrument through which a decision to construct the Rideau Canal was finally made after many years of discussion.

There were, naturally, no local newspapers when the canals were built, those that serve St Andrews, Lachute, and Hawkesbury – three settlements that did exist at that time – starting only in 1874, 1877, and 1911, respectively. The *Gazette* of Montreal was already well launched on its distinguished career, but naturally it did not carry any reports from the little construction job 'up the Ottawa.' No records made by local residents have yet been located. Unfortunately, therefore, nothing is known about the personal relations between the officers of the Royal Staff Corps and the few local residents already settled in the vicinity of the canal works. This makes more valuable a letter that Major John Hancock has found in the third volume of the *Naval and Military Magazine* for July 1828. On page cxxvii of this obscure publication, it is recorded that, at a meeting of the principal inhabitants of the township of Grenville, on 1 November 1827, the following address was resolved upon, addressed to Captain William King, RSC:

Sir, – we, the inhabitants of Grenville and its vicinity, take much pleasure in meeting together at this time to testify our unfeigned approbation of your conduct during your command here, and to acknowledge the orderly behaviour of the detachment while acting under you. That while you conducted, with singular zeal and laborious exertion, your public duties, you possessed the uncommon and happy talent of cultivating the good-will, and securing the best affections of the natives of all classes, and the poor emigrant, who never failed to experience relief from your humanity, all of whom now come forward spontaneously to regret having no better means of demonstrating their gratitude for, and admiration of the many virtues, and accomplishments, public and private, with which you are dignified, than this simple expression of the sense we entertain of them, which if we did not publicly make known, we should consider ourselves justly chargeable with being insensible to merit and devoid of gratitude.

That you may arrive safe in your native land – that your merit may be duly appreciated by your King and country, and that you may long enjoy health and happiness, is the sincere wish of the inhabitants of Grenville and its vicinity.

Signed in their name by
> Archibald McMillan,
> > Chairman of the Meeting.

The tribute corroborates all that can be sensed of the character of Captain King from the official correspondence for which he was responsible, so similar is it in every respect to that of Henry Du Vernet.

Study of all the official records that now remain leads one inevitably to the conclusion that Du Vernet was held in similar high esteem by the small local population. But no record of this has yet been found, nor have any private 'papers' of the commanding officer come to light other than the occasional private note within official letters. Since he wrote such delightful communications to his superiors, and since he was resident at Grenville and then Carillon for almost all of fifteen years, with no modern 'diversions' to fill his time, it would seem most probable that he kept a diary, as did so many other literate men in those years. Again, however, no trace of any diary has yet been found, although the search continues among members of the now-widespread Du Vernet family. If ever it is found, it will be one of the very few records touching upon the lives of the scattered settlers in the Carillon-Grenville area in the early nineteenth century. There seem to have been no local 'scribes.' Newspaper reports concentrated (as did all other Canadian newspapers at that time) upon events in Europe, especially in Great Britain. The only local references so far found (in a Montreal paper, for there were none in the lower Ottawa Valley) have been about acts of violence such as the murder by two rivermen, of unusual strength, of a quiet lumberjack!

There was, however, one notable figure of the time who did keep a private journal which has been found: the ninth Earl of Dalhousie, first lieutenant-governor of Nova Scotia, and then from 1818 to 1828 the governor-in-chief of British North America, a decade during which the Ottawa River canals were being built. He was a cultured Scot of unusual vision, devoted to the welfare of the new land of which he was the governor. Assiduous in visiting as much of the Canada of his day as possible, he appreciated in a quite remarkable way the importance of canals to the development of the country. Accordingly, as has already been seen, he visited the site of the Ottawa River canals on several occasions, always stopping to see the progress of the work on his way up and down the Ottawa in 1826, 1827 and 1828 when the much larger Rideau Canal was being built by Lieutenant-Colonel John By and the Corps of Royal Engineers. And from the start of his service in 1816 in Nova Scotia until he left Canada in 1828 he kept a personal journal.

The original is now one of the treasures of the Scottish Register House in Edinburgh. It gives such a vivid picture of early Canada, especially of some of the leaders in Canadian life at that time, that it is greatly to be hoped that the whole journal (about 250,000 words) will one day be published, suitably annotated and illustrated with some of the vivid sketches and watercolours of his official 'draftsman' Major J.E. Woolford, an accomplished artist, an example of whose work we were unfortunately unable to illustrate in this book. Some parts of the journal have been published in three small books, but it requires the journal printed in its entirety to give the full flavour of the sagacity and acute observations of this truly impressive governor. It is not a daily diary, entries clearly being written when time and opportunity permitted, and is accordingly succinct with, quite naturally, only a minimum of reference to the lives of ordinary Canadians.

There are some local references, however, and so this chapter may well be brought to a close with an extract (printed with the kind permission of the present Earl of Dalhousie) from the journal for September 1826, while the governor was on his way up the Ottawa to assist John By in deciding upon the site of the entrance to the Rideau Canal, and while Captain King was still holding the fort for the absent Du Vernet. It so clearly reflects Dalhousie's humanity and is typical of the way in which he regularly put aside his personal wishes if in this way he could help others. Writing at 'Grenville Camp' on 22 September 1826, the Earl says:

I find a quiet hour to note a very busy and very queer day yesterday. We started from Montreal at 6 a.m. in two large stage coaches of Dickinson the contractor. Our party consisted of Lady D. & myself, Colonel Durnford R. Engineers, Capt. Byng R.A., Capt. Stewart R.N., Major Elliot and Lt. Hope, Mr. Commissary Finlay & his son, one footman and Lady D's maid. Breakfasted at Ste Annes, 27 miles, and precisely at 10 o'clock embarked in our two canoes or rather bateaux. We stopt at the Indian village on the Lake of Two Mountains where the priest, Mons. Humbert of the Seminaire of Montreal and several others had prepared an early dinner for us. All was done in the kindest manner possible and we left there again at 2 p.m. M. Humbert explained to me in his private room some measures of severity he had been obliged to take to prevent the intermarriage of Indians with Canadian women, generally the parties being of loose bad character on both sides. He anxiously solicited my sanction to his driving them from the village in such cases, and I readily gave him my fullest approbation.

There may be 400 Indians at that point – Iroquois, Algonquins, and Nipisings. The two latter are extremely jealous of the former tribe. Each nation hunts on distinct and separate tracts. They cannot agree, and cheat each other in every way imaginable.

It was about 6.00 p.m. when we reached St. Andrews in the seigneurie of Argenteuil, belonging to Sir John Johnson. We intended to have proceeded immediately to the Camp at Grenville, but Mr. W. Brown had assembled the Yeomen and Militia in honour of the Governor's visit, and had invited a large party to dinner. We were therefore obliged to accept his invitation to remain the night. I sent Durnford and Hope forward to camp to announce the cause of my delay.

Mr. James Brown is a substantial proprietor farmer there, but a democrat in politics and not very highly esteemed by his neighbours. I had, however, no cause to know or meddle in these matters & all were very happy. An address was read to me by Revd W. Abbott to which I replied very shortly. A great deal of lively fun passed between Stewart and Brown, both sailors. We joined the Ladies at tea and then I was informed by Stewart a marriage had been arranged in the family for that day but had been postponed on account of my visit. Old Brown however insisted in the Eveng on calling forth the parties, and accordingly entered the room after tea with the Clergyman, W. Abbott. Mr. Castle, the Surgeon at Chambly was the Bridegroom, and the youngest Miss Brown the bride, [who] thus taken by surprise declined the ceremony at that time, & after some bustle exceedingly distressing, it was put off. This morng. we were to start early to breakfast at Camp, & examine the works of the Canal. I had walked out before 6 o'clock & our carriages were at the door at 7, when old Brown came to me saying that tho' defeated last night, he was determined to command this morng. & insisted on the marriage being celebrated in the presence of the Governor-in-Chief before I left his house. Accordingly Dr. Castle and Miss Ann Brown were married at 7 a.m. this morng. amidst the heavy sobs and streaming tears of this poor pretty girl. She is only 17; he a very nice gentlemanly young Doctor. Beginning in tears, I very sincerely hope it may still prove a very happy marriage.

We started immediately under an escort of a troop of volunteer cavalry commanded by Major de Hertel & Capt. Maclean, two very active clever fellows. At least 50 men attended mounted on all sorts of beasts, their swords being oak saplings. [A] very absurd exhibition it was, but they rode like devils, & would not listen to my entreaties that they would spare their horses and retreat. They pushed on, some of them dead done, to the Camp where I gave them their breakfast, and they all returned home in great glee. I have thanked them, & promised to establish the troop and give them swords. They are young, good looking fellows, but such a troop of cavalry, I suppose, was never seen before.

5

The Grenville Canal, 1827–34

The officers and men of the Royal Staff Corps had laboured steadily during the eight working seasons from 1819 to 1826 in their isolated location in the virgin forests on the shores of the Ottawa. News from the world without would have reached them throughout the summer by the limited mail service then available. Only when they returned to winter quarters in Montreal or Chambly would they be truly in touch with normal activities. They would have heard of the death of King George III in 1820, bringing to an end his long reign. He was succeeded as king by George IV, whose reign opened with the tragedy of Queen Caroline. The 'radicals' who supported her position pointed the way to the beginnings of the agitation for parliamentary reform which was to characterize the next decade of British public life. In the United States John Quincy Adams had been elected president, succeeding James Madison, by the crucial vote in the House of Representatives on 9 February 1825. The Earl of Liverpool continued to guide British policy, as prime minister, throughout the whole period, the Duke of Wellington similarly continuing as master-general of the ordnance. Only at the British Foreign Office was there a change, George Canning being appointed foreign secretary in 1822 following the suicide of Castlereagh. His rather flamboyant character resulted in some redirection of foreign policies, but in the main he carried on along the lines developed by his predecessor.

International relations were disturbed when France invaded Spain in 1822–3, and President Madison rebuffed British overtures for joint action. Unusual naval moves by the French in the West Indies in 1823–5 caused the British some concern, as did the intentions of the United States with regard to Cuba. British garrisons in the West Indies were reinforced. In order to check on the situation in the Caribbean, the Duke of Wellington sent out to the West Indies in 1823 a commission of engineer officers, under Colonel Sir

James Carmichael Smyth, RE, to report on the situation. They recommended no major changes, but their report must have impressed the duke, since, when U.S.-British relations were put under further strain during 1824–5, the same commission was directed to proceed to British North America in order to examine and report upon its defence. Carmichael Smyth was now a major-general. The other members of the commission were Lieutenant-Colonel Sir George Hoste and Captain J.B. Harris, both of the Corps of Royal Engineers. This was the commission briefly mentioned in the preceding chapter.

They received their instructions from the Duke of Wellington on 11 April 1825, sailed from Liverpool on an American packet on 17 April, and reached New York on 17 May. They proceeded directly to Quebec, where they arrived on 25 May, reporting to Sir Peregrine Maitland, the acting governor-in-chief. They then personally inspected the entire border defences of British North America from Drummond Island near Sault Ste Marie to Halifax, a distance of over 1,200 miles, noting that only bad weather prevented them from visiting Prince Edward Island and Grand Manan Island in the Bay of Fundy. Their report is about 50,000 words long, entirely (naturally) handwritten. It was unanimous and was signed by all three members of the commission in Halifax on 9 September, almost exactly five months from the day on which the Duke of Wellington had signed their instructions. When it is recalled that the Atlantic crossing by sailing ship took a full month, and that their travel in Canada had to be by canoe or bateau whenever possible, the primitive roads being used only for significant portages, the speed with which they completed their task is indeed remarkable, even by modern standards.

The report was naturally a secret document at the time.[1] It appears that only twenty-five copies were issued. A few of these were even more highly classified, since they contained in addition a confidential report by Captain Harris on the routes that might be followed if the United States were to be invaded from British North America, following a visit which he had paid alone to the United States. Among the vulnerable points that he studied on the ground was the newly opened Erie Canal (now the New York State Barge Canal). There is a copy of the report, including this additional top-secret section, in the Metropolitan Toronto Reference Library. It makes fascinating reading even today, one of its unpublicized gems being this statement: 'We cannot avoid expressing upon the subject of York our regret, that it should ever have been selected as the Capital of Upper Canada. It offers no advantage that we are aware of either of a Civil, Military or Commercial Nature.' The commissioners much preferred Kingston. They discuss the three obvious invasion routes from the United States and so deal fully with defences along the Richelieu River; the Niagara Frontier and its defence; communication between Quebec and Fredericton (even considering the possibility of a 'Rail Road' from Temiscouata to the St Lawrence – this in 1825!); and coastal defences in New Brunswick and Nova Scotia.

Of the 137 pages of the report, eighteen are devoted to the alternative military route between Montreal and Kingston and associated waterway matters. The clarity with which they review the whole problem is testimony to the care with which they studied the situation on the ground. It is remarkable that this commission pointed out emphatically for the first time that the Grenville Canal by itself would be useless for military purposes. A lock at Ste Anne and canals to circumvent both the Carillon Rapids and the Chute à Blondeau were essential before the Grenville Canal could be used to provide access for small gunboats and other vessels up to the mouth of the Rideau. It now seems clear that this strange gap in British appreciation of the overall alternative route stemmed from the sudden death of the fourth Duke of Richmond in 1819. We have already seen that he left a bare minimum of instructions, pending his own anticipated visit to the Long Sault. Had he lived, his consequent report to the Duke of Wellington would in all probability have mirrored what Sir James Carmichael Smyth and his colleagues saw so clearly. But the eight lost years would have to be made up, and so the commission noted that 'when therefore, the Grenville Canal is completed, which will be (as we already have had the honour to explain to your Grace) in 1827, there will remain only the Ste Anne's and Carillon Rapids, and the Chute à Blondeau to be turned, and which will probably as already explained, be done for about £50,000. There will then be an uninterrupted communication to the mouth of the Rideau.'

The members of the commission were pleased with what they saw at Grenville: 'The Canal is extremely well executed, and all the details and arrangements appeared to us to be highly to the credit of the Officers concerned.' They noted that £32,000 had already been expended on the Grenville works, with £8,000 more scheduled for the 1825 working season. Despite the fact that one lock only had been finished, they estimated that only £20,000 more would be required to complete the canal, giving a total cost of £60,000. They reckoned that a total of £50,000 would be required to build the two other Ottawa River canals and the lock at Ste Anne and noted that this amount 'must be advanced to get the better of the Carillon, Chute à Blondeau, and the Ste Anne's rapids, before any benefit can be derived from the money now expending at Grenville.' Accordingly, their total estimate for the money still required to complete the alternative route between

Montreal and Kingston, including £169,000 for the Rideau Canal, was £239,000. (When all the works were finished, the total cost amounted to over £1,000,000.) The commission discussed the possibility of seeking some financial assistance from the provincial governments but indicated that they did not regard this procedure as practical, concluding that 'expecting it is undertaken by His Majesty's Government, we are afraid it will never be executed' and they give salient reasons for their opinion. As if to reinforce their expressed opinion, they say also that 'It has occurred to us, that the only possible mode of having the [Rideau] Canal executed, will be for the British Government to undertake it, and to complete the whole of the water communication from the Ste Anne's Rapids near Montreal to Kingston by the Ottawa and the Rideau upon the same scale as already has been commenced upon at Grenville.'

This reference to the 'same scale' refers to the size to be adopted for the locks. The commission grappled also with this difficult problem. In dealing with the cost estimates that had already been made for the Rideau Canal, they noted that the estimate then in general use was based upon locks measuring only eighty feet long by fifteen feet wide. Their own estimate of cost allowed for locks of the same size as those planned for Grenville and already in use on the Lachine Canal (which had just been completed by a commission financed by governmental grants). They saw clearly that 'it would be better indeed that they (lock sizes) should agree exactly ... [even though] ... this of course, would cause an additional expense.' Their report to the Duke of Wellington was, therefore, a thorough response to his original instruction; it finishes with these words: 'Your Grace will judge of the proper degree of weight to be assigned to each [recommendation], and arrive at that conclusion which, doubtless, will be the most advantageous for His Majesty's Service' and the commissioners sign their report by saying that 'We have the honour to be, My Lord, with the utmost respect, Your Grace's most faithful, most obliged, and most obedient humble servants.' They were indeed.

Wellington did not take too long to study the report and all its implications, since, on 6 December of the same year (1825) he addressed a long memorandum to Earl Bathurst, the colonial secretary, heartily endorsing the Carmichael Smyth recommendations, with this general conclusion:

I do not entertain the smallest doubt that if the communications and works proposed by the Committee are carried into execution, His Majesty's dominions in North America ought to be, and would be, effectually defended and secured against any attempt to be made upon them hereafter by the United States, however formidable their power [whereas, if the recommendations are not adopted] we cannot expect the inhabitants, upon whose loyal and gallant exertions we must in the end depend for their defence, will do otherwise than look for the security of their lives and properties to a seasonable submission to the United States.[2]

Demands for economy were, however, very much in the air in Great Britain, and so the Treasury would not agree to even an initial grant of £100,000, half for the canals and half for works at Halifax and Kingston. Wellington was also anxious to keep all such defence measures secret. The combination of these two viewpoints led to a grant of only £25,000 for the canals alone. This sum was to come from the Colonial Office funds and so could be authorized by the secretary of state without previous reference to parliament. The decision was made to commence work on the Rideau Canal. Wellington appointed Lieutenant-Colonel John By, RE, then on half-pay, to direct this great construction project. And Henry Du Vernet was ordered to return to Canada to resume his direction of the building of the Ottawa River canals.

Captain King must have been delighted in July 1827 to welcome back to Grenville his fellow officer, now Major Du Vernet, and to pass back to him responsibility for the works, with all the extraneous worries that they now involved. King was put in direct charger of the completion of the first lock, while Du Vernet was soon involved not only in the overall direction of the Grenville works but also with the start of work on the Carillon Canal and that at Chute à Blondeau. Since these two smaller works were quite separate from the Grenville Canal and were finally constructed by contract, it will be convenient to consider their construction separately in the following chapter. The end of the 1827 working season came early, owing to the early onset of winter, but Du Vernet was able to report at the end of the year that the (regulating) lock was now complete, the excavation between it and the second lock now deepened by two feet for a length of over one mile, leaving a length of only 180 yards yet to be excavated to full depth.[3] There had been seventy men working in the quarry on the property of Mr Mears (on the south side of the river), with enough stone cut and dressed for the fourth and fifth locks, ready to be hauled in winter to the river's edge and later floated across to the lock location. Excavation for the second and third locks was well advanced, and some stone was ready for backing masonry. Sand had been shipped from the Rouge River, seven miles above Grenville. At Grenville a large blacksmith's shop had been built and a carpenter's shop completed for the fabrication of lock gates. A bridge had been built across the excavation to give access to Mr Grece's property, and some smaller buildings had been erected at the lower end of the canal route.

Provision of the bridge did little to calm Mr Grece, who continued, throughout the construction period, to be an impossible man to satisfy. On the other hand, Du Vernet reported to the military secretary on 9 November that, with Captain King, he had visited Mr Thomas Mears and they had agreed upon a price of £100 for the stone being obtained from the Mears quarry.[4] Lieutenant Hopper continued his duties as storekeeper and so problems with the Commissary Department were generally in his hands but, such were the 'communications' of the day, that he had to write to the governor's military secretary in October about the signing of warrants he needed for payment of accounts, Captain King having been previously the signatory; now he professed himself 'ignorant of what is necessary.'[5] The need to haul the heavy blocks of stone for the construction of the locks led to an increase in the use of horses. By the end of the season, Du Vernet had to appeal to the governor for an increase in the ration of forage, asking specifically that more oats be supplied in view of the heavy work the horses were doing.[6] He had put some out to grass pasture to fatten them up, but, 'one, a chestnut, is so complete a *garron* – lean, lame and stubborn' that it was useless and so 'should be disposed of and another obtained in his place.' The system was such, however, that a decision on the matter required an examination of the horse by a board of review; for this purpose the animal had to be brought down river to Montreal.[7]

Accidents further complicated the project. On 20 September a premature explosion of blasting powder badly injured a civilian miner employed on the works for five years, by name John Ritchie.[8] He had been under the care of David Jearrad, the assistant surgeon, at the small job hospital and had drawn only rations since the accident. Ritchie had appealed directly to the governor for a pension, his appeal being naturally referred back to Du Vernet for his opinion.[9] Despite his humane attitude to the men working for him, the practice of the day is reflected in Du Vernet's reply to the effect that if Ritchie were granted a pension, then so should a lot of others who had been injured on the works. Ritchie was a persistent man; even though he was again at work in 1829, his emotional appeals continued until long after the canal was completed.[10]

Other serious problems, however, claimed the attention of the commanding officer, notably a decision on the size of locks to be used for those not yet finished on the Grenville Canal and for those on the Carillon and Chute à Blondeau canals when they were constructed. It will be recalled that Du Vernet had to start work on the Grenville Canal with a minimum of instructions, owing to the death of the Duke of Richmond. He had no working drawings to refer to but was guided by the dimensions adopted for the Lachine Canal. Initially authorized in 1815, this important link in Canada's early waterway system was built between 1821 and 1825. It had six locks, and these were built 100 feet long by twenty feet wide, with five feet of water over the sills.[11] These were the dimensions used for the construction of the first three locks in the Grenville Canal (approximately, as will later be seen). They allowed for the passage of the largest bateaux then in use, the assumption being that vessels would be hauled through the canal by horses walking on a tow path. But the first steamboats had already appeared (see p. 46) and they might well invalidate this assumption.

The one man who saw clearly the transformation that the use of steamboats could effect was Lieutenant-Colonel John By of the Royal Engineers. He had arrived in Quebec on 30 May 1826 to take up his position as engineer in charge of the building of the Rideau Canal. In moving to Montreal from Quebec, he would have seen the small fleet of primitive steamboats then being developed for use on the St Lawrence by John Molson, the first one launched in 1809. Steamboats were far from being widely accepted, however; the first one had appeared on the Ottawa River only in 1822, so that John By's percipience was remarkable. As early as 13 July 1826 he wrote to General Gothar Mann a truly far-sighted letter, from which this fairly extensive quotation is warranted:

I have the honor to report that on examining the Military defences of Canada, it appears self-evident, that by forming a steam boat navigation from the River St Lawrence to the various lakes; would at once deprive the Americans of the means of attacking Canada; and would make Great Britain mistress of the trade of that vast population on the borders of the Lakes, of which the Americans have lately so much boasted, and to secure this trade have expended immense sums of money in cutting canals, which canals would in the event of our steam boat navigation being completed, ultimately serve as so many outlets for British Manufactured goods. I therefore feel it is my duty to observe that all the canals at present projected are on too confined a scale for the increasing trade of Canada; and for Military service they ought to be constructed of sufficient size to pass the steam boats best adapted for navigating the Lakes and rivers of America, which boats measure from 110 to 130 feet in length, and from 40 to 50 feet in width, drawing 8 feet water when loaded, and are capable of being turned to Military purposes without any expense as each boat would carry four 12 pounders and 700 men with great ease ... The number of these steamboats now building on the banks of the St Lawrence is one of the great proofs of the increasing trade and prosperity of the country. I therefore strongly recommend the Welland, the Rideau, and the Grenville Canals being constructed on a scale sufficient to pass these steam boats ... The expense of enlarging the Grenville Canal will be trifling when compared with the magnitude of the advantages to be gained by an uninterrupted line of steam boat navigation from Quebec over the Lakes of Ontario, Erie, Huron, Michigan, and Superior, which is to be effected by a trifling work at the Falls of St Mary's ... I therefore beg to state that from the price of Labour at this moment I conceive, that to pass the large size steam boat as before recommended the ... Rideau Canal will cost £400,000; the Grenville Canal will cost £100,000 ... I hope I shall receive orders to commence these works [the Rideau] with promptitude and vigour, as that would relieve thousands from distress, and reanimate both Provinces, which certainly appear to feel the pressure of the times.[12]

The complete letter, comprising ten legal-sized pages, is a masterly presentation showing at once the character of the writer and the grasp he had of the overall situation with regard to the defence of British North America – and this after being back in Canada (where he had served earlier as a young sapper officer) a mere six weeks. It was the opening salvo of a politely waged argument between John By, the man on the spot, and the more conservatively minded senior officers in London. The major decision was made with regard to the locks on the Rideau Canal, but, as Sir James Carmichael Smyth repeatedly pointed out, 'the augmentation of the Rideau Locks without the whole series of Canals and Locks from Montreal to the Rideau (being) similarly enlarged, would afford no military advantage whatever.[13] Accordingly, the studies by which the decision on the Rideau locks was finally reached must be summarized, since this decision determined the size of all the locks on the Ottawa River canals yet to be built.

General Mann referred John By's letter to Sir James Carmichael Smyth for an opinion. Writing on 23 August 1826 from his home at Nutwood Bygate, Sir James poured cold water on By's enthusiasm, saying that larger locks were not necessary, that gunboats would be able to pass through twenty-foot-wide locks, that steamboats could not be used in the canals because of danger to the banks, and that in any case the expense involved if John By's proposals were followed would be 'prodigious.'[14] There the matter rested until Colonel By was able to provide more specific information. He made his first journey along the full route of the Rideau Canal in May 1827, having now moved his headquarters up from Montreal to the Ottawa end of the canal; the small construction camp thus started is today the capital city of Ottawa.[15] Later that summer, members of his staff made longer journeys along the full line and did the necessary surveys, so that it was possible to prepare a complete set of working drawings for all the locks and impounding dams in the fall and to estimate the total cost of the canal on the basis of this more accurate site information. (These valuable documents are now among the Dalhousie Papers in the safe keeping of the Scottish Register

House in Edinburgh.) Knowing that the new estimate of the total cost – £474,000 – would alarm the authorities in London, John By arranged for the plans and estimate to be taken over to London by one of his most trusted assistants, Lieutenant Pooley, who took also all the arguments for the larger locks, the official estimate being based on locks 100 feet long by twenty-two feet wide. The new estimate did cause concern, but Pooley must have been an able representative of his chief, since not only was the increased expenditure approved, but a committee of senior engineer officers was appointed to study the plans that Pooley had brought and to make a recommendation as to the size of locks.

Sir James Carmichael Smyth was of course one member of the committee, but the chairman was Major-General Alex Bryce, and the other members were Colonel J.T. Jones and Lieutenant-Colonel E. Fanshawe, all officers of the Corps of Royal Engineer.[16] They wasted no time, and so were able to report back to General Mann on 28 January 1828. They commended the work that John By had already done; they approved of the provision of larger locks, accepting By's arguments about the probable use of steam-boats, but they recommended a size intermediate between his suggestion of locks 150 feet long and the Lachine length of 100 feet. Surprisingly, they also suggested that consideration might be given to the use of timber for building the locks 'as a temporary expedient' as was done elsewhere, clearly being conscious of the then current pressure for economy in governmental spending.[17] The respective estimates were, in round figures – Colonel By: £474,844; the committee: £407,531; the committee, using wooden locks: £330,118. But their report was not unanimous. Somewhat naturally, Sir James Smyth disagreed, since, taking into consideration all the locks on the alternative route (including those on the Ottawa River canals), as he so consistently urged, the total cost appeared to him 'to be too gigantic and expensive an undertaking even seriously to be thought of.'[18] John By knew of the committee and so wrote a very polite letter to Sir James from Montreal on 10 December, advancing again his strong arguments in favour of the larger locks, but his efforts were to no avail.[19]

The committee's guidelines were based only on a study of the plans that Lieutenant Pooley had brought to London from Canada, and his assistance to the committee was acknowledged. The Ordnance Department therefore recommended to the colonial secretary (now Huskisson) that another committee should examine the problem on the spot, with Lieutenant-Colonel By.[20] This suggestion was accepted along with the recommendation that the larger locks recommended by the committee be used if they did not cost too much, and with the further suggestion that all the work that John By had so far done should be carefully checked – the entire letter being one of the most delightfully written and cautiously constructive of all documents on the subject of this technical problem in the distant forests of Canada.[21] The sound thinking of the day is further illustrated by the fact that Lieutenant-Colonel Fanshawe, a member of the 'London Committee,' was appointed a member of the 'visiting committee' together with Lieutenant-Colonel Lewis and the chairman, Sir James Kempt (at that time lieutenant-governor of Nova Scotia, later for two years the administrator at Quebec, following the departure of the Earl of Dalhousie).

Sir James Kempt advised Lord Dalhousie that on 7 May he would leave Halifax by road for Pictou, where he would take a vessel for Quebec on 20 May; he could not leave earlier because of the amount of ice in the 'Gulph' of St Lawrence.[22] He would thus arrive at Quebec just before the end of May, but so efficiently did this committee do its work that, after a full inspection of the Rideau Canal route, they were able to sign a unanimous directive to John By in Kingston on 28 June.[23] Sir James confirmed this to Lord Dalhousie in Montreal on 3 July, saying that he had to return immediately to Halifax 'with your Lordship's gracious permission.' John By was with the committee in Kingston, since he was able to tell the Governor and General Mann, when sending them copies of the directive, that he had been given it on the evening of the 29th June. The committee was most favourably impressed by all the work that John By had been able to accomplish and said so.[24] The members made a number of constructive suggestions about the building of the Rideau Canal, including a strong recommendation that as much land as necessary at Bytown – the name given to the main construction camp – should be annexed (the implementation of this suggestion greatly benefiting Canada's future capital).

They told By to carry on and construct all the Rideau locks to the compromise size of 134 feet long by thirty-three feet wide with a depth of five feet of water over sills. He did so, and the locks that are still busy today after a century and half of service meet these dimensions.[25] This decision carried with it the implication that no towpath would be necessary; none was provided, all navigation through the Rideau being by steamboats from the start, in recent years superseded by oil- and gasoline-powered craft. Their estimates were, for locks 150 feet by fifty-feet wide (By's suggestion), their agreed dimensions, and the original size of 100 feet by twenty feet: £597,676, £576,757, and £544,676, in round figures, respectively. Given this most emphatic green light, John By forged ahead and had the canal (with fifty-two dams and forty-seven locks) substantially completed by the end of the 1831 working season; his own first voyage from Kingston Mills to Bytown was made in May 1832.

Lord Dalhousie advised Major Du Vernet about the new size of locks after receiving the advice of Sir James Kempt's committee, but it was too late for any change to be made on the Ottawa River canals before the 1829 working season. In his progress report for the year 1828, written in Montreal on 8 December, Du Vernet says:

In consequence of the Instructions received from His Excellency the Governor, for making the Locks for Steam Boat Navigation, the Scaffolding and Railways that were fixed, the Sills that were in readiness, and also the Gates which were in a state of forwardness for Locks on the *smaller scale* became useless – and it was moreover found necessary from the increased dimensions of the Locks to carry their Excavation further into the rising or ground, in order to give greater strength to the Embankments which work was entirely in slaty Rock. Although the greater part of the Sill Stones for Locks No. 4 and 5 on the larger scale have been cut, and a quantity of Ashlar Stone, Lime and Sand conveyed to the spot for commencing building, it was thought advisable to delay the work until the Spring when there will be nothing to impede its progress.[26]

This extract from a longer than usual year-end report shows that there was still considerable work to do before the canal would be ready for use, but substantial progress had been made despite 'the unusual height of the River, which continued throughout the season,' high water levels naturally interfering with work at the two ends of the canal.

It will be useful to review briefly the status of the work at the end of the 1828 season.[27] In summary, the upstream regulating lock was complete with its gates; the iron work of 'the dimensions required for the Strapping' could not be obtained in Canada and so had to be brought over from England, resulting in a delay. The cofferdam guarding the entrance had been removed, but two additional feet of rock had to be excavated in the approach channel to the regulating lock. Houses of stone had been built here and at the two other finished locks, ready for the lock-masters. The long stretch of canal to the next lock was reasonably complete and could be used, necessary sluices and waste-water spillways having also been completed. The second lock was also ready as was the next long stretch of canal prism, although the banks for one section, 1,000 yards long, had sunk because they had been built over a swamp and so had required some building up. The third lock was complete and functional, but there was still much to be done on the excavation of the lockpits for the two pairs of locks as well as at the lower entrance to the canal. A large quantity of stone for these locks had been quarried and finished, and had been ferried across the river in scows during the summer; it was planned to bring more stone across the river during the winter over the ice that formed above the rapids. Frequent references to the towpath show that the hauling of vessels through the canal was still contemplated (and was done throughout most of the useful life of the canal). But Du Vernet complained that 'the Towing Path which has become almost the highroad, the road so denominated being impassable the greater part of the year' making considerable repairs necessary. And he also referred to the fact that during the summer 'larger squads of Miners and Laborers were employed excavating Locks 6 and 7,' showing that the old limitation on expenditure to £8,000 a year had been removed.

Sir James Carmichael Smyth had been helpful in ensuring this new liberality. After the consideration of the 1825 report, the Duke of Wellington made one of his typically brief requests. He wrote from his home at Stratfield Saye on 10 August 1826: 'I want to have considered and decided upon if possible before the Cabinet shall meet on the 5th of next month, how much money we shall require to lay out the communications in Canada in the year 1827. I would include those on the Niagara Frontier. Beg of General Mann to communicate with Sir James Smyth on this subject.'[28] Sir James provided General Mann with a succinct overall review of the situation as he then saw it. He had revised his idea about the completion of the Ottawa River canals and stated that they could not be completed before 1832. After referring to the £10,000 that had been approved for 1825, he suggested that the annual expenditure on the Ottawa should be raised to £15,000.[29] This increase was eventually granted, so that first Captain King and then Major Du Vernet were able to accelerate the tempo of the work on the Grenville Canal, as well as oversee the building of the two smaller works.

Problems with communications remained, however; for Du Vernet advised the military secretary to the governor in January 1829 that he had never 'received instructions relative to the breadth of the Canal,' and asked if he should allow sufficient width for two vessels '30 feet across the Paddle Boxes' to pass each other throughout the length of the canal or to provide passing places.[30] This question was referred to the commanding Royal Engineer in Canada, Colonel Durnford, who advised that he 'can, of course, shortly ascertain from Colonel By the intended width of the Rideau Canal, but think it would be better for Major Du Vernet to pay a visit or write to the Colonel, from whom he would get such information as will be sure to prevent any sort of mistake.'[31] He also referred to the time 'when the

Locks already completed at Grenville come to be altered to the corresponding dimensions' as those that were to be used for the remaining locks.

This matter of changing the size of the upper three locks, as we shall shortly see, was to have a long history. Attention must now be directed, however, to the surprising suggestion of Colonel Durnford that Du Vernet should communicate with John By. One would expect this to have been a normal procedure, especially since the two men and their respective work forces were only sixty miles apart, and this in virgin territory. Access to the Rideau Canal works was up the Ottawa River, and so all travellers to and from what was soon to be called Bytown would have to pass the Grenville camp when making the last portage round the Long Sault. And yet there seems to be no reference in either the Rideau Canal records or those of the Ottawa River canals to any contact whatever between the two jobs until this suggestion of Colonel Durnford. Indeed, in discussing means of operating the Grenville Locks, Du Vernet proposes the use of small capstans 'as adopted for the Locks of the Dock at Antwerp and at Ostend' with not a word about those of the Rideau Canal just sixty miles away.[32]

The official records provide no explanation of this remarkable situation, but the history of the Royal Staff Corps may suggest a possible explanation. Appendix A reveals that the Staff Corps was established by the Duke of York because he was dissatisfied with the service he was getting from the Corps of Royal Engineers. Officers of this famous corps would have been less than human if they were not somewhat affronted by the duke's action. It seems clear that the memory of this royal reflection upon the work of the Royal Engineers was not forgotten. Whether it had any bearing on the disbanding of the Royal Staff Corps in 1839 cannot now be ascertained but this is certainly a possibility. Officers were transferred to the Ordnance Department in 1829, but the Staff Corps work on the Ottawa River canals continued until the project was completed. Before looking at this transfer, however, there is one clue in the official records that is so significant that it must be quoted in full, not only to give the flavour of correspondence in those days, but also to demonstrate further aspects of the character of Major Du Vernet. In this case he was obviously so annoyed that he disregarded protocol and in March 1828 wrote directly to the Earl of Dalhousie in these words:

My Lord,
Having learnt that extra allowances have been granted to the Officers employed on the Rideau Canal, it appears that I should ill fulfill my duty towards those I have the honour to Command were I not to solicit your Lordship's attention to the Grounds

afforded by a similarity of Duties and Situation for an extension to them of the indulgence which has been allowed to the Royal Engineers.

The knowledge which your Lordship possesses of the nature of the works upon which the Royal Staff Corps has been employed in this Country renders it unnecessary for me to point out the deprivations, inconveniences and expenses resulting from the unimproved state of the country which has been the Seat of their labours. I must, however, beg permission to remark on the unusual closeness of attendance and exertions which have been required from the Officers in consequence of the entire superintendence and direction having been exclusively performed by them a consideration which I trust will weigh with your Lordship when I venture on suggesting that the participation in the liberality of Government from which I cannot suppose we are intended to be excepted may be extended retrospectively in favour of those individuals upon whom the severe and most laborious duties have fallen.

It may not be irrelevant to mention that when the Grenville Canal was first commenced under the auspices of His Grace the late Duke of Richmond a prospect was held out to the Officers of the nature I have alluded to and that the issue of additional pay to the Officers of the Royal Staff Corps when employed on particular duties had been of frequent occurence and is still the practice in the Service.

Having been with the exception of about two years and a half in Command of the Detachment since the year 1819 ample opportunity has been afforded me of judging the Zeal of the parties whose interest I am pleading with your Lordship of this I am happy to have it in my power to speak in the fullest terms of approbation.

I have the honour to be, My Lord, your Lordship's obedient humble servant ... etc.[33]

It was fortunate that Du Vernet could thus address a governor whom he knew personally, who clearly held him in high esteem, and who had paid regular visits to the Grenville works. Lord Dalhousie had to refer the request to London; we shall shortly see that it received support from an unexpected quarter.

Economy was the watchword in British governmental circles at this time. Great Britain was in a period of most interesting transition. Trade unions had just been given legal status. Parliamentary reform was very much in the air, to be effected by the Reform Act of 1832. The House of Commons was taking an increasing interest in governmental expenditures, to such an extent that a select committee of the House questioned any further expenditure upon military canals in British North America. Wellington was now prime minister, having assumed office in January 1828 following the short term of Lord Goderich. He was to serve only until November 1830, when he was succeeded by the second Earl Grey, under whom the great Reform Bill was passed into law. As prime minister, Wellington appeared before a select committee of the House of Commons, and in answer to a question as to what would be the probability of defending Canada 'if neither the water communication or the works mentioned in theses estimates were executed,' he made this significant reply:

I should say that the defence of Canada would be impossible. I have never been in that country, but I must add that I have been astonished that the officers of the army and navy employed in that country were able to defend those provinces (in the) last war; and I can attribute their having been able to defend them as they did only to the inexperience of the officers of the United States in the operations of war, and possibly likewise to the difficulty which they must have found in stationing their forces, as they ought to have done, upon the right bank of the St Lawrence.[34]

The moneys requested were granted; the construction of the Rideau and the Ottawa River canals continued until all were completed; but one major change was effected in March 1829.

On the last day of that month, the master-general of the Ordnance and the Board of Ordnance decided, and minuted in their records, that the Royal Staff Corps should be transferred to the Ordnance Department.[35] Five companies were involved, of which two were in Canada, engaged on the Grenville Canal construction. Their status on this work and in their corps was to be unchanged, but they were to be considered as placed under the direction of the commanding Royal Engineer in Canada. It would be interesting indeed to know the reactions of Major Du Vernet and his fellow officers to this news; some indication is given by the fact that until the very last letter he wrote in 1833, Du Vernet always headed his letters from the Royal Staff Corps office at Grenville, or Chatham, when it was moved downstream for convenience in the supervision of the two small canals. Communications were, as usual, faulty. Almost three months after the transfer, Du Vernet had to write to Colonel Durnford saying that 'I have the honour to state that I have not received any instructions upon the System to be pursued in the payment of the two Companies under my command, transferred to the Ordnance, or upon any other arrangement consequent upon that event.'[36] Durnford sent a kindly reply on 10 July, suggesting that Du Vernet should select a suitable man as temporary paymaster and send him up the river to Bytown so that he could be shown how to use ordnance forms until such time as he, Colonel Durnford, heard how the master-general and board wished to operate.[37] It was not only Du Vernet who was neglected in this distant outpost!

The lower entrance to the Grenville Canal (Grece's Point) after reconstruction, September 1909

Earlier, however, Colonel Durnford had paid his first official visit to the Grenville works, on 4 June 1829, to the instructions of the governor to whom he reported, through the military secretary. The governor had asked a number of specific questions, for example, upon the passing places to be provided on the Grenville Canal. All these queries Colonel Durnford answered with precise comments, saying with regard to the passing places that they were 'I think very judiciously proposed by Lieut. Col. Duvernet' (his promotion had come on the first day of 1828).[38] Durnford suggests that it would be advisable to procure 'the whole of the banks of the river to the road for about 200 yards down the river under the probability of its being required for works to defend the lower entrance.' Use of the word 'probability' is significant. He also advocated the building of an appropriate office and dwelling for Colonel Duvernet (he never did get the spelling correct), 'so as to enable him to attend with greater facility [to the overseeing of the Carillon Canal] his present residence being 12 miles distant from this part of the work.' When the canal was finished, it became one of the lockmasters' houses. He endorsed Du Vernet's suggestion that a road should be built from the present road down a small ravine to the upper entrance to facilitate the watering of their cattle by local residents. The tone of the whole report shows clearly the good rapport developed between the two men. It includes also this brief statement of progress: 'Nos. 1, 2 and 3 locks on the Grenville Canal are completed and in use for Departmental purposes of passing sand, etc., down the Canal nearly as far as Nos. 4 and 5 Locks which latter as well as Nos. 6 and 7 have foundations nearly cleared out, and Lt. Col. Duvernet informs me he expects to finish the masonry of 4 and 5 and to make considerable progress in 6 and 7 during this season [1829]. Locks 1, 2 and 3 are completed on the scale of the Lachine Canal and will consequently require altering.' This reference to the narrowness of the locks was to be a continuing refrain in official reports for several years yet to come.

Instead of requesting Henry Du Vernet to send one of his very small staff up the Ottawa to consult at Bytown about official procedures, Colonel Durnford asked John By if he would leave his urgent tasks on the Rideau Canal and travel downriver to visit the Grenville works. He did so in June, reporting to the commanding Royal Engineer on 30 June 1829 in a letter which warrants being generously quoted:

I have the honor to report that in obedience to your order of the 20th inst., I have laid before Lieut. Colonel Du Vernet the whole of the documents relative to the two Companies of the Royal Staff Corps, under his command, being employed in the Ordnance Service upon the principle pointed out by the minute of the Master General & Board under date 31st March 1829.

I have the honor to report that I have examined the ground, and the plans and Estimates for the proposed works at Grenville, the chute à Blondeau, and the Carillon Rapids, and respectfully beg to state that I am of opinion the grounds cannot be better laid out for the required works to overcome the obstacles to the navigation of the Ottawa River, at the Chute à Blondeau & Carillon Rapids than has been done by Lieut. Colonel DuVernet, and great praise is due to that officer for his zeal and judicious arrangements for carrying on these works, the whole of which appear to be so well conducted that nothing is wanting except his being put in possession of the ground, and in addition to the grant of £30,000 for the present year, he should have authority to expend the same sum in the years 1830 & 1831 respectively for without this authority he will find difficulty in forming contracts, as no man will like to enter into the expenses necessarily attendant on such works without a promise of their being completed in a certain time or being paid a much higher price to cover his first disbursements ... [a shrewd comment showing John By's experience with construction contract work] ...

The various works at the Grenville Canal, Chute à Blondeau and the Carillon Rapids, requiring the Officers of the Royal Staff Corps to be separated from each other they are unavoidably exposed to great privations & hardships, and there being no relief from this arduous duty during the working season I strongly recommend these Officers being placed on the same footing as the Officers of the Royal Engineers employed on the Rideau service, and that the allowance of 10/- Sterling per day should commence on the day of their breaking ground for works at Chute à Blondeau and the Carillon Rapids. I respectfully solicit your recommending the same to His Lordship the Master General & Right Honble Board.[39]

Whatever may have been the reservations of the officers of the Royal Staff Corps, and especially of their commanding officer, when they heard of their transfer to the Ordnance Department, all must have been encouraged by the strong support given to them and their work by Colonel Durnford and Lieutenant-Colonel John By. As long as these two men served in Canada, they gave Henry Du Vernet their full support and assistance, as will be seen, for example, when the development of the Carillon Canal is described. Their support was timely, since on 8 September 1828 the Earl of Dalhousie had sailed for England, his long term of service to British North America completed. For the next two years, the governor's position was occupied by Sir James Kempt as administrator; he was already familiar with the canals being constructed. He served until October 1830 when Lord Aylmer arrived, to act first as administrator and only after February 1831 as the governor and commander-in-chief. Du Vernet was therefore fortunate in all the men in Canada to whom he had to report; there were still to be many occasions when he needed their interest and assistance. One of the first appeals he had to direct to Sir James Kempt, still through the military secretary, followed upon the death on 9 October 1828 of Lieutenant Thomas Marshall Harris, one of his faithful officers who had come over originally with the two companies that arrived in Halifax in 1815.[40] His widow was pregnant and had her first small child to look after, so Du Vernet asked if she might draw the allowances of the rank of her late husband, since she was unable to return to Great Britain. Harris's death was generally regretted; he was the first officer of the Staff Corps, since its days in Halifax, to die in Canada.

Despite the fact that Lieutenant Hopper still served as storekeeper, the commissary-general was soon making life difficult even for the commanding officer, to such an extent that an appeal to the governor's office was necessary. On 10 October 1828 Du Vernet had to write to ask if the order with regard to supplies for the Grenville works, passed in 1819, might still be used, since the Commissary Department was again demanding approval of each order by the Commander of the forces before it would issue any supplies.[41] If this procedure had to be followed 'for every trivial article that may be immediately required a delay of a fortnight or three weeks may take place before they will be supplied and may cause a very serious inconvenience.' When it is remembered that around Grenville were merely the houses of the few first settlers, permitting local purchase of forage and fresh meat only, the frustration of the commanding officer can well be imagined. Du Vernet had to make another appeal in February 1829 when the Commissary Department demanded an itemized list of all stores issued between 1819 and 1828.[42] This was supplied, the total value being just under £5,000! A board of survey (consisting of three or four officers) was required for all regular reviews of stores. The report of one such board made in the spring of 1829 lists even items such as 'Quills 325; Red tape, pieces, 18.'[43] One hopes that this is an indication that the officers concerned had not lost their sense of humour.

The non-payment of bills by the commissariat was yet another problem that came to the commanding officer's attention; Du Vernet was served with a legal notice (dated 29 March 1829) for the payment of £50 to Archibald McMillan for work alleged to have been done with men and oxen in 1822 and 1823.[44] The solicitor-general fortunately told Du Vernet to pay no attention to the summons.[45] It must have been some slight compensation to find that Commissary-General Routh himself had to address the military secretary in June 1829 to ask if Du Vernet might be authorized to repair the road from opposite Pointe Fortune (at the downstream end of the Carillon Canal) as far as its junction with the road built by the Royal Staff Corps along the full length of the Grenville Canal, since it was in such bad shape compared with the Staff Corps road, and the commissary supplies for both the Rideau and the Grenville canals had to be transported along it.[46]

With the increased expenditures now permitted for the Grenville Canal, financial matters demanded more attention, to such an extent that Du Vernet had to make two winter journeys from Montreal to Grenville in order to check on estimates and annual accounts – and he had to submit expense accounts to the military secretary for what these trips had cost him.[47] The inquiries about payment for the men of the Staff Corps resulted in the London Ordnance Office's requesting the ordnance paymaster on the Rideau Canal to be responsible also for payments to the men at Grenville.[48] Paymaster Rudyard replied, loyally, that he would do so but pointed out that the duty involved regular journeys of seventy-five miles each way (by canoe) and the handling of £30,000 each year, a sum that was more than he could manage.[49] The payments were based on these typical rates of pay: lieutenant-colonel: nineteen shillings threepence; Captain: fifteen shillings eightpence; first lieutenant: nine shilling; sergeant: two shillings sixpence;

privates: two shillings to one shilling threepence. All salaries were per day, without extra 'working pay' such as had been requested.[50]

Despite administrative difficulties, the work progressed steadily but slowly. By the end of the 1829 season, Locks Nos 4 and 5 were practically complete, masonry having been carried up to the copings, with paving around still to be done.[51] Excavation for Locks Nos 6 and 7 had been carried down to a depth of five feet below river level, protected by a cofferdam. An attempt had been made to continue with excavation during winter weather, as had been first suggested by Captain King in 1825, but this had been found to be impracticable. Wrought ironwork for all the lock gates and lock machinery was complete, and a bridge had been built to give access to Greece's Point. As could be expected this concession did not satisfy Mr Grece who wrote in April 1830 suggesting instead a floating bridge, built as the superstructure of a scow.[52] Later that same summer Grece wrote again submitting what Du Vernet termed 'an absurd claim (from) old Mr Grece (who) was dead but left a claim of £9,000 against the Government for a few acres of uncleared land used for the Grenville Canal.'[53] His heirs wanted to put the claim under arbitration, and so the presence of Mr Brown was requested, since, according to Du Vernet, he is 'not a competent judge of property and some of the Tenants speak no other language than Gaelic' – an interesting commentary on the settlers who were steadily taking up lands around the canal.

Early in the 1830 season another complication arose. On 23 April Colonel Du Vernet had to write to George Hamilton at West Hawkesbury (now building up his lumber business) asking if it were true that Hamilton had stopped a barge going upriver to the mouth of the Rouge River to get sand, this being the only location from which suitable sand could be obtained for the works.[54] What a contrast is this exchange of letters to the acrimonious correspondence with Mr Grece. Mr Hamilton replied on 24 April that the report was quite correct, but that he would lose his saw logs if the boom were opened; he expected that they would be out of the way in from five to six weeks.[55] He added that he owned both banks of the Rouge River but would permit sand to be taken, suggesting that it could readily be carted to the downstream side of the boom, adding 'this as a Political Economist I can tell you will not be as great a loss to the Public as the loss of my saw logs.'

Indicative of the increased tempo of the Grenville project is a list of the civilians engaged on the works in July 1830.[56] There were a total of 368 men engaged by the Staff Corps for carrying out the work directly, that is, not working with contractors as would be the case on the two smaller canals. They had six carts and ten horses but apparently no oxen, as had been

Upstream (western) end of the Grenville Canal in 1929: the entrance can be seen in a sheltered bay away from the head of the rapids; the route of the Portage Railway can just be discerned amid the trees to the right of the roads in the lower right-hand corner, the CNR line leading to the bridge coming from it.

employed at the start of the project. Of the men 249 were classed as labourers, the next two groups in size comprising twenty-eight stone cutters and twenty-two masons. There were only ten smiths and eleven miners, indicating that the arduous work of excavating in rock was approaching its end. Ten drivers were available for the horses and twenty-one carpenters, sawyers, and wheelers (wheelwrights). The most surprising figure is that for the overseers of whom there were seventeen, but when the large area over which the works were spread out is considered, including the quarry on the south side of the river, one can readily understand the need for these foremen (as they would be called today).

Colonel Durnford visited the canal in late August 1830 and duly reported to the military secretary; he found the Grenville Canal complete as far as

Downstream (eastern) end of the Grenville Canal in 1929, looking westward: the two pairs of downstream locks can be seen in the centre foreground; the location of the little Chute à Blondeau canal is just downstream of the bottom of the photo.

the lower locks (nos. 6 and 7) which he expected to see finished in 1831.[57] But he reports also on the active progress with the Chute à Blondeau Canal and lock, with clearing along the route of the Carillon Canal also in progress.[58] This was, therefore, a time of transition. In anticipation of the completion of construction, one company of the Royal Staff Corps had returned to England in the summer of 1829, reducing the detachment from a strength of 104 to fifty-eight. When work actually started on the building of the Carillon Canal, the canal headquarters were moved downriver from Grenville to Chatham, the name adopted from the township in which Carillon is situated but not now in use for any settlement.

On 20 July 1831 a letter was sent to Colonel Durnford advising him that he had been appointed commanding Royal Engineer at Portsmouth, so he left for England before the end of the summer, after fifteen years' distinguished service in British North America.[59] His place as commanding Royal Engineer in Canada was taken by Colonel Nicholls then the senior Royal Engineer at Halifax.[60] In November 1831 thirty-one members of the Staff Corps were discharged, and eight were sent back to England. The few remaining men, apart only from the officers, returned to England in August 1832. Du Vernet himself remained on the works until November 1833 when he, too, returned to England.

This gradual winding down of the operations on the Grenville Canal would be inexplicable if it were not for the fact that, as its construction approached completion, work on the Carillon Canal, by contractors but under Staff Corps supervision, was approaching its peak. It was now generally realized that full use of the Grenville Canal could not be made until the two smaller downstream canals were also ready. This fact clearly influenced the final steps in finishing off the Grenville Canal, always a difficult matter to schedule on any construction project. And to these factors was added a virulent outbreak of cholera in the summer of 1832 when, otherwise, all the works might have been completed. It was reported to the military secretary by Colonel Nicholls on 5 September 1832, when he said that 'in consequence of the Cholera having carried off many of the Contractor's workmen and many more having left the works with alarm,' Du Vernet could not possibly get the works finished that season as had been hoped.[61] In a later report, made in October 1832, Colonel Nicholls refers to the 'malignant Asiatic cholera.'[62] Fortunately, the officers of the Staff Corps escaped from this dreaded disease, although Lieutenant Hopper, the storekeeper, died in the summer of 1833, the only other casualty during this long period during which the Royal Staff Corps had been engaged on the Ottawa River canals.[63] Hopper was a professional soldier who had served with distinction during the war in Spain in 1810 but was badly injured and taken prisoner. Recovering, he came to Canada as adjutant of the 89th Foot Regiment and fought at the battles of Crysler's Farm and Lundy's Lane. He was placed on half-pay in 1815 but still suffered from his injuries. A petition from his wife led to his appointment to the Staff Corps. The Grenville Canal could be used by Durham boats by August 1832, but there were clearly many details still to be finished off.[64] Completion of the two smaller canals could not be effected until late in the 1833 season. It was not until 5 May 1834, therefore, that the new storekeeper at Grenville could report to Colonel Nicholls in Quebec that 'the Ordnance Canals between Carillon and Grenville were opened on 30th, ultimo to the public in general.'[65]

Commercial development was now well started along the shores of Lake Ontario to which access from Montreal was still possible only up the St

Lawrence River using the rough portage roads around the many rapids and the small canals at Coteau. It is not surprising, therefore, to find that a group of merchants in Kingston, knowing that Colonel John By had completed the Rideau Canal and was planning his own first through voyage from Kingston to Bytown (which started on 24 May 1832), was moved to address a loyal, exceedingly polite, and beautifully written petition to the governor, Lord Aylmer.[66] Dated 7 May 1832, it urged that efforts should be made to finish the Grenville Canal in one season, with good superintendence: 'It is now upwards of twelve years since the Grenville Canal was commenced ... and the Rideau Canal, six times its magnitude, was completed in five years under Colonel By.' The submission closed by stressing the great value of the Ottawa-Rideau route to the development of trade with the west. Not a word was mentioned about the defence of British North America; how quickly the times were changing!

One can only sympathize with Henry Du Vernet's having to bear the brunt of criticism such as this, on top of all his other concerns; the petition was naturally sent to him for comment. He explained to Colonel Nicholls that he could have the canal open for Durham boats (as noted above) but only by working the lock gates for the lower locks with ropes, since he had received only two of the necessary capstans on order from Montreal.[67] He added that repairs to the sluiceway and waste weir will take more time, because they now were distractions from his principal task at Carillon. Landowners continued to be his most distressing diversion, however, and there were now more of them, their corporate views doubtless influenced by Mr Grece Junior, who seems to have been even more troublesome than his father. On 20 September 1830 Grece led nine of his fellow settlers (including five Camerons) in signing a long appeal about the value of their riverside farms 'of the highest fertility.'[68] It will have been noted that Henry Du Vernet, despite all provocations, always managed to write letters that were correct and polite. His comment on this latest effort of Mr Grece brings him as close as he ever got in official letters to displaying his irritation. Responding to Colonel Durnford of 24 January 1831 he wrote: 'If any inference is to be drawn from the extravagant demands made in the later Arbitration, Mr. Grece's property as well as that of the other proprietors similarly situated must be greatly improved instead of injured by the said Canal.'[69] An arbitrator had been sent up from Beauharnois to try to work out some agreement, without too much success; the details of these arguments of long ago do not appear to warrant recording. Nothing would satisfy Mr Grece. He wrote again to the military secretary on 9 March 1831, this time complaining that his land had been flooded when the canal prism was first filled.[70] He was at it again in November, and his complaints continued long after the canals had been completed and were in use.

He was not alone in his unreasonable attitude. If only to illustrate the petty difficulties Du Vernet had to deal with while directing the canal works, there may be mentioned as the last such example from the Grenville Canal a letter sent directly to Lord Aylmer on 21 May 1832 by Owen Owens, a new settler later to be well known because of the store he established.[71] He stated that he had suffered 'vexations, grievous loss and ultimate ruin' through the removal by the Royal Staff Corps of a bridge across the canal, in consequence of which 'every load of Manure or produce has to make a circuit of 1200 yards' additional to that permitted by the bridge. As usual, the petition was sent to Du Vernet for his comments. He explained to the military secretary on 5 June 1832 that the 'bridge' was only a temporary structure of a few rough logs, allowed as a concession to Owen Owens, who had been told repeatedly that it would have to be removed when the canal was opened.[72] Owens had refused to act, so men of the corps had taken it out. Connection with the high road had admittedly been broken, 'if an opening in the Woods & a slough full of Boulders can be considered a road.' Further, Owen Owens had not mentioned in his petition that he could now use the tow road to his great advantage. All told, 'it is evident that one or both his representations   must be incorrect; and is an oversight of his neighbour and advisor, whose trivial and exaggerated complaints I am now no stranger to.' Mr Grece was all too well known!

The canal was finally finished. For the first seven years, as was seen in the last chapter, expenditure was limited to £8,000 each year. This limitation was removed in 1827 although strict control was still exercised on the amounts spent so that they were in accord with what had been authorized by the British Government. Numerous requests were sent to Du Vernet for reports on his progress. After being asked to make semi-annual reports, without any regard for the fact that mid-summer was when construction activity was at its peak, he was led to say to Colonel Durnford on 2 August 1830: 'I take the opportunity of suggesting the necessity of having a person appointed to assist me as a Clerk; the only one I have hitherto had being a Corporal of the Detachment and the increased number of Returns and writing renders it impossible for me to comply with the whole [request] without further assistance.'[73] Polite, as always, it was clear that he was frustrated, not with his commanding officer, but with the officials who were demanding so much 'paper work' regardless of the extensive nature of his duties. In the summer of 1830 he was involved in works that extended all the way from Grenville to Carillon, a distance of about twelve miles over which he had to travel on foot or on horseback.

Adding to his concern was a further breakdown in communications. Writing to Colonel Nicholls on 14 May 1832, in response to another inquiry about costs, he said: 'I further beg leave to state that I do not even know the amount granted by Parliament for the service of the Ottawa Canals for the two last years.'[74] Surprisingly, he had to repeat this disclaimer in a reply to officers of His Majesty's Ordnance, written from Chatham on 28 February 1833, saying that he had never been told what parliament had granted for the Ottawa canals after the report from a committee of which Colonel Durnford was chairman (which will be noted when the Carillon Canal is described).[75] Small wonder that he betrayed some impatience, but, like the good soldier that he was, he got on with the job, knowing that it was required of him that he get all three Ottawa River canals completed as quickly as possible.

He must have completed the works without any serious overrun of expenditure, since, unlike Colonel John By, he was not called upon to explain any excess of expenditure over what had been authorized. Unfortunately, the actual amounts expended in the years 1831 and 1832 do not appear in the official records still surviving, and there is available only an estimate (by Du Vernet) for the money necessary to complete the Grenville Canal in 1833. Table 1 presents a summary of the annual costs that are available, from which it may be deduced that the total cost of the Grenville Canal, with its seven locks, was in the neighbourhood of £200,000.

It will be appreciated that if Henry Du Vernet had not been required to divert most of his attention to the greatly delayed building of the two downstream canals, he could have had the Grenville Canal ready for use in 1832, if not indeed in 1831. The construction period would still have been fourteen annual seasons for building a canal with seven simple locks and a total length of only five and three-quarter's miles. At first sight, such a record would seem to indicate a rather poor performance. When it is recalled, however, that for eight of those seasons annual total expenditure was limited to a mere £8,000, the picture takes on a different perspective. The most surprising feature of the work is that unlike almost all other early canals in Canada, the Grenville Canal had to be excavated throughout its length (including the lock chambers) in solid rock. And there was no modern construction equipment, such as rock drills, available. Everything had to be done by hand – the holes drilled by hammering on drill steel held in place by the second man of a team, blasting with crude black powder, and 'mucking,' or removing the broken rock, using only wheelbarrows which themselves had to be made on the job. The total volume of rock excavated in this primitive manner was approximately 400,000 cubic yards, a figure that will be noted with amazement by all readers familiar with

TABLE 1
Cost of the Ottawa River canals

Year	Expenditure	Total	Reference (PAC)
		Grenville Canal	
	(£.s.p.)	(£.s.p.)	
1819	6,197-14-5	6,197-14-5	c.40, 50
1820	6,901-19-10¼	13,099-14-3¼	c.39, 169a
1821	6,906-3-2¼	20,005-17-5½	c.47, 183
1822	7,089-11-0¾	27,095-8-6¼	c.40, 113
1823	7,447-17-6½	34,543-6-0¾	c.41, 2
1824	8,770-2-8¾	43,313-8-9½	c.41, 38
1825	7,498-7-1½	50,812-3-11	c.47, 36
1826	8,062-1-8	58,874-5-7	c.42, 180
		All three canals	
1827	12,174-7-5¾	71,048-13-0¾	c.50, 97
1828	11,092-17-7¼	82,141-10-8	c.50, 97
1829	31,778-9-4	113,920-0-0	c.50, 279
1830	32,213-6-8	146,133-6-8	c.49, 177
1831	?	?	
1832	?	?	
1833	13,737-1-11¾	208,748-0-0	c.56, 90

modern construction, as they contemplate the human effort required to complete this quite prodigious job. Instead of being a poor effort, therefore, the building of the Grenville Canal, in the untamed wilderness on the banks of the Ottawa River, was a most notable achievement.

When Henry Du Vernet left his home on the Ottawa for the last time, in the late fall of 1833, he carried away one disappointment. All three canals were finished and ready for use, but he knew that the upstream three locks of the Grenville Canal would constitute a bottleneck for transport on the Ottawa. He had constructed them, as directed, to the dimensions used for the original Lachine Canal. The other four locks had been built, also as instructed, to the larger size approved for the Rideau Canal. Despite continuing suggestions from all who inspected the Grenville works, the three smaller locks had not yet been rebuilt to the larger size. The dire effects of this inaction will best be seen when the use of the canals is considered in chapter 7. Indicative of the urgings to have the reconstruction done while canal construction was still in progress was the appeal in the last letter addressed to the governor's military secretary by Colonel Durnford as he was about to leave for England.[77] Writing from Quebec on 21 September

1831, Durnford reported that Du Vernet was making considerable savings on the Ottawa Canal works because of reasonable contract prices for the Carillon Canal, and he asked if the savings thus made could not be applied towards widening the upper locks on the Grenville Canal. He added that he had made only a hasty perusal of the report of the committee of the House of Commons but had seen that it fully supported the idea of reconstructing the upper Grenville Locks; so he urged that contracts be entered into for their enlargement. But even this appeal was in vain; the three 'little locks' as they were naturally called, were to remain just under twenty feet wide for many years to come.

This defect was in no way the fault of Du Vernet; his record is clear, as an able engineer, and 'officer and gentleman' in every way, and a most kindly man. Despite all the problems with the Carillon Canal, in January 1832 he wrote to Colonel Nicholls, pleading for permission for the men of his command who had been discharged in the previous October to be allowed to settle on their grants of land, since many of them were destitute, having been discharged so late in the year.[78] In 1831 he had obtained permission, through the governor, for the granting of land to men of his command upon their discharge, if they had served a minimum of three years; he submitted his first list in September of the same year.[79] Even here administrative difficulties were encountered. The commissioner of crown lands excused his failure to act on the grants in a letter to the military secretary dated 4 February 1832, on the grounds that Colonel Du Vernet had not furnished him with a list.[80] Colonel Nicholls lost no time in telling the governor through his secretary, two days later, that the list had been submitted on 29 October, before the men were discharged on the 30 October.[81] Three lists were submitted by Du Vernet.[82] The names on the lists are included as Appendix B; some of their descendants are still residents in the vicinity of the canals.

Upon his return to England, Du Vernet completed his long service with the Royal Staff Corps, even though he now reported to the Ordnance Department, and he was placed on half-pay on 1 July 1834. He was promoted to the rank of full colonel on 23 November 1841, this recognition a contrast to the treatment of John By who never did receive such a promotion. The little canals on the Ottawa River to which Du Vernet devoted such attention have been flooded, as will later be seen, but two of the original locks remain, at the downstream end of the original Carillon Canal. Here is where a long delayed memorial to Lieutenant-Colonel Henry Abraham Du Vernet, Royal Staff Corps, might appropriately be placed.

6

Chute à Blondeau, Carillon, and Ste Anne-de-Bellevue

The Grenville Canal could not be put into fully effective use until the two smaller canals downstream were also complete. It will be recalled (p. 25) that one mile below the foot of the Long Sault, and thus of the Grenville Canal, there was the Chute à Blondeau, a small rapid with a fall of about four feet. Three and two-thirds miles further downstream the Carillon rapids, dropped a total of about ten feet. Durham boats could be hauled and poled up these rapids on the south shore of the river, but, as Captain Mann had noted in his 1818 report, they would have to be bypassed by canals if through navigation of larger boats were to be provided for. Looking back from the vantage point of the present, it is still puzzling to think that the building of the Grenville Canal proceeded for over six years before the necessity for the two smaller canals was officially recognized. The delay can be explained only when the strange start of work at Grenville is remembered, ordered by the Duke of Richmond but was unconfirmed in writing, the necessary works to be decided upon when the Duke paid his anticipated visit to the site, a visit never paid because of his tragic and untimely death.

Henry Du Vernet was aware of the necessity for the smaller canals and reported on them in one of his regular letters as early as 1823,[1] but it was only after his return to the works in 1827 that he was able to take any positive action about their construction.[2] In a letter to the military secretary written from Montreal in January 1828, he explains that 'I always understood improvements were intended at the Chute à Blondeau and Carillon Rapids but it did not appear to me that it had been finally decided upon. The sudden death of the Duke of Richmond prevented matters being properly arranged at the commencement ... [so that] ... I did not give myself any trouble about the Chute à Blondeau till I returned to the country last summer.'[3]

His lack of action, without any official encouragement even to consider the smaller canals, is understandable when it is recalled that for the first seven years he was restricted to spending no more than £8,000 in any one year; that was little enough money for what had to be done at Grenville. One wonders whether Du Vernet ever discussed the two smaller canals with the governor, when Lord Dalhousie came up the Ottawa on one of his regular visits. Even if he did, no action resulted. The delay in starting work at Carillon, in particular, was the direct cause of the completion of the Ottawa River canals two years after the Rideau Canal had been put into use throughout its length, so that the commanding officer is not to be blamed. As will be seen, once he did have his instructions, he lost no time in doing all he could to get the necessary work started.

THE LOCK AT CHUTE À BLONDEAU

Du Vernet was able to report to the military secretary in December 1827 (before the transfer of the Royal Staff Corps to the Ordnance Department) that he had been down several times to look over the Chute à Blondeau, describing the rock bar across the Ottawa – 'the Water falling as over a Rolling Dam' – and outlining the canal that would be necessary across a small rocky peninsula to provide the navigation lock.[4] He described the rock as 'hard claystone rock lying in large oblong blocks,' the strata as horizontal, and the quality as unfit for building stone. Based on a lock pit 165 feet long by forty feet wide, with four feet of water over the sills, he made a reasonable estimate of the rock excavation required, suggesting a total of 29,080 cubic yards, with 5,500 cubic yards of cut stone required for the masonry lock structure. (As built, the small canal involved a total volume of excavation of 32,600 cubic yards). The one lock was all that would be necessary to raise and lower vessels the four-foot drop of the rapids, but the dimensions suggested by Du Vernet show that he was not yet in direct communication with Colonel By about the Rideau Canal. It was significant, however, that as early as 1827 he was recommending much larger locks than he had built on the Grenville Canal. The lock, as built, was about 130 feet long and thirty-two feet six inches wide. Du Vernet's anxiety to get on with the work he knew to be necessary is shown by his urging upon the military secretary the necessity for starting the works as soon as possible, since all excavation would be in solid rock. In January 1828 he advised Colonel Darling (the military secretary) that he could carry on both works (that at Grenville and the two small canals) at the same time, 'the Chute à Blondeau (canal) not re-

The Chute à Blondeau Canal: a view showing the upper part of the deep rock cut in September 1909 after its lock had been removed, following construction of the second crib dam at Carillon

quiring many persons to superintend it.' He gave two preliminary estimates of cost for Chute à Blondeau, of £8,057 and £7,212.[5] But nothing happened.

The inaction during the year 1828 is difficult to understand, apart from the fact that the Earl of Dalhousie was coming to the end of his term as governor and must have been greatly preoccupied with political problems in Quebec. In London, all attention must have been concentrated upon the economy measures that led to in the transfer of the Royal Staff Corps (and so of the Ottawa River works) to the Ordnance Department. But no action was taken, with the result that it was not until 29 January 1829 that Du Vernet was able to send this letter from Montreal to the military secretary at Quebec:

I have the honour to inform you that the Plans and Estimates for the proposed Canals at the Chute à Blondeau and Carillon Rapids required by your Letter of the 16th. Instant will be forwarded by the Stage to Quebec this evening.

These Canals I conceive cannot be executed in less than three Seasons and as the means under my control will not admit of my furnishing Military Overseers to Superintend the increased number of men likely to be employed divided as they will be, I conceive the completion of the Works will be accelerated particularly the excavation by its being performed by Contract but whether it would increase or diminish the expense I do not feel capable of giving a correct opinion not having been employed when the Work has been done in that manner.[6]

The somewhat unusual wording and punctuation are due to the fact that this letter is quoted from a hand-copied version of Du Vernet's letter rather than from one of his original letters, as is the case with most of the other extracts. The reference to absence of experience with the contract system for carrying out public works (instead of by direct labour under the supervision of the designing engineers) is at once an indication of Du Vernet's frank approach to all his problems and a reflection of the relative newness of this development in military construction practice. Separation of engineering design from actual construction operations, conducted on the basis of a tendered price, can be traced from about the beginning of the nineteenth century in North America, although the method had been followed in Europe for some time prior to that. The system was well established enough, however, for all the major works involved in the Rideau Canal to be constructed by contractors, under the general direction of and to the designs of Lieutenant-Colonel John By and his assistant engineers. The Grenville Canal, on the other hand, had been built by a labour force employed directly by the Royal Staff Corps officers under Du Vernet. His suggestion of contract work on the Chute à Blondeau Canal and the Carillon Canal, however, was acted upon.

Both Du Vernet's lack of experience with contract work and his desire to expedite the construction of the Chute à Blondeau Canal are reflected in an interesting suggestion which he advanced to the military secretary in a letter dated 12 June 1829 (presumably written in haste, its composition being not as meticulous as usual):

With regard to the Chute à Blondeau Canal which is on a much more limited scale (than the Carillon Canal which he had just dealt with) and at a trifling distance from the present Works, with a good Water communication I should have less difficulty in undertaking it; moreover I conceive that as the excavation is entirely through Rock, that Tenders for the Contract would be high, the expense would be lessened by bringing into use the Tools and Materials belonging to the present establishment, taking into considerations these circumstances, I am induced in this instance, to suppose that following our present plan would be the cheapest, which if approved of, I am ready to commence on.[7]

Just one month later, Colonel Durnford was able to advise the military secretary that 'I have particularly recommended that the Contracts may be so worded as not to prevent Lt. Col. Du Vernet accelerating the work by means of any men he can spare.'[8] The judicious wording will be appreciated. Colonel Durnford probably realized, as those with modern construction experience will do, that one sure way of getting into trouble on contract work is to mix up day-labour operations with the work of a contractor, on the same job. It does not appear that any such overlapping was even attempted.

The contracts were awarded by the commissary-general, a factor that added to Du Vernet's problems, some of which arose from his unfamiliarity with the contract system. The first contract, for the construction of the relatively simple Chute à Blondeau canal and lock, was awarded to a firm headed by a Mr Cook.[9] The work was a straightforward job, consisting of the excavation, all in solid rock, of a straight canal prism and the construction of one masonry lock. The excavation had to be completed before lock-building could begin. Cofferdams were necessary at the two ends of the canal to exclude the water of the Ottawa River until the works were completed and ready for use. The excavated rock, as already noted, could not be used for the lock, cut stone having to be quarried on the south side of the river upstream and brought over to the site of the works. The lock later became superfluous when the Carillon Canal was rebuilt (as will be explained in chapter 7). Although the lock gates and fittings were partially removed after this reconstruction, in the latter part of the nineteenth century, the short rock cut could still be seen, just as it was finished, until the building of the Carillon hydroelectric dam in 1960. Looking at the depth of the rock cut was then a vivid reminder of the extensive human labour that went into the building of these small canals, since, as with the Grenville Canal, all this rock had to be removed by hand work. The shattered rock had to be man-handled into wheelbarrows for disposal in spoil banks along the sides of the cuttings, the outlines of which could still be discerned, under their covers of vegetation, until all were flooded out in 1960.

Sir James Kempt was now the acting governor; he was familiar with the sites of the two smaller canals and had inspected the Grenville Canal. With his personal endorsement, therefore, he was able to transmit the plans and estimates to the Board of Ordnance.[10] Approval was given and the contract with Cook signed in the early summer of 1829. It was at this time that the

Royal Staff Corps was placed under the Ordnance Department, with the consequent visits of both Colonel Durnford and Lieutenant-Colonel By to the Grenville works and the other two sites. Their visits probably reassured Du Vernet; the two engineer officers were accustomed to contract work and would have been able to advise him how such projects should be directed. The work at Chute à Blondeau must have got off to a good start, since in his progress report for the 1829 working season, the commanding officer was able to state that about one-third of the rock excavation had been completed, with some indication that work was continuing into the winter.[11] As the cut became deeper, progress would naturally be slower (in view of the fact that all shattered rock had to be removed from the cut by hand). When Colonel Durnford paid one of his regular visits to the works in the fall of 1830, therefore, he found that only two-thirds of the excavation had been completed, but much of the cut stone required for the lock had been delivered to the site.[12] Reports show that hopes were entertained that the canal and lock would be completed by the end of the 1832 season, but this goal was not achieved, not only because of the cholera epidemic, already noted,[13] but because the works were flooded, presumably by the overtopping of one of the cofferdams due to a sudden increase in the flow of the Ottawa River and consequently a rise of its level.[14]

The canal was completed in the 1833 working season. The delay was not serious, because its effective use depended upon the completion of the Carillon Canal, to which attention will shortly be devoted. As is so often the case with contract construction operations, the contractor submitted a claim for extra payment after the works had been accepted as complete, Mr Cook requested about £1,500.[15] One of his claims was that there was more rock to excavate than he had expected, a claim that has been made on innumerable excavation contracts since that time. A further claim is of interest, since it discloses something of the crude pumping arrangements that had to be used for keeping dry excavations such as this small canal. The rock had been found to be so fissured that leakage occurred through the seams in the rock: 'A water wheel upon the adjoining rapid and attached to the pumps by a connecting rod for the purpose of keeping the Works clear of water, equal to the power of 48 men per day and which was considered sufficient for drawing off and keeping out the water from the originally intended quantity to be excavated, was rendered of no use in winter by its being frozen up.'[16] Readers familiar with construction practice will see that Mr Cook was stretching matters considerably in making a claim based on the fact that water froze in the winter! His claims were placed before a board of three arbitrators, but they could not agree. The commissary-general therefore suggested that Mr Cook should be given one-third of his claim (£500), a most surprising proposal which showed the ignorance of this official in supervising contract work. Colonel Nicholls lost no time in pointing out that any such award would invalidate all future contracts.[17]

This part of the story, unfortunately, cannot be completed, because the records still available do not show what, if anything, Mr Cook did receive in payment in addition to his contracted sum. The records for the Chute à Blondeau Canal are the least complete of those for the three canal works. This situation is, perhaps, understandable, since the job was quite the smallest, the total cost having been finally estimated as only £11,580.[18] Mr Cook's tender appears to have been for £13,806, but even this amount is small in comparison with the costs of the Carillon and Grenville companion canals. The only additional cost was for the land that had to be expropriated. Both the Chute à Blondeau and the Carillon Canal were located not on crown lands, but on land that had been part of that originally granted when Chatham township was established in 1788. This factor was recognized from the start of the two works; the arrangements then made will be considered in connection with the Carillon Canal. Legal opinion with regard to the site of the Chute à Blondeau Canal was obtained (from the solicitor-general) before Mr Cook started his work; it was clear that the land used would have to be purchased from the owner, who bore the famous name Simon Fraser – not the explorer, however, but a retired lieutenant of the 42nd Regiment (on half-pay) living at Terrebonne.[19] On 23 January 1831 he addressed a reasonable and politely worded petition to the Honourable Roderick McKenzie, of which the following is an extract:

At (the) peace of 1802 your petitioner was induced to retire at half pay by a promise of 3,000 acres located to his father for military services on the Ottawa River; that in 1812 your memorialist obtained letters patent for this grant which has now been in (the) possession of his father and self for 40 years ... [The works have] deprived him of the carrying place at the Chute à Blondeau on which there is a valuable Mill Site ... you were present when Lord Dalhousie of his own accord mentioned the Canal to me stating that if it did any injury to my property. His Majesty's Government would certainly indemnify us.[20]

Before summarizing the progress of this petition, it should be explained that the land taken for the building of the canal amounted to seven acres three rods and twenty-four perches which, valued at $15 per acre led eventually to a settlement of £29-12-6 local or Halifax currency, equal to £25-13-6 sterling.[21] Despite the minuscule amount involved, the petition was handled in the usual way, submitted to the administrator, whose military secretary asked Major Du Vernet for his opinion.[22] Not surprisingly, the latter reported that Lieutenant Fraser had made no attempt to construct a mill at the site he spoke of, so that land only was in question.[23] Since money was involved, the claim had to be submitted to London; Lord Aylmer (now the governor) did so on 5 February 1833 indicating his full support for Du Vernet's opinion.[24] Fraser was, however, a determined man. At about the same time, he supported his claim by stating that, when he built his mill, he would pay back what he had received plus $10 per acre for the clearing that had been done for the canal and that he had engaged a civil engineer, Mr Manly, to design his mill.[25] He did not agree with Du Vernet that the '3 foot drop' was insufficient to drive a water-mill. In response to a request from Colonel Nicholls in October of the same year, Du Vernet reported that Mr Brown of Beauharnois (who served as a land valuer on several claims) had been to the site in 1830 and had met Fraser but found that he could not reason with him.[26]

Fraser was at it again in 1834, but by this time the Board of Ordnance in London had solemnly declared that it fully supported Lieutenant-Colonel Du Vernet and granted the sum mentioned.[27] The idea of the Ordnance Board itself having to concern itself with a claim valued at £25 is a good indication of the difficulties encountered by the men dealing with such matters on the spot, even as it is also evidence of the care with which all financial expenditures were now being watched by 'Downing Street.' The paymaster for the Ottawa River canals was finally authorized to pay Fraser the £29-12-6 Halifax currency, in an order dated 24 March 1834, more than three years after the original petition was presented.[28]

THE CARILLON CANAL

It is necessary to go back in time by a few years in considering the building of the Carillon Canal, since at first sight its long neglect and so its late start are puzzling. The scale of construction of the Carillon Canal was intermediate between that of the Grenville Canal and that of Chute à Blondeau. It served to demonstrate the sound engineering sense of the officers of the Royal Staff Corps in matters of design. The drop in the Carillon Rapids to be overcome by the canal was about ten feet, a difference in elevation requiring at the most (in those days) two locks. In his first plans, Du Vernet showed the locks located in a canal prism running along the shore of the river from a small bay giving a good entrance to a suitable spot near the foot of the rapids. On the basis of this outline plan, original estimates were

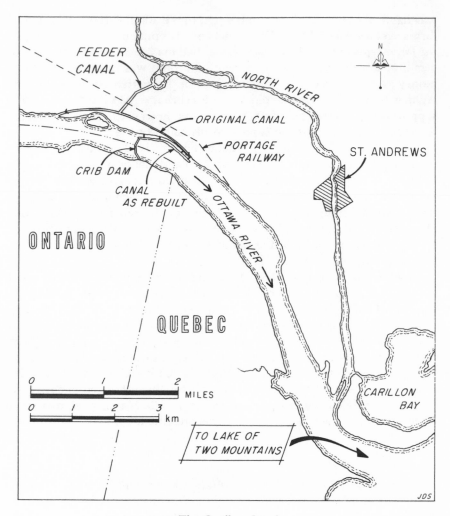

5 The Carillon Canal

prepared and submitted. It was such a plan that Du Vernet had included in his original report of 1823. It was revived again in 1827 and featured in the proposal submitted by Du Vernet in January 1829 to the acting governor and forwarded by him to London.[29]

   The best layout for the Carillon Canal clearly continued to be a matter of concern to the commanding officer. He wrote a few weeks later pointing out to Colonel Durnford that all the excavation, for a canal located parallel and

The second Carillon Canal, looking upstream (westward), showing the crib dam built in association with the 'new' canal; the entrance to the original canal can be seen to the immediate right of the start of the 'new' entrance channel, the route of the old canal following approximately that of the main road; the abandoned route of the Portage Railway may be discerned just to the right of the village of Carillon in the lower right-hand corner, coming from the wharf seen in the photo on page 176.

close to the river bank, would be in solid rock.[30] If passing places had to be provided for vessels between the locks, the cost would be increased appreciably above his first figures. Based on locks only 110 feet long by thirty-two feet wide, Du Vernet estimated that the cost of the canal would be about £60,000.[31] This estimate was approved by Downing Street when submitted by Sir James Kempt, but Du Vernet was ordered to confine himself in 1829 to the sum approved for the Ottawa River canals (£32,213-6-8). In answer to the inquiry from Canada about carrying out the Carillon works by contract, the only reply from Sir George Murray, was: 'I am not aware of any objection to the execution of a proportion of the Work by Contract.'[32]

A few weeks later, in a general report to the military secretary, Du Vernet says with reference to the Carillon Canal: 'I should recommend its being tendered for contract, not only with a view to expedition, but also from not having the means in my power of otherwise superintending the Work.'[33] Colonel Durnford approved of this proposal but reminded the military secretary that it must be understood that the Royal Staff Corps could not expend more than was already available in their 1829 allowance. Regarding supervision, he had to add that 'I am not aware of the strength of officers at Lt. Col. Du Vernet's command ... but all contract work must be under his especial supervision and some other officers acting under him.'[34] Here is further evidence of the complete separation of operations of the Royal Engineers and the Royal Staff Corps in Canada, until the full implementation of the move of the Staff Corps into the Ordnance Department. It was at just about this time, however, that Colonels Durnford and By paid their visits to the Ottawa River canal works; thereafter, liaison was no problem. As a result of his visit, Colonel Durnford suggested one change in the location chosen for the Carillon Canal, that it should be moved in somewhat from the edge of the river.[35] With his approval and that of John By, following his visit to the works, Du Vernet must have felt encouraged even if (as is obvious from his letters) he was becoming impatient at the delay in getting the Carillon works started.

In a long report to the military secretary, dated 10 July 1829, Colonel Durnford reviewed sympathetically all three Ottawa River works, suggesting that the line of the Carillon Canal should be cleared (since the landowners had not yet done more than their initial clearing of the virgin forest) and that the location for the downstream end of the canal should be resurveyed.[36] Acting promptly, Du Vernet had the work started, and he prepared two estimates of cost – but just for the excavation, presumably because the cost of the locks would be the same irrespective of location. He based his estimate on a cost of three shillings for removing one cubic yard of rock and so arrived at two totals, one for the shortest line, with 15,598 cubic yards, and one for the longer line, with 69,767 cubic yards, the great increase being due to the rise in the level of the land adjacent to the river. His respective totals were £2,340 and £10,465 in round figures.[37]

Tenders for the work had been called by the commissary-general; seven were received and were sent to Colonel Du Vernet in mid-September for his comments. He reported to Colonel Durnford on 23 September that the lowest bid was that of Mr Hartwell but said that since Hartwell had failed in his contract on the Rideau Canal, his tender could not be accepted.[38] The second-lowest was that of Mr Wright, but his total sum was greater than the official estimate. Further negotiations must have taken place in Montreal, since we have the details of one more tender submitted on 2 November 1829 to the deputy commissary-general by the firm of A.C. Stevens.[39] Stevens asked for £150 for the necessary cofferdam at the foot of the canal; one shilling one penny per cubic foot of finished masonry in the locks; and a graded scale of prices for excavation: eight shillings per cubic yard for the lowest six feet, five shillings sixpence for the next eight feet of depth, and three shillings only for what was above that to the surface, or the first three feet from the surface. Du Vernet's comments on this tender are especially interesting. He told Colonel Durnford on 23 November that he had tested the ground conditions every 100 yards along the full length of the canal (as would be done in modern engineering practice), and on the basis of what he found, he estimated that the average cost of rock excavation, if Stevens's tender was accepted, would be six shillings one penny, or more than twice the firm's estimate; accordingly, the tender should be immediately rejected.[40]

It will be seen that the entire working season had been lost by these negotiations. It is not surprising, therefore, to find the commanding Royal Engineer suggesting to Du Vernet (on 4 December) that he might perhaps start some work on the Carillon Canal by day labour (i.e., under his direct control) while new tenders were called.[41] It was really too late in the year for this to be done, and the only progress that could be reported at the year-end was that the route of the canal was being cleared of forest.[42] One can well imagine the thinking that had occupied Du Vernet's mind during this period of waiting and so appreciate his request, made to Colonel Durnford on 10 January 1830 in response to the suggestion of starting work by day labour: 'Having always felt an indecision about the Carillon Canal which your suggestion of altering the proposed site has greatly increased ... [he requests] ... a Committee of responsible officers to look over the whole project' and to consider what should be done about land and further tenders.[43] In sending on this suggestion to the military secretary, Colonel Durnford stated that he did not think that a committee was necessary, advising rather that new tenders should be called. But he must have been persuaded to change his mind, since he presided over a committee consisting of Lieutenant-Colonel By and Captain Boteler of the Royal Engineers, and Lieutenant-Colonel Du Vernet and Captain George D. Hall of the Royal Staff Corps which met at the site on 23 February 1830. The holding of a winter meeting in those days, with no conveniences for travel or for heating buildings, is indicative of the urgency that was now featuring considerations of building the Carillon Canal. The committee had soundings made through the river ice at possible locations for the downstream entrance, as a result of which they recommended a slight change in the line already cleared.[44] They prepared a revised estimate for the completion of all the Ottawa River works.

Colonel Durnford reported the findings of the committee to the military secretary in a letter from Chatham written on 8 March 1830.[45] He promised to send later details of the estimates they had prepared, along with a plan; these papers are still available, the plan of the canal being a fine example of the excellent drafting done by the Royal Staff Corps, even in their isolated location.[46] The cost estimates included the following: for building the Carillon Canal, £72,318-3-7¾ (that three farthings is pleasing to a modern eye!); pay for the establishment of the Royal Staff Corps for three years (the estimated duration of construction), £23,761-11-8½; and for changing the three upper locks on the Grenville Canal to the now standard dimensions, £54,245-19-2.[47] The committee urged that the rebuilding of these three locks and adjacent parts of the Grenville Canal to accommodate vessels that could sail through the Rideau Canal was absolutely essential, and that this remedial work should go ahead simultaneously with the building of the Carillon Canal. It was yet another in the steady succession of recommendations for this most necessary work; once again, however, the suggestion was not accepted.

Colonel Durnford wrote a supplementary letter to Colonel Couper, the military secretary, on the same day, advising him that just as the committee's report was finished, Lieutenant-Colonel Du Vernet had suggested an entirely new concept for the canal, using a small feeder canal from the adjacent North River to supply an upper section of the canal into which vessels would have to lock *up* when they entered the upstream lock, and then down through two locks as they entered the Ottawa River at the downstream end.[48] The accompanying diagram illustrates this novel suggestion. The great advantage of this layout for the canal would be a considerable reduction in the amount of rock to be excavated, and therefore in the time necessary for construction. This resulted from the lie of the land, since high ground adjacent to the river made deep cuts necessary if the canal followed the 'obvious' course of running parallel to, and not too far from, the bank of the Ottawa. Du Vernet advised his fellow officers that he had carried out rough surveys, finding that there was a drop of six feet between a loop in the North River and his proposed upper level; this would be sufficient to supply water to the canal. Such a supply would be necessary to replace the water lost when the locks at the two ends of the upper level were operated, two lock-chambers-full of water being discharged into the river whenever a vessel was locked through.

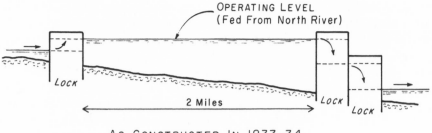

AS CONSTRUCTED IN 1833-34

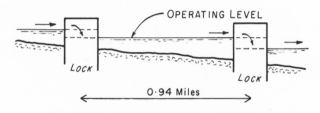

AS RECONSTRUCTED IN THE 1870s

Diagrammatic sketch of locks on the Carillon Canal

This remarkabale proposal showed clearly the engineering ability of Henry Du Vernet. No record has yet been found of any other early canal with this arrangement, which contributed so much to ease of construction and economy, despite adding to operating costs and times of transit. The upper section of the first Welland Canal (1825) was constructed above the level of Lake Erie, but this was done for a different reason (failure of soil strata), and it was not a 'run-of-river' canal as was the Carillon. The committee were naturally impressed by this ingenious proposal, clearly the result of much thinking on the part of Du Vernet, but they were unable to check on its validity because bad weather in early March made further survey work impossible. Within a week, a remarkably short time for those days, the military secretary addressed to Du Vernet a most interesting questionnaire about the new proposal, headed *Considerations*, to which the commanding officer dutifully replied on 11 April.[49] In answer to a query about the locks, Du Vernet said that the number (3) would be more than in the original design (2), but that the savings to be effected in the amount and cost of excavation would more than counter-balance the cost of an extra lock. If a dam were built on the North River to deflect water into the feeder canal, the military secretary asks, would this result in any flooded land? To this and to other questions Du Vernet gave clear and unequivocal replies, showing that he had thought through most carefully his unusual proposal.

His answers must have been deemed satisfactory, since he was ordered to prepare revised plans and new estimates of cost.[50] These were finished so quickly that on 29 May 1830 Colonel Durnford was able to send them to the governor through his secretary along with his full endorsement and an urgent request that authority to proceed be granted, with the necessary funds, as quickly as possible. The urgency with which his request was made is understandable, since he was well aware of the splendid progress that was being made with the Rideau Canal works under John By. The Rideau Canal was well on the way to completion. By the end of the 1831 working season it was all but complete, and was actually opened throughout (by Colonel By) in May 1832. And here was the Carillon Canal, a vital link in the over-all Montreal to Kingston alternative route, not yet started. No wonder that John By should have commented in a letter to his chief dated 2 July 1830 (about Rideau Canal matters) that neither the Carillon Canal nor the lock at Ste Anne had been started.[51]

Another indication of the general uneasiness about the delays was the action of Lieutenant Charles Stoddart, who had arrived in Canada only in August 1829. He wrote directly to Colonel Durnford, recommending that the downstream end of the Carillon Canal be carried into the North River instead of into the Ottawa River, as all plans had shown. Such 'cutting of corners' could not be condoned; on 15 June Durnford wrote to Du Vernet asking him to tell Lieutenant Stoddart that he was never to write to him directly unless Du Vernet, for some reason, refused to send on his communications![52] Stoddart was an interesting character, as this incident suggests. He served later in Persia, where he was executed in 1842, having been imprisoned for almost a year before.

Nothing more appears in the records about this 'excess of zeal' (for that is what it appears to have been). In June it was possible for Du Vernet to report that he had started clearing the new route for the canal and had employed men for 'piling and burning the logs, [and] clearing and deepening the Rivulet by which means I shall drain the swamp.'[53] To this he added the rather plaintive comment that 'Emigrants are arriving in such numbers in search of employment that I am completely beset by them, but I will engage no man for the present.' This decision reflected his knowledge that tenders were being invited by the commissary-general, in Montreal, for carrying out the works to the new plan. In one of his letters to Colonel Durnford, about Thomas Philips, the contractor for the Black Rapids Dam on the

Rideau Canal, John By explained that Philips would not submit a tender for the Ottawa River work, since he considered that 'the officers of the Royal Staff Corps had not been accustomed to contract work on a large scale and that he felt confident that he would be interfered with more than he would like.'[54] John By, being the man he was, added that although Philips was an excellent workman, 'I have observed that he has a very peculiar temper and cannot at all times agree with his own Partner, Mr White.'[55] Other contractors, as will shortly be seen, were not so particular, since a number of tenders were received. Du Vernet's final plans, however, were undergoing the usual and necessary scrutiny. It is not surprising, therefore, to find that the same joint Royal Engineers / Royal Staff Corps committee met again at Carillon on 17 August for a final review of the revised plans, just before contracts were let.[56] While there, the members heard the first rumblings of the local objections to the building of the little feeder canal.

The whole area was in the seignory of Argenteuil, the new seigneur being Sir Charles C. Johnson (a son of the Sir John Johnson who was the son of Sir William of Indian fame). Much of his land had been subdivided and the banks of the North River were well settled, the first settlers having arrived in about 1785. The seignory contained an important water-mill on the North River upon which depended, according to the seigneur, 'settlers for twenty miles around.'[57] The upper part of the little feeder can still be seen today. To stand by its side and look at the 'little ditch' (which is the only way in which it can be described) and then to recall all that happened when its construction was proposed, makes one wonder if the whole business did not merely provide a delightful diversion from the quiet and simple life of those early settlers. When it is further recalled that flow down the feeder would be intermittent, the amount of water taken being merely that required to fill the locks when they were used, whereas the North River had a good continuous flow of water, it is difficult to understand why so much commotion was caused by such a simple proposal. It is equally incomprehensible how the officers who had to deal with the complaints managed to do so without showing what must have been their real feelings, all communications being conducted with the greatest courtesy and consideration. The committee, for example, included in their August report the very sensible comment that the amount of water that would be taken by the little feeder would not be as much as the water already going to waste over the mill dam. They naturally advised against using the North River, as was proposed locally, for the downstream section of the Canal. But they had to add that 'the Mill being a seignorial privilege which progressively improves as the population increases ... we beg to observe that this [the destruction of the mill seat, as was suggested] becomes a question of Law, upon which we cannot presume to offer any opinion, or how far, or whether the Government has power to divert water from the North River.'[58]

News of the committee's opinion must quickly have reached the local residents, since the barrage of complaints started five days after the date of their report. It began with a moderately worded request that the canal should be taken into the North River, instead of into the Ottawa River, signed by about 300 local residents, most of them Scottish.[59] This idea was supported in a beautifully written petition to the governor, signed by George William Hoyle on behalf of the seigneur, and headed St Andrews, 28 August 1830.[60] It requested that the canal be routed through St Andrews, not 'in the continuance of the Grenville Canal through the Carillon Rapids, notwithstanding the almost impracticability of the same.' Reference is made to 'the distressed condition of the Seignory' and to the 'many thousands of settlers on the banks of the North River.' It was followed by an even more remarkable memorial, one of the largest documents now in the Public Archives of Canada.[61] It is over six feet long, again beautifully prepared, and signed by about 500 inhabitants of the seignory. It pleads for a complete change in the design of the Carillon Canal, urging not only that it be diverted into the North River at St Andrews, but also that it should then utilize the North River for forty miles, in which only a small rapids at Chute Mills would have to be bypassed, then intersecting the Rivers L'Achigan and L'Assomption, and so into the St Lawrence at Berthier, thus giving an outlet for the fertile country through which it would pass. It would 'open an unbounded field for immigration' and 'afford a short and secure conveyance for Military Stores in case of a war with the United States.'

The early settlers in the lower Ottawa Valley were sound and worthy men; they had to be endowed with common sense and good judgment in order to make their homes in the forests and succeed with their new life. How such men could have subscribed to such a 'hare-brained' idea is impossible now to understand. There was a portage between the headwaters of the North and L'Achigan rivers but it was far upstream of their navigable portions. The proposed route would have bypassed the Island of Montreal completely.[62] Enough delays had already plagued the construction of the Ottawa River canals. The scheme proposed by the 500 would have taken several years to execute, even if granted top priority, and would have cost several times the sum that had already been spent on all three Ottawa River canals. Small wonder that no more about this ludicrous proposal appears in the records. That some of the local settlers saw the folly of the proposal is indicated by the content of yet a third memorial, dated 15 September 1830, and signed by about 200 settlers, one of whom was J.J.C. Abbott, later to be the first Canadian-born prime minister of Canada.[63] This document merely requested that the mills on the North River should not be interfered with and that water for replenishing the canal should be abstracted from the Ottawa River instead of from the North.

Du Vernet was able to assure Colonel Durnford, when his opinion was solicited, that the use of the little feeder canal would not affect the operation of the Mills at St Andrews.[64] The first suggestion – of taking the canal into the North River instead of into the Ottawa – had been carefully studied by Du Vernet and Captain Hale, who found that it would cost much more than the official plan. Permission to proceed was therefore solicited and eventually granted.[65] From the absence of any further reference to these proposals in the surviving records, one can assume that, after the initial alarm about the little feeder had died down, sounder thinking prevailed. Since Du Vernet and his fellow officers were now stationed at Chatham (now Cushing), they would be in close contact with residents of St Andrews and so, one can hope that they had the chance of explaining how little water, relatively, would be used by the feeder, thus allaying initial suspicions.

Another local resident of note, who did not sign any of the petitions, may also have helped in this process of explanation: he was Charles James Forbes, now the deputy commissary general.[66] Born in Hampshire, England, on 10 February 1786, Forbes had an adventurous career, first in the Royal Navy, later in the British Army, serving on duty in the Mediterranean Sea area and acquiring a knowledge of other languages which later served him in good stead. He was present at the battle of Waterloo, going thereafter to Vienna to take charge of the money lent by the House of Rothschild to pay Prussian troops. Thereafter his career was in the commissariat service. He came to Canada in 1825, serving first in Halifax before being moved to Montreal as Deputy to Commissary-General R.J. Routh. Sent next to the West Indies, he had there two attacks of yellow fever and so was invalided back to Canada.

During his first stay in Montreal, he had found the climate there unsuitable for his children and so had purchased an estate in the seignory of Argenteuil, on the hillside directly north of the foot of the Carillon Rapids. There, in 1827, he had built a large stone house, well named Bellevue, since the view of the Ottawa River from its windows and gardens was magnificent. He spent time at Bellevue when not on duty in Montreal, finally retiring there and living the life of a country gentleman until his death on 22 September 1862; Mrs Forbes died seven years later. In this gracious house Forbes entertained many leading men of the time – the Earl of Dalhousie, Sir

James Kempt and other governors, George Simpson of the Hudson Bay Company, Bishops Stuart and Mountain; and Louis-Joseph Papineau was always a welcome guest. After Forbes's death Bellevue was sold with 700 acres to the Ottawa River Navigation Company. At a later date it was bought by the Roman Catholic Church and today serves, with some extensions, as a special school. The beauty of its surroundings and the splendid views from its grounds remain.

Deputy Commissary-General Forbes must have been an interested observer of all the work on the Carillon Canal. His concern over its progress is shown by a proposal he advanced on 28 September 1829 for the building of a commissary storehouse at the foot of the Carillon Rapids. Du Vernet was asked to prepare plans and specifications for a suitable building and an estimate of its cost; he submitted these to Colonel Durnford in the early summer of 1830.[67] The building, rectangular in plan, plain and dignified in appearance, was to be eighty-four feet long and forty-four feet wide, with three storeys, twenty-three feet high above a basement formed of rubble masonry walls. Du Vernet estimated the total cost as £946-17-5, one of the items being 236 'toises' of rubble stone in the basement walls. Colonel Durnford submitted the documents to the military secretary, saying that authority for the building would have to be obtained from England unless the commander-in-chief would authorize its construction.[68] In this he was backed, surprisingly, by the commissary-general who said that 'the Magazine is necessary immediately, there being no cover for any Stores whatsoever, either Ordnance or Commissariat, at the Carillon. The reference to England would be most inconvenient and expensive ... if the works are to go forward.'[69] Later Commissary-General Routh changed his mind (as had happened on other matters involving expenditure of money), suggesting that perhaps a wooden building would suffice or that a building might be rented; Charles Forbes, knowing the exact circumstances, wrote to his chief explaining again the need for the building, to such good effect that authority was obtained; the building was constructed.[70] It stands today virtually in its original state, for which reason these details of so small a part of the Carillon works seem warranted. After serving a variety of functions, the commissary building is now the headquarters and the museum of the Historical Society of Argenteuil County. Once inside the building, it takes but little imagination to forget the things of today just outside and to visualize something of the use of the building while the Carillon Canal was being constructed.[71]

His letters and action suggest that Forbes was a kindly man, meticulous in his duties but tempering his decisions with reason. The commissary-general

The original Commissariat storage building at Carillon, now the Museum of the Historical Society of Argenteuil County

was of a rather different character; some of his communications give one the feeling that he was just 'trying to be difficult,' especially so in some of his actions in relation to the Rideau Canal. But the two men were close colleagues, and the fact that Forbes had his residence at Carillon must have been helpful in dealing with the perennial problem of land owners. Many of the men, if not all, who owned land that would be affected by the Carillon Canal would be known to Forbes. Accordingly, it is not too surprising to find the commissary-general recommending to the military secretary, as early as 21 March 1829, that a commission should be established to report upon the land required for the two smaller canals, so as to avoid the troubles that had plagued the building of the Grenville Canal.[72] A few days later, the deputy commissioner wrote to the solicitor-general, Charles Ogden, asking for advice about the procurement of land, very probably at the suggestion of the governor.[73] Ogden's reply is a delightful example of

legal verbiage, but he says, in effect, that the land must be purchased out-
right, although in reaching this decision he invokes both the king of France
and the king of England.[74] Action followed; on 25 May Du Vernet submitted to the military secretary a table showing all the land required, totalling
about sixty acres, with the names of the owners.[75] He reports that he had
spoken with all the 'Proprietors' and that all had indicated their willingness
to co-operate. On 18 May an order in council was passed at Quebec authorizing the take-over of the land required, using Du Vernet's table, and referring to the original grants that permitted the land to be thus expropriated by
the king 'for Work of Military Defence.'[76]

This order would seem to have cleared the way and removed all difficulties, but the land had to be valued. Once again, the owners suddenly developed inflated ideas of the worth of their properties and proceeded to petition accordingly. The first appeal was addressed to Du Vernet by James
Fuller on 15 June 1829, stating that the canal would deprive him of a good
mill site, and that his land was worth at least £10 an acre.[77] Five of the
owners appealed shortly afterwards to the acting governor, Sir James
Kempt, having had their properties valued by another group comprising
John McDonnell, JP, M. Davis, T. Barron, and J. Brock.[78] They allowed
each man £15 per acre, apart only from the land of Solomon French for
which they allowed only £10 an acre.[79] In addition, they allowed £50 a lot
for the loss of river frontage (the valuation being made for the original line
of the canal) £200 for a stone house, up to £50 for smaller buildings, and
£150 for a lime quarry and kiln. James Fuller's name does not appear in the
valuation report, but he kept up his appeals, without success. As late as 3
March 1835, after the canals were in use, he was still writing bitterly about
not being granted £1,000 for the loss of his potential mill (wherever it was to
be), adding that 'had the Ottawa Canal been used exclusively for Military
Works of Defence, I should have little to say but it is notorious that these
Canals are now applied by His Majesty's Government to the purpose of
Trade and Profit.'[80] Although this smacks of special pleading, it is an interesting commentary from a local resident of the time upon the changing
character of the Ottawa River canals so soon after their completion.

Somewhat naturally, Du Vernet could not agree with the compensation
requested in the petition from the owners. On 23 June he wrote to the military secretary stating that in his view the land was not worth more than £5
per acre, some of it having been purchased (so he had heard) for £4 per
acre.[81] He requested that someone other than himself be called upon to make
an official valuation. He was authorized to make such an appointment and
so reported on 30 July (now to Colonel Durnford) that he had assembled the

proprietors, who had nominated Messrs Gates and McGill of Montreal and Mr Mears of Hawkesbury.[82] Du Vernet had pointed out that these men were merchants and that all possible conflicts of interest had to be avoided. He had therefore nominated Mr Brown of Beauharnois, Mr Simpson of Coteau du Lac, and Deputy Commissary-General Forbes 'who has a perfect knowledge of the Locality.' To assist with the valuation, the deputy provincial surveyor (Alexander Stevenson) was sent up to the canals at the end of July to survey all lands required for the two canals. Du Vernet had shown him around and provided an assistant, but on 7 October he complained that he had not yet seen any report.[83] It was provided in November, showing a total area of fifty-six acres 2 rods and 6 perches, (the document, incidentally, was signed by Joseph Bouchette, the deputy surveyor-general).[84] No record can now be found of the final result of this initial valuation, but this matters not, because of the major change in the routing of the canal, the land question had to be reviewed afresh in any case. By far the most influential landowner was now Theodore Davis who, having heard of the proposed feeder canal (to run through his land), wrote to Du Vernet on 2 April 1830 saying that he would not object to the feeder if he were paid for the land but that he objected to Charles Forbes's being an arbitrator because of 'misunderstandings existing for a length of time.'[85]

While waiting for Du Vernet to submit his detailed plans for the new arrangement of the canal, Colonel Durnford advised the military secretary that Forbes would have to be told of Davis's objections to him, suggesting that this task should be done by the commissary-general himself, a good indication of the discretion that characterized the personal relations of these senior officers.[86] Negotiations about the valuation of the land now needed, about 100 acres, dragged on throughout the summer. It proved impossible to reach agreement with the landowners as to mutually acceptable arbitrators. Theodore Davis must have been one of the real impediments to progress, as is shown by an eleven-page statement of complaint which he prepared and signed on 19 November 1830, on his own behalf and that of other residents of Chatham.[87] In it he explains that Lieutenant-Colonel Du Vernet 'is totally unacquainted with agricultural pursuits,' because he did not appreciate that value of fences, some fence-posts having been destroyed. Davis goes on to say, however, that

Col. Du Vernet's zeal for His Majesty's Service has not only induced him to entertain erroneous opinions, but also to make hasty assertions without sufficient information or due deliberation ... The Colonel is probably not aware that it is not easy for a Magistrate in a remote Country place, without any other assistance than the authority given him by law, to enforce the Laws, order and obedience among two or three hundred of the lower order of Irishmen; as for a Colonel to maintain strict discipline in the Corps which he commands.

Small wonder that Du Vernet exhibits, on occasion, slight signs of frustration.

It was finally decided early in 1831 to settle the matter by legal action. Hearing this, Mr Davis wrote to the attorney-general in Montreal on 11 March 1831 saying that, understanding that legal action was to be taken 'to compell him to surrender or deliver to H.M. Government part of my lands ... all that I look for is just compensation,' adding that Mr Mears was still his arbitrator.[88] The case was tried before the Court of Kings Bench in Montreal, the court appointing Messrs Grant, Somerville and Rice to be the 'Arbiters.'[89] These men visited the site in late 1831 and were shown round by Du Vernet, but judgment was not rendered until 28 April 1832.[90] Davis was awarded £3,327 for his fifty-six acres of land, and the four other owners involved receiving sums ranging from £177 to £505, for a total of £4,494. On 14 May Du Vernet advised Colonel Nicholls that as far as he knew no sum had been included in the estimates for the canal to cover this award.[91] On 23 October Lord Goderich had to advise the governor from Downing Street that His Majesty's Treasury did not include any sum for such a purpose in the 1832 estimates, so that the owners would have to wait until 1833 for payment.[92] Even the three arbiters had not been paid by May 1833, when they, too, had to appeal to the governor.[93] It was indeed a leisurely legal world.[94]

Compared with land negotiations, the actual building of the canal was straightforward. It involved excavating pits for the one upstream lock, which would have a lift of thirteen feet, and for the two downstream locks in tandem with a combined drop of twenty-three feet, and the canal prism between them, a total length of just over two miles. Much of the excavation was in rock, but, because of Du Vernet's judicious suggestion, the average depth was only ten feet with an extreme depth of twenty-two feet. The masonry locks had finished dimensions of 128 feet in length and thirty-two feet six inches in width, providing a depth over the sills of five feet six inches. The revised estimate of cost was £70,000.[95] All the work was done by contract, the excavation being awarded as one contract (to a Mr Waid, of whom nothing is known), the masonry to the firm of William McKay and Alexander Crichton (Masons and Contractors of Montreal). Du Vernet was in Montreal for the opening of the tenders received which took place on 31 August 1830.[96] It was just three months later that the strength of his detachment was reduced to less than sixty. With this small establishment, Du Vernet was responsible for finishing the Grenville Canal by direct labour and for supervising the three contracts, one at Chute à Blondeau and the two larger undertakings on the Carillon Canal. It is small wonder that there are clear indications in the surviving papers of some neglect of written records. When it is recalled that these works were spread out over a total distance of twelve miles, it is indeed surprising that such records as do exist are as good as they are.

Before he returned to the United Kingdom, Colonel Durnford was able to report to the military secretary that he was well pleased with the work going on at Carillon, this being at the end of the 1831 working season.[97] For the final stage of the construction of the Ottawa River canals, Lieutenant-Colonel Du Vernet did not return to Montreal for the winter but stayed on the job at Grenville. The contractors carried their operations into the winter months. It must have been distressing for Du Vernet to be forced to appeal on 5 November 1831 for a supply of fuel for the winter:[98] 'The Reduction of the Establishment to one Company doing away with the Situation of Quarter Master Sergeant, the allowance to that Non Commissioned ceased on the 31st., ult., but as his duties for the detached situation of the Company remain the same,' so would they please, therefore, hurry up with the fuel. He had also to make a corresponding appeal for greatcoats, supplying a detailed accounting of those used before asking if they can have sixty-one new ones.[99] But the work went on. There was some delay with the excavation but apparently no undue trouble. Protests continued, naturally, one received in March 1832 from the seigneur of Argenteuil relating to the very small dam (or weir) that had to be built on the North River on one side of Île au Chat to ensure diversion of water into the feeder canal.[100] It was during the summer of 1832 that the most serious delays occurred, owing to the cholera epidemic. This outbreak is not mentioned in Du Vernet's letters still on record, but an account of its effects on the works can be found in a report sent by Colonel Nicholls to the military secretary.[101] In July, Du Vernet wrote a strong protest to Commissary-General Routh (since he was responsible for the contract arrangements) about the delay in the masonry work at the upper lock, saying that he was 'determined not to be trifled with longer' by McKay and Crichton.[102] In doing so, however, he displayed his unfamiliarity with contract work, as was very kindly pointed out to him by Deputy Commissary-General Forbes.

One can so readily sympathize with Lieutenant-Colonel Du Vernet and his fellow officers in having to supervise civilian contract work after their entire professional careers had been spent on projects subject always to

The remains of the entrance locks to the original Carillon Canal, completed in 1834, as first seen by the author in 1959; trees have now been removed and the site has been well restored by Parks Canada.

military discipline. They must have been shocked, for example, when men working for McKay and Crichton forcibly entered a house near the lower locks and did damage for which £600 compensation had to be paid.[103] The rough conduct of the civilian workers was even acknowledged by one of the supporters of the claim for extra payment that was predictably lodged at the end of the work. John Fotheringham, writing from Montreal on 24 April 1835, had to admit that 'their personal deportment (McKay and Crichton) was not what it ought to have been which gained them the ill will of the officers.'[104] But the explanation that the deputy commissary-general gave in his letter of 12 July 1832 dealt with more serious aspects of the contract work.[105] He explained to Henry Du Vernet that 'we failed to deliver over to them the Lock Pits, in time to permit of their completing the Contract ... They complained, and with great reason, of this obstruction to their undertaking, which, I am sorry to say, was of a nature to throw the responsibility of non-execution, with its concommitants, entirely upon the Government Officers.' Although Forbes clearly understood the niceties of contract interrelations, someone responsible for the original contract arrangements did not – possibly the commissary-general? Forbes went on to explain that 'it would be understood in a Court of Justice, that, when we made a Contract with Messrs McKay and Crichton to complete the whole of the Carillon Locks by the 31st October 1831, we effectively placed a Barrier to their doing so, by having agreed with Mr Wait to complete the Lock Pits by that day only.'

Small wonder that there were problems in contract administration. Not only was there this overlapping of contractual periods, but much trouble was experienced in keeping dry the lock pit for the upstream lock. Since the bottom of this excavation was naturally below the level of the river (so that vessels could eventually sail into the lock), a cofferdam had to provide a temporary barrier to the river water.[106] The primitive pumping arrangements then available have already been noted: if water did get into the excavation, it was a long and tedious task to get it out. Du Vernet had to record again, at the end of the 1832 working season, that the masonry work for the upper lock was still far from complete.[107] The work dragged on into the summer of 1833, despite all the pressures to finish it, and there was clearly trouble with the lower downstream lock, since McKay and Crichton were still engaged at 'puddling at the back of the Lower Entrance Lock' in May 1834, after the canals had been officially opened for regular traffic.[108] By this time, Captain Richard Hayne, RSC (who had arrived in 1828), was the 'Officer in charge of the Ottawa River Canals,' Henry Du Vernet having returned to England in November 1833.[109]

Although he did not see the canals fully in use, Du Vernet left with the

knowledge that they were essentially complete, to be ready at the opening
of the 1834 navigation season, after the long years of effort, the many frustrations, and the remarkable difficulties provided by some of the local residents. Captain Hayne had the troublesome task of dealing with the complex
claim for extra payment made by McKay and Crichton. Enough has already
been said to show that they had legitimate grounds for extra payment
because of delays and extra pumping; to these factors was added an argument about the precise measurement of the masonry work that had been
completed. There will now be little interest in the details of the discussions
that preceded the final settlement; they seem to have taken up more 'paper'
than the actual building of the locks! But some of the masonry in question
can still be seen, the only remains of the original Carillon Canal being the
rather dilapidated masonry of the two downstream locks, now most fortunately preserved in the small park at Carillon that will be mentioned in the
last chapter. Those interested can still see how skilful was this handiwork of
a century and a half ago.

The serious delay in completing the Carillon Canal was not only a worry
to the contractors and to the supervising engineers, but a matter of great
concern to those charged with overall responsibility for the defence of
British North America. In his letter of July 1832 Charles Forbes had this to
say:

As the Rideau Canal is now in operation, and of course the necessary Lock Keepers
and Lock men are employed at a vast expense, it is a matter of the utmost importance that the intermediate Canals between this and Bytown should be completed
likewise, in order that the expense the Government must necessarily be put to, or at
least a portion of it, might be re-imbursed to the Military Chest, by inducing the
Trade thro' the Ottawa, instead of by the St Lawrence.[110]

Here is clear indication that the civilian use of the canals was recognized in
official quarters, a fact that was confirmed when the commissary-general
sent copies of the foregoing exchange of letters to the military secretary. In
his covering letter he explained that

The difficulties which have been experienced by the Forwarders at Montreal in procuring Bateaumen, to send on the Emigrants, and the reluctance I have to interfere
with those exertions, have induced me to send the Indian Presents and a Remittance
of Copper Money by way of the Carillon and Grenville, through the Rideau Canal
to Kingston, and because it appeared to me expedient that Government should be
the first to encourage the new Route.

He continued with a note on the impossibility of forcing 'loaded Bateaux or Durham Boats up the Rapids, by the main stream of the Ottawa to the mouth of (what is properly called) the Grenville Canal.'[111]

These were the realistic views of the Commissariat officers, but that the Ottawa River canals were still regarded as part of the military waterway between Montreal and Kingston is clearly shown by a request made by the commanding Royal Engineer in Canada. Writing to the military secretary on 22 November 1833, knowing that the Ottawa River canals were now ready for use, Colonel Nicholls asks about the use of one lot of land for fortifications to protect the Canals 'where it is proposed they remain and be put under the Superintendence of the Commanding Royal Engineer, Rideau Canal.'[112] The British government had now expended a total of £208,748 on building the three small canals and four times that amount on the Rideau Canal. Once the works were complete and the reservations of His Majesty's Treasury about slight over-expenditure on the Rideau Canal had been satisfied, the military canals were accepted by the British government as a sound investment as part of the measures taken for the defence of British North America. There was continuing concern, especially by the Duke of Wellington, as will be seen in chapter 7, about the three narrow locks on the Grenville Canal, but the other weak link in the chain of communication between Montreal and Kingston – the rapids at Ste Anne – seems to have escaped official attention.

THE LOCK AT STE ANNE-DE-BELLEVUE

Between the smooth water of the Lake of Two Mountains, which reached up to the Carillon Rapids, Lake St Louis, joined to Montreal by the Lachine Canal since its completion in 1825, there were the small rapids at Ste Anne-de-Bellevue and Vaudreuil, separated by Île Perrot, with a fall of about three feet for most of the year. Although this was not a large drop, it was concentrated and so sufficient to interfere seriously with vessels that had to pass, to such an extent that a group of Montreal forwarders had constructed a simple wooden lock adjacent to the shore at Vaudreuil as early as 1816. The St Andrews Trading Company built the lock, under the supervision of Theodore Davis, one of the landowners at Carillon with whom Henry Du Vernet had to deal. No details can now be found of this structure, but it was in regular use for about thirty years, so that it must have been of substantial construction. Until relatively recent years, some of the timbers used in its construction could be seen in the clear water of the rapids at Vaudreuil. It is probable that the existence of this privately owned lock, which did enable vessels to pass from Lake St Louis to the Lake of Two Mountains, was responsible for the continuing lack of official attention to the necessary permanent lock at Ste Anne as a part of the Montreal to Kingston military route.

It was certainly not forgotten. When Du Vernet submitted plans for the two smaller Ottawa River canals to the military secretary in 1829, he stated that he could not give an estimate for the cost of the necessary lock at Ste Anne, since he had no plans or reports upon which to base such calculations.[113] There is a tantalizing reference in a private letter written at about this time from Charles Forbes to Colonel Couper, the military secretary, in which he says that the Seminary of Montreal had lost £6,000 in attempting to 'build a sluice' (lock?) at Ste Anne.[114] The appointed contractor had failed because of the hard rock, and the work was abandoned. In a tabulation prepared early in 1830, the lock at the Ste Anne Rapids is included, with a sum of £40,000 assumed for its cost.[115] During the winter of 1830–1, Henry Du Vernet visited Ste Anne and prepared a large plan showing possible routes for a canal, without locks, designed to circumvent the rapids.[116] The plan, still in existence, was dated 8 March 1831; notes upon it give useful information about the fall in the rapids. Since the drop varied from nothing, at time of extremely high flood flows in the spring, to the normal three feet, Du Vernet's lock-less canal was not really practicable. He must have appreciated this fact, since on 12 July 1831 he was able to submit to the military secretary a set of plans and estimate of cost for a masonry lock at Ste Anne.[117]

No action was taken, however, and if the pressures to get the Ottawa River canals completed are recalled, this is perhaps understandable to a degree. The wooden lock at Vaudreuil was now owned by the Ottawa and Rideau Forwarding Company, which purchased in 1832 the first two steamboats in use on the lower Ottawa River. They proceeded to restrict passage through the lock to their own vessels, but for a short time only, since a valiant riverman in 1841 found a passage through the rapid up which vessels could be winched. Thereafter the monopoly was broken, but by this time work had commenced at Ste Anne on the building of a masonry lock. In 1839 the governor, through his military secretary, requested that the plans and other documents relative to the proposed lock at Ste Anne then in the hands of the military be passed to the Board of Works of the government of Lower Canada.[118] In a letter dated 5 February 1841, Commissary-General Routh (still in Canada) refers to 'the projected work by the provincial government at the Ste Anne Rapids in the ensuing spring.'[119] Work was finally started by the government of Lower Canada; its Board of Works awarded a contract in August 1839 for a masonry lock 190 feet long by forty-five feet wide. This was a time of transition, however; Upper and Lower Canada were united into the province of Canada in February 1841, and all public works in both provinces were taken over by the new Board of Commissioners of Public Works, of which H.H. Killaly was the first chairman. Accordingly, the lock at the Ste Anne was finished under this organization, but the Royal Engineers were also involved.

Captain Benjamin Stehelin was the Royal Engineer officer now resident at Carillon. On 31 March 1841 he wrote to the chairman of the Board of Works saying that the contractors at Ste Anne had done nothing beyond cutting ice and bringing pumps from Cornwall; would the board please do something?[120] On 1 July of the same year, the chairman wrote as follows to Captain Stehelin: 'Your Ste Ann's contractors are certainly as snarlish and unpleasant gentry to deal with as I have ever met' (the firm in question being Wilkinson and Company).[121] After the take-over by the commissioners, the secretary to the new board wrote from Kingston on 27 April 1843, again to Captain Stehelin, telling him that there was an error in one of the lock walls, and that they would not require a superintending engineer after the end of the month.[122] No engineer officer would take such an insult sitting down, and Stehelin stated in a long, six-page letter dated 8 May 1843 that he had been appointed directly by Lord Sydenham during a visit by the governor to Carillon in September 1840.[123] As for the error, this he describes as a 'malevolent act against my foreman.'

The lock at Ste Anne was therefore finished under the direction of the commissioners for public works, with some assistance from the Royal Engineers, and was first used in June 1843. In August of that same year, the new governor, Sir Charles Metcalfe, wrote from his Montreal residence to Lord Cathcart, the commander of the forces, as follows:

Concurring with your Lordship's views, I should rejoice in the transfer of the Lock at Ste Anne's Rapids to the charge of the Officers who conduct the management of the Rideau and Ottawa Canals on the part of the Imperial Government, but I much fear that the cession of the Ste Anne's Lock by the Colonial Legislature without a direct compensation, is not to be expected, and that the cost of the necessary enlargement of the three under-sized locks on the Grenville must devolve exclusively on the Imperial Government. I will nevertheless agitate the question.[124]

The transfer of responsibility, when it did take place, was the other way round, but the critical place that the Ottawa River canals occupied in official considerations of the defence of British North America continued to the end of the century.

The first vessel to pass through the Grenville Canal, however, had been not a naval vessel nor one with military supplies, but the *St Andrews*, a small trading vessel, reflecting the importance that the Ottawa River and Rideau canals were to occupy in the economy of the awakening country in their first years of operation. The first vessel through the Ste Anne Lock was likewise civilian. From June 1843, therefore, it was possible to sail all the way from Montreal to Kingston by way of the alternative route, lifted and lowered in well-built masonry locks, just as the duke of Richmond had foreseen a quarter of a century before. But only eight years later, the St Lawrence canals were finally completed, and all trade to the Great Lakes and the west was gradually diverted to the St Lawrence route, leaving the Ottawa and Rideau route, while still strategically important, to handle merely local traffic to and from the Ottawa and Rideau valleys.

7

Under the British flag: 1834–56

During the years of Henry Du Vernet's second stay in Canada, while he and his detachment were struggling to get the three Ottawa River canals completed, momentous events were taking place in the United Kingdom, the United States, and elsewhere in British North America. In 1830 King George IV died, generally unregretted as a person, although as monarch he was probably the most artistic king since Henry VIII, the Royal Academy and the British Museum being two of his foundations. He was succeeded by William IV, who reigned for seven years only. The Duke of Wellington became prime minister of Great Britain in 1828. Under his short administration some notable advances were made, but he could not accept the pressures for parliamentary reform and resigned on 16 November 1830. Although the Reform Bill was passed by the House of Commons in the following year, it was thrown out by the House of Lords. Introduced again under the administration of Earl Grey, it was finally passed by both British houses, but only under the threat of creating enough new members of the House of Lords to ensure its acceptance in the upper house. This was a pivotal event in British history. Passage in 1833 by the British parliament of the act abolishing slavery throughout the British empire was to have possibly even wider repercussions, as did the start of the British trade union movement at about this time. In 1837 King William IV died and was succeeded by Queen Victoria. And at the start of this time of transition, the Stockton and Darlington Railway had been opened on 27 September 1825, perhaps the most significant event in the early part of what would be called the Industrial Revolution, an event of special importance to all canal building.

In North America the uneasy truce between the United States of America and the British colonies continued. The impossibility of settling the dispute about the international boundary between New Brunswick and Maine (mediated in 1831 by the Dutch) was symptomatic of the lingering animosity. The Maine boundary question was finally settled in 1842 by Daniel Webster and Lord Ashburton (as Canadians can never forget). Andrew Jackson was re-elected as president in 1832 and was succeeded in 1837 by Martin van Buren. Jackson had the pleasure of seeing the entire national debt of his country paid off in 1835. Under van Buren expansion to the west was accelerated, but even in those years the problem posed by slavery was beginning to have political overtones. Strong action taken by the U.S. authorities against Canadian 'rebels' was indicative of growing rapprochement, and the Rush-Bagot agreement for the demilitarization of the Great Lakes continued to be scrupulously observed.

It was in Upper and Lower Canada, however, that local political developments were approaching a critical stage, leading to the outbreaks in both provinces in 1837. Quickly put down, the 'rebellions' indicated a state of affairs that could not be allowed to continue. The British government selected the Earl of Durham ('Radical Jack'), then in his forty-sixth year, to come out as the new governor in 1838, with power to suspend the constitution and to make a full investigation of what the future of the Canadas should be. He was recalled to Great Britain only five months after he had reached Quebec for reasons that are, today, difficult to appreciate. He sailed for England from Quebec on 1 November, so soon after his happy arrival on 27 May. During this short period he spent some time in Montreal and visited Upper Canada (where he spent eleven days), even though doing so involved the still arduous journey up the rapids of the St Lawrence River. He did not see the Ottawa Valley but doubtless heard of it in his many talks with citizens of all ranks. He obtained such a clear grasp of the situation in the Canadas, and in colonial territories generally, that the report that he prepared has been described as 'one of the finest state papers in the English language.'[1] Landing in Plymouth on 30 November, he set to work at once on the preparation of the report which was completed on 31 January 1839. But this remarkable man died on 28 July of the same year, at the age of only forty-seven.

The injudicious remarks in the report about French-speaking Canadians of Lower Canada have had the effect of making Lord Durham a figure of obloquy to many Canadians. His regrettable comments of 140 years ago have never been forgotten and so have unfortunately obscured the statesmanlike character of most of his great report, a document that firmly laid the foundations for future self-government of all British colonies. It has been said that 'he gave to the world a state paper on colonial matters which will live to all time,' and Canada was one of the beneficiaries, the Confederation of 1867 being, in some ways, an outcome of the 'Durham Report' as it is so widely known.[2] The earl's grasp of all the major aspects of life in early Canada and of the potential for development that he saw so clearly is truly remarkable when one recalls that he spent only five months in this land. Transportation was one matter that he saw to be crucial to the peaceful growth of the country. He observed the beginnings of the St Lawrence canals at Cornwall and must have heard of other canals, such as those on the Ottawa River. As he sailed past the mouth of the Ottawa before entering the St Lawrence from Lake St Louis, it is entirely probable that this second great river was pointed out to him; the delay in building the lock at Ste Anne-de-Bellevue would be a natural topic of conversation. Be that as it may, he expressed surprise in his report that there was only one short railway then operating in the whole country. One of his objections to the reservation of lands for support of the clergy was that they constituted an obstacle to the development of good transportation routes. But his most forthright comments had to do with canals:

While the Assembly (of Lower Canada) was wasting the surplus revenues of the Province in jobs for the increase of patronage, and in petty peddling in parochial business, it left untouched those vast and easy means of communication which deserved, and would have repaid, the application of the provincial revenues. The state of New York made its own St Lawrence from Lake Erie to the Hudson [the Erie Canal], while the Government of Canada could not achieve, or even attempt, the few miles of canal and dredging, which would have rendered its mighty rivers navigable almost to their sources.[3]

This is the only specific reference to canals in the report. Its rather over-enthusiastic wording gives a clue as to the appearance of some of the ill-considered remarks elsewhere, but the overall strong impression that water transportation in the Canadas had made on the earl's brilliant mind explains why it was that he had commissioned a special study of all the Canadian canals then in existence or in prospect. No mention of this study appears in the report or in its appendices, an omission perhaps explained by the speed with which the report was completed after his entirely unexpected recall to England, which resulted in the curtailment of many of his plans. Lieutenant-Colonel H. Phillpotts of the Royal Engineers was the officer selected to make this study; he had worked on the building of the early St Lawrence canals and his fine training as a sapper officer stood him in good stead as he carried out his investigation. At the start of his published report, he states that:

The following Report, called for by the instructions of His Excellency the Earl of Durham, will embrace three distinct lines of communication: (I) The communication of Lake Erie to the sea by the Welland Canal, Lake Ontario, and the River St Lawrence; (II) The communication from Lake Simcoe to Lake Ontario by the Rice Lakes and the River Trent; and (III) The communication from Lake Huron by the French River and Lake Nipissing, to the Ottawa River. the first of these being the most important, and my attention having also been more immediately called to it, as well as by my instructions as by the directions which I have subsequently received from His Excellency Lieut.-General Sir John Colborn, I proceed to report upon the communication from *Lake Erie to the sea by the Welland Canal, Lake Ontario, and the River St Lawrence*.[4]

This splendid report was published in 1842 in volume V of the *Professional Papers* of the Corps of Royal Engineers. This is now so rare a volume that it is small wonder that the 'Phillpotts Report' is so little known. No trace has yet been found of the other two parts of what was planned as the complete report, but the introduction to this first major part shows what a careful study Colonel Phillpotts had made of the whole problem of water communication in the Canadas, including the Ottawa River canals. He refers briefly to the building of the Rideau Canal by the Royal Engineers under Lieutenant-Colonel John By (mentioned by name), and of the Ottawa River canals by the Royal Staff Corps (with, as usual, no mention of Lieutenant-Colonel Du Vernet). He notes that the new lock at Ste Anne is expected to be built 'next year by the Provincial Government' (i.e., 1843) and then proceeds to compare the waterway from Montreal to Kingston by way of the Ottawa River and Rideau Canals, with that by the direct route up the St Lawrence. The change in thinking about the choice of routes, even on the part of a senior officer of the British army, is so remarkable that a full quotation seems to be called for, so that the future of the Ottawa River canals may then be viewed in the context of the thinking of the time. This is what Phillpotts said:

The question will at first sight naturally be asked by all persons not well acquainted with the subject, why the above mentioned canals, which now afford a safe communication to Kingston, and to which the British Government have already so largely contributed will not answer every purpose? and why therefore they should be called upon to assist in completing the works on the St Lawrence? To which it may be answered, that although the Ottawa and Rideau Canals are most useful in a military point of view, and in the event of a war with the United States they would be invaluable, yet they are so circuitous, and so much impeded by lockage, that they will not answer for commercial purposes; at least they never can compete with the American canals for the trade of the Western States. Some of the locks on the Ottawa Canals are at present too small for steamers; and even if they were enlarged to the size of the Rideau locks, they would be altogether too small for the steamers which navigate Lake Ontario and the Upper Lakes, and therefore a trans-shipment at Kingston would be necessary; consequently a canal on that scale, even if it were made along the line of the St Lawrence, would never draw off the trade of the Western States to the sea-ports of Lower Canada to the extent that it may be made to if completed on the scale here proposed. For unless we open an uninterrupted navigation for *large freight steamers*, capable of conveying a cargo of at least 300 tons, *without any trans-shipment* before they arrive at Montreal or Quebec, we have no chance whatever of securing any great portion of that vast and important trade which may, if properly encouraged, be most undoubtedly induced to come by this route, and thus confer incalculable advantages on the inhabitants both of Upper and Lower Canada ... [with this percipient addendum] ... And I fully believe that nothing would tend so much to quiet the different parties in both provinces, and to produce contentment in the minds of all the well affected portion of the population, as the speedy completion of this very important communication, of which I now proceed to enter upon the details.[5]

If one increases that figure of '300 tons' a hundred times, much of Colonel Phillpotts's quoted statement could well have served as a manifesto for the St Lawrence Seaway and Power project completed in 1959! The clarity of his vision is also shown by the qualifying footnote that appears in the report, with reference to the lockage on the two routes to Lake Ontario and their respective lengths. He points out that on the Ottawa route there is a rise of eight-two feet from Lachine to the entrance to the Rideau Canal, then a rise of 292 feet three inches to Upper Rideau Lake, followed by a drop of 165 feet four inches to Lake Ontario, all in a total distance of 237 miles. The route up the St Lawrence has a total length of only 190 miles with a total rise of 209 feet. This significant difference was naturally well known to all who planned the Ottawa River canals and the Rideau system, but their thinking was dominated by requirements of defence. It is an indication of the change in thinking that Colonel Phillpotts, himself an engineer officer, should have stressed the commercial advantages of the St Lawrence route and given only a lukewarm acknowledgment of the defence aspects of these water transportation systems. But the Rideau and the Ottawa River canals were still military waterways, their construction was paid for completely by the British government, their operation was still its responsibility, and the operating staff were officers and men of the Royal Engineers. They were to remain so until the year 1857. And even in recent years, the Ottawa Rivers canals were still known to local residents as 'the military canals,' as the writer has himself heard when talking with older residents of the Grenville area.

We saw at the end of the first chapter of this book that the Royal Navy ceased to have any presence on the Great Lakes in 1838. The meticulous observance of the Rush-Bagot agreement throughout all the years since then had made unnecessary any change in this situation. The threat of naval action remained for many years, however, so that those responsible for British defence planning were very glad to have the Ottawa-Rideau route complete, just in case it should be needed. It is not without relevance to note that one of the last-ditch arguments of the opponents of the St Lawrence Seaway in the United States was that, if built, it would permit ships of the Royal Navy to enter the Great Lakes, thus threatening the peace that had by then existed between the two countries for a century and a quarter.

The advantage of the St Lawrence route was well appreciated by those living along its shores. Work had therefore started on the first Cornwall Canal, to circumvent the Long Sault (of the St Lawrence), as early as 1834; the records suggest fairly definitely that this move was in direct response to the completion of the Ottawa-Rideau route, even though the Ste Anne lock had still to be built.[6] The troubles of 1837 slowed up progress, and work was not fully resumed on the Cornwall Canal until 1842, when the newly created Board of Public Works undertook its completion. Work was so far advanced by the fall of that year that, before the season closed, a Captain Stearns managed to sail the small steamer *Highlander* through the still unfinished canal and then up the rapids further up the river, finally reaching the harbour of Kingston. This was the beginning of the end for the Ottawa-Rideau system as a through commercial route between Montreal and Kingston. When the board completed the first Soulanges Canal in 1845 and then the Williamsburg canals by 1851, the die was cast and the St Lawrence route began its long career as the major artery to the Great Lakes. Thereafter, the Ottawa River canals would serve only local traffic between Montreal and Bytown-Ottawa, although, as will be seen, they continued to be a key part of British defence planning for the North American colony of Canada, and later for the new dominion, even after Great Britain had surrendered its responsibility for defence to the government of Canada.

Throughout the two decades following the completion of the Ottawa River canals, they continued to give good service to traffic up and down the Ottawa. And until 1851, when the St Lawrence canals were finally completed, the Ottawa-Rideau route was also the St Lawrence seaway, since small ocean-going vessels could sail up to Montreal from the Atlantic, then through the Lachine Canal, and so up the Ottawa River and through the Rideau Canal to Kingston. Officially under the Board of Ordnance from 1829, as has been seen, the operation of both the Rideau and the Ottawa River canals was made the responsibility of the Corps of Royal Engineers. Superintending engineers, after Colonel By's departure in 1832 were Lieutenant-Colonel Bolton (to 1843), Lieutenant-Colonel Thomson (to 1847), Captain C.E. Fort (to 1853), and Captain Chayter to the time of transfer to the commissioners of public works of the province of Canada. For a short time after the departure of Colonel Du Vernet, Captain Richard Hayne was in charge of the Ottawa River canals; he, too, continued to sign himself as an officer of the Royal Staff Corps. Eventually Captain Ben S. Stehelin, RE, was appointed superintending engineer.

These officers had to deal not only with the operation of the canals but also with some residual problems from the time of construction. Claims for damages to land continued, especially from Mr Grece. One record made by Captain Stehelin to his commanding officer on 18 June 1841 relates that 'about 36 hours after the opening of navigation of the Grenville Canal, Mr Grece accompanied by another person came to me while the Northwest Canoes were passing the detached lock of the Carillon Canal.'[7] This interview was about the bridges over the Carillon Canal; it finished up, as did so many of Mr Grece's encounters, with a first-class row. The reference to 'Northwest Canoes' is a strange lapse, since the North West Company had amalgamated with the Hudson's Bay Company as long ago as 1821, all traffic thereafter being that of Hudson's Bay Company's canoes, notably the annual spring journey of Sir George Simpson, the illustrious governor of the honourable company.

Even more surprising were the continued efforts of Richard Ritchie (see p. 91) to obtain a pension because of the injuries he sustained in 1827 when working under Captain King. In July 1839 he addressed another formal petition to Sir John Colborne, the governor who had succeeded Lord Durham and served throughout that year.[8] The appeal related how he had lost an eye in the accident, was now losing the other eye, and had eight children to support; it continued thus: 'Last year (your petitioner) joined a Company of the Grenville Royal Volunteers with his son (yet a boy), both having been actuated by an earnest desire of rendering themselves useful in that capacity, should their services be required, which points out to your Excellency that your (petitioner) rears up his children in the principles of loyalty and attachment to the Crown, of which he himself is well known to be possessed.' Despite the illogical nature of the appeal, it had to be forwarded across the sea to Whitehall, and formal letters continued to be exchanged.[9]

These personal problems, however, were completely overshadowed by the continued frustrations caused by the narrow widths of the three upstream locks on the Grenville Canal, *still* not rebuilt despite the many recommendations that they should be brought up to the standard dimensions of the later locks on the Ottawa River canals and of all those on the Rideau Canal. Even the Duke of Wellington, in his retirement at his country residence, Strathfield Saye, was concerned about this far-distant engineering defect. He was still consulted by the British government, and in two confidential letters to Lord Hill, dated 12 and 14 April 1841, he relates that he has 'seen a person who has lately travelled by Inland Navigation from Montreal to Kingston and back again.' The second letter reveals that the person was his son Charles. No record of this journey has yet been found, but it was clearly on the basis of his son's information that the duke stated that 'It appears that the Canals between Montreal and Bytown ... are not as wide as the Rideau Canal from the Ottawa to Kingston. It would be very desirable, therefore, that all the canals from Montreal to Bytown should be widened, as soon as possible, to the size of the Rideau Canal ... This work was always reckoned upon, and was estimated.'[10] And as late as 1845, at the age of seventy-seven, he asked in a special letter written on 25 August from his stately home to Lord Stanley, the secretary of state for war and colonies: 'I entreat your Lordship's attention ... to the necessity for immediately reforming the Locks on the Grenville Canal.'

The duke was near the end of his life when he wrote thus, in response to a request for his views on the defence of British North America. Despite his worry about the locks at Grenville, it is gratifying to read of his satisfaction with the works in general: 'However expensive the work upon the Rideau (and Ottawa) nobody now doubts the wisdom of the plan, its efficiency, and above all its economy.' The economy of the whole system, however, was seriously restricted by the limitation upon the size of vessels that the three Grenville locks imposed. Typical of the many protests still on record is a petition from the grand jury of the district of Dalhousie (in which Bytown was located) to the commanding officer of the Royal Engineers, in February 1844, begging that the three locks at Grenville be enlarged and asking if the commander-in-chief of the forces (the governor) would let them know the views of the government on this matter.[11]

The establishment of the Board of Public Works of the province of Canada has already been recorded; the commissioners, too, were concerned about the 'little locks.' On 26 March 1844 to the civil secretary of the board, the chairman, H.H. Killaly, wrote:

That these locks should have been permitted to remain, for such a length of time, of dimensions so much smaller than all the others upon the same line of communication between Lake Ontario and Lake St Louis, has long been a source of public dissatisfaction, inasmuch as thereby the value of that communication to the trade has been materially lessened ... and it may be questioned if all the locks of this – the Rideau and Ottawa navigation – had been of uniform capacity whether the extensive and costly improvements of the St Lawrence route would have been undertaken by the Province for a considerable time to come ... I am further of opinion that the permitting these locks to remain of the small dimensions, must continue to be not only a serious drawback to the amount of revenue which might otherwise be derived from this navigation, but will tend also to retard the improvements of the River beyond Bytown.[12]

This percipient comment from one of Canada's outstanding early engineers confirmed what others had been saying. The St Lawrence canals would almost certainly have been built in any case, as an alternative to those on the Ottawa-Rideau route, but the early efforts to complete the Cornwall Canal do seem to have been accelerated by dissatisfaction with the military canals.

Some notice must finally have been taken of the growing complaints about the little locks, since on 5 March 1846 Colonel Holloway (now the commanding Royal Engineer in Canada) was able to report that the master-general and Board of Ordnance had notified him on 2 February that the lords commissioners of Her Majesty's Treasury had sanctioned the issue of the necessary order for granting the sum of £23,650 in anticipation of the vote of Parliament towards 'enlarging the Grenville Canal and building the new locks in the year 1846-7.'[13] But Parliament did not vote as expected, and so, once again, nothing was done. Nor would this essential reconstruction job be undertaken for another quarter of a century.

Few records remain that relate to the actual users of the three locks and the nuisance that the narrow channels must have caused, and there are not many accounts of journeys up or down the Ottawa during this period. One of the few is a copy of an extract from the log of the 'H.M. Steamer *Union*.'[14] This vessel is believed to have been the first steam-operated vessel on the Ottawa River. Constructed by Thomas Mears at Hawkesbury in 1822 and named then the *Union of the Ottawa*, the vessel was sold in 1830, the name being then shortened to *Union*. Eventually it was bought for government use but, as the log makes clear, it was a most unreliable vessel. As originally built, it was little more than an elaborate barge with a Boulton and Watt steam engine mounted on the deck. The log does not give the captain's name, but he was clearly a patient man. The boat left Montreal at 4 p.m. on 13 August 1841, was towed through the Lachine Canal by four horses, and arrived at Lachine at midnight after 'experiencing considerable difficulty in passing the Locks, from there not being more than just the length of the vessel and in two instances, not more than her height under the bridges.' The *Union* did not leave Lachine until 5:30 the next afternoon, since, in an attempt to reverse the engine, the 'rest of the rocking shaft' was broken, and then the tubes of the boiler were found to be leaking; the boiler had to be drained and the tubes repaired. It was eight o'clock in the evening when it reached the Cascades (just below Vaudreuil).

After an early start on 15 August, it went through the private lock at Vaudreuil but found a depth of only three feet of water (two feet ten inches at one point), so ballast had to be removed to get the vessel through. It was helped by the steamer *Ottawa*, took on one cord of wood, left at 2:15 p.m. on 16 August and reached Carillon at 5:30. The passage through the Ottawa River canals on the following day is thus described in the log:

Took on Board one cord of firewood and at 7. a.m., steamed up the Canal, at the western end of which, in consequence of the Cofferdam not having been removed, we were obliged to lighten and employ Steamer *Mohawk* to get over, there being barely 3 feet of water on it – towed up to Chute-à-Blondeau 2½ miles – at the western entrance of the Lock took the ground – with assistance of Steamer got over without lightening – the Bottom very soft mud – at 4:30 arrived at Greasey's point (distance 1½ miles) entrance to Grenville Canal, found the Channel much obstructed by two large rocks, which if removed, would make the entrance commodious, experienced considerable delay from a Batteau aground on one of the Rocks there not being Room to pass, got our Anchor away and hove her off, which permitted us to proceed, hired four horses to tow up the Grenville Canal and arrived there at 8 P.M.

Thirteen hours for passage through the three canals was not fast travelling, but improvements must have been made by the Royal Engineers, because later accounts do not mention delays such as the *Union* experienced.

In 1841 Colonel R.H. Bonnycastle (later Sir Richard) travelled the Ottawa-Rideau route and later described his journey in a well-known book (*The Canadas in 1841*). He pays glowing tribute to John By and his work on the Rideau Canal, but his reference to the Ottawa River canals is brief in the extreme:

The Carillon Rapids ... have been overcome by a government military canal in con-nexion with the Rideau ... Between it and the Grenville Canal is another interruption of nearly a mile, called the Chute-à-Blondeau, but this is comparatively trifling. Twelve miles from the Carillon was a more serious impediment ... and here it was necessary to create a canal of six locks. It however happened, that owing to its being decided to render the Rideau navigation a steam-boat channel, an alteration took place in the size of the locks of some parts of these works, which was ordered after some of them had been finished on the same scale as the La Chine Canal. Thus, steam-boats could not pass through the Grenville Canal, and an outlay must be re-quired in conjunction with that at Ste Anne's, or Vaudreuil, to render the line navigable from La Chine.[15]

Small steamboats, as has just been seen, could pass through the Grenville Canal, but this slight inexactitude may be overlooked along with the absence of any reference to the Royal Staff Corps, when it is recalled that this was the record of an officer of the Royal Engineers. (Gaps in the quota-tion are names and brief records of distances.)

Another justly famous Canadian travelled from Montreal to Kingston in 1845 on one of the small steamships that had already been introduced to provide a through passenger service on this route. He was a young Scots-man, Sandford Fleming (later Sir Sandford), outstanding railway engineer, builder of the Intercolonial Railway, inventor of Standard Time, designer of Canada's first postage stamp, with many other notable achievements in his seventy years of service to Canada. In his diary he recorded that the boxes over the side paddle wheels of the small vessel had to be removed in order to get the boat through the three little locks, an exercise that clearly made a profound impression on the young engineer's mind![16] It is somewhat remarkable that Sandford Fleming did not notice, or at least did not record, that there was a rough road running parallel to the three canals, from Carillon to Grenville. As passenger traffic developed in the 1840s, a simple type of stage-coach was operated over this road so that passengers could be spared the slow (though interesting) passage through the canals and locks. And in 1854 the road and the canal were paralleled by a railway, one of the most remarkable of early Canada.

The story of the 'Portage Railway' comes in the later civilian period of the history of the Ottawa River canals, but the existence of the road is a clear indication that the canals were being well used early in their service to

Canada. To get an overview of the development of commercial traffic, it is necessary to go back a little in time and recall that it was the introduction of steamboats, of steadily increasing power and size, that changed for all time the character of traffic on Canadian waterways. The first steamboat on the St Lawrence was the *Accommodation* of John Molson, launched in 1809; the first on the Ottawa in 1822 was the *Union of the Ottawa,* one of whose later adventures is recorded on p. 154. Earlier, Philemon Wright had been operating for some years his own regular packet service from Grenville to Hull using, probably, a Durham boat. Below the Long Sault, 'Judge' Macdonnell of Pointe Fortune had started a similar service between St Andrews and Montreal.[17] It seems probable that one of the very early steamboats was built for this service, since in 1816 there was organized the St Andrews Steam Forwarding Company and it was this small group that built the wooden lock at Vaudreuil (see p. 141). Just as the Ottawa River canals were approaching completion, a group of far-sighted Montreal businessmen headed by John Molson banded together to form the Ottawa and Rideau Forwarding Company, which bought up the few existing steam vessels and the St Andrews Company, thus taking possession also of the lock at Vaudreuil.

Once the canals were opened for public traffic in 1834, traffic did indeed develop as expected, and it was not long before the monopolistic position of the new company at Vaudreuil caused problems. On 19 April 1834 William Morris, a leading citizen of Perth, then the main community in this part of eastern Upper Canada, wrote thus to the governor's military secretary:

so long as the Ottawa Forwarding Company have the exclusive contract of a Lock near the Lake of Two Mountains they will monopolize the whole navigation of that River, and it has occurred to me that as the manager of that Company will not permit any persons to pass the Lock in question with boats from this quarter that his Lordship may justly direct that the boats of that operation should not be allowed to enter any of the Government Locks so long as the public is prevented from using their private lock upon the payment of reasonable tolls.[18]

Somewhat naturally, this suggestion does not appear to have been accepted by the governor. The company continued to own and operate the lock, but with mounting irritations.

Their position was not threatened until 1841, when an intrepid river man, Robert Ward Shepherd, found a channel near the Vaudreuil Lock up which barges could be 'snagged,' as had been the limited practice up the rapids at Ste Anne when the river level was high enough. But this solution was short lived, since, as has been seen, the new masonry lock at Ste Anne was opened for use in June 1843; thereafter the lock at Vaudreuil fell into disuse. It was from 1843 until the opening of the final St Lawrence canal in 1851 that the 'Ottawa route,' as the main route from Montreal to Lake Ontario, saw its greatest days. Traffic developed so rapidly that it was soon reported that 'steamers upon the principle of the screw propellor, as well as others [presumably paddle-wheelers] were about to navigate the whole route, carrying burdens the same as a barge' and that one steamer was already in use for carrying passengers only.[19] It was not only Montreal businessmen who were alive to the possibilities that the Ottawa route would present, but also those in the St Lawrence towns. Early in 1841 the brothers Jones, writing from Brockville, had appealed to the commanding Royal Engineer to have the fixed bridges across the canals raised, since they were building a steamboat which otherwise would have to have its funnel and wheelhouse changed if this were not done, because there would be insufficient clearance.[20]

Somewhat naturally, statistics of the early traffic on the Ottawa River canals are almost non-existent, the earliest continuously recorded figures starting in 1852. There is one record of the traffic using the canals in 1845, however, and it shows that 354 steamboats and 903 barges passed through, presumably in the two directions.[21] These vessels carried 484 'cabin passengers,' 19,381 tons of merchandise, and 4,715 tons of iron and fish, the distinction being made because the latter items were not charged tolls. In 1846 it was necessary for the commanding Royal Engineer to request the governor through the usual channel to extend the regulations governing the operation of the Rideau Canal to the Ottawa River canals in order 'to protect the works from improper conduct of the Masters of Vessels.'[22] The increase in the volume of traffic must have been spectacular for the time, since by 1856, the year in which the canals were finally transferred to the ownership and control of the provincial government, the traffic is reported to have been:

Upstream: 1,458 vessels carrying 10,784 tons of freight and 1,377 passengers;
Downstream: 1,188 vessels carrying 158,617 tons of freight and an unspecified number of passengers.

Statistics do not make for easy reading, and so all the available figures have been combined into tabular form and will be found in appendix C, from which the growth in traffic over the years, despite the opening of the direct St Lawrence route, can readily be traced.

The striking contrast between the upstream and downstream volumes of freight is explained by the growing lumber trade of the Ottawa Valley. Sawn lumber was now being milled at both Ottawa and Hawkesbury and shipped to Montreal and other markets by barge. At the peak of this trade, towards the end of the century, there were as many as 250 barges and fifty tugs in use. The barges were pulled by tugs downstream from Bytown-Ottawa and Calumet. They were hauled through the Grenville Canal by horses using the towpath between Grenville and Greece's Point; a special tug then hauled the barges down to the upstream lock of the Carillon Canal, through which they were also pulled by horses, a separate stable being kept at Carillon for this purpose. Thence tugs again took charge for the sail across the Lake of Two Mountains. Correspondingly, large timbers were going down the Ottawa River in immense quantities in the form of great rafts, formed by linking up carefully made cribs. These rafts were guided through the rapids by expert rivermen whose skill became legendary, a fascinating part of the history of the Ottawa. Some indication of the quantity of timber moved down the Ottawa is given by the fact that the cribs passing Bytown varied from 8,310 in 1840 to 14,131 in 1846, the average for a nine-year period being 9,300. (These figures come from an annual report of the commissioners of public works, not from the military records). Each crib would hold at least 200 large timbers, so that on the average almost 2 million timbers went down each year. The lumber trade is a fascinating part of the story of the Ottawa River, but, other than the fact that sawn lumber comprises so much of the freight transported through the canals, it is beyond the scope of this book. Readers who are interested may be referred to the author's *Ottawa Waterway* for a general treatment of this remarkable chapter in the development of Canada's lumber industry.

Tolls were charged on freight and passengers using the canals from the time of opening and thereafter until the abolition of all tolls on Canadian canals in 1903, on the very sensible grounds that it was then costing more to collect the tolls than they yielded. The rates thus levied so long ago are of little interest today, but the total income from tolls on the Ottawa River canals for the year 1845 amounted to £4,113-4-1. The initial tariff of rates was protested, with the result that the officers responsible urged the governor to halve the rates on many items. Very bulky items of freight were charged too much, while other rates would, if reduced, advance 'the clearing and settlement of the Ottawa River.' The list of items reflects the pioneer life of the small population then living on the banks of the river. It included beef, pork, beer, and cider; staves and oak, pine, and elm timbers. Firewood on rafts for the use of ships was to be free; and the rate on tanner's bark, ashes, and potash was halved. This last item reflects the cutting down of the forest by the early settlers; trees that were not sold for timber were burned to obtain the ash, then needed to make soap and explosives. And immigrants 'forwarded at the cost of Government' were to be carried free.

Settlers were indeed arriving and were using the Ottawa River canals almost from the day of their opening. In June 1834 the Kingston *Herald* explained that

Persons who can take the River line (i.e. the St. Lawrence route) of boats and stages, will gain time by taking that route, as they will reach Montreal from Kingston in less than a day and a half, and return in two days. But for Emigrants, who, if they ascend the St. Lawrence, must come in Durham boats, the Rideau route is greatly preferable. Coming from Lachine to Kingston in barges, they are preserved from frequent drenching rains, from heavy dews by night, and a burning sun by day, and they will generally accomplish the passage in less time than by the river.

This was tribute indeed, coming from the city of Kingston, local rivalries being what they were in those days. The use of covered barges towed by steam tugs quickly became well established, some barges going through the entire route from Montreal to Kingston (for which a fare of twelve shillings sixpence was charged), the tugs confined to the different navigable stretches of the rivers.

This is a far cry from the intended use of the canal system for defence purposes, but settlement was a vital part of the opening up of the Ottawa Valley, and in this the Ottawa River canals played their part. A brief summary of settlement may therefore be given before we turn back to the actual operation of the canals while they were still the responsibility of the British government. The small towns of St Andrews and Lachute were well established when construction of the canals started; they had been founded in 1785 and 1797, respectively. In 1796 Nathaniel Treadwell had come up the Ottawa, eventually to establish his settlement just above the Long Sault in one of the only two seigniories ever founded in Upper Canada, the settlement becoming the town of L'Orignal. Louis Joseph Papineau, that formidable figure of early Canadian politics, travelled up the river in 1803, after purchasing the seigniory of Montebello, where he later built his manor house, still to be seen today, in which he entertained many of the early leaders of Canada. The Hamilton brothers came in 1808 and purchased from Thomas Mears (of St Andrews) the first mill of what was to become their great lumber industry, the foundation of Hawkesbury on the south shore of the river at the head of the Long Sault. Archibald Macmillan followed in 1810, establishing himself at what was soon to be the village of Grenville on the north bank of the river. In later years, Macmillan and Hamilton would communicate across the river by a system of flags, arranging in this way for their social meetings on appropriate Scottish festival days.

They sometimes joined John Macdonald of Pointe Fortune, the settlement at the downstream end of the rapid section of the river, opposite Carillon, which had been established in 1788 and named after Colonel William Fortune to whom the original land grant was made. John (Judge) Macdonnell was later joined by his brother Miles, famous in Canadian history because of his part in Lord Selkirk's adventures at the Red River settlement. In 1804 Captain Jacob Schagel was one of the first settlers at what became Carillon, and one of his first jobs was to fulfil a contract for carrying freight from Carillon to Grenville over what could only have been a rough trail through the bush. He also operated the first ferry between Carillon and Pointe Fortune. When construction of the Ottawa River Canals started, therefore, the four small settlements at the two ends of the 'canal stretch' of the Ottawa, on both banks, were well established as the staging points for the portaging that was so necessary along the stretch of the river. They were simple places with little to offer the officers and men of the Royal Staff Corps, although they did provide some human contacts which must have been extremely welcome for the men in the construction camps.

It is an interesting aspect of the settlement of the Ottawa Valley that these four settlements, at the 'corners' of the canal area, still exist today despite all the changes in the intervening century and a half. Pointe Fortune, Carillon, and Grenville remain as pleasing small villages; Hawkesbury alone has become a large town, the earlier lumber mills succeeded by a major pulp and paper plant (now closed). Other early settlements, however, have not lived up to their early promise. Lemuel Cushing, for example, came up the Ottawa in 1823 from Trois Rivières and established himself on a small creek just downstream of the Chute à Blondeau, which soon became known as Cushing Creek. Within a short time, a saw-mill, stone-cutting shop, a blacksmith's shop, and finally a grist-mill were in operation on the creek, which flowed down from St Philippe; the village of Cushing became a centre of activity for the whole of the canal area. Cushing himself served as a justice of the peace for over fifty years and was a leader of the community in every way. His grist-mill must have been especially welcome to the few early settlers around. It is recorded that Alexander Cameron, who had come over from Lochaber in Argyllshire in 1808 to settle at a spot half-way up the shore of the Long Sault, walked to the mill at Lachute (about twelve miles) with a sack of grain on his back and then walked back to his little cabin the same day carrying now the milled grain.[23] His son was known as 'Big Allan' and served as a pilot on the Ottawa River for forty years.

Stores sprang up and prospered once the canals were in operation. Perhaps the best known was that of Owen Owens, a settler from Denbigh in North Wales, who established himself at Stonefield, the name that had come to be used for the few houses around Lock No. 3 on the Grenville Canal. The name was appropriate, since the land around was (and still is, to some extent) strewn with large glacial boulders. At one time, five assistants were needed in Owen Owens's store, but with changing times, trade dropped off until the store closed in 1936, and the building was demolished before the flooding of 1962. There was another busy store at Cushing, as well stocked (so it was said) as any between Ottawa and Montreal; and another one was established at Carillon. Grenville also had a store, an early hotel, and the first post office of the district, which dispatched mail by coach to Montreal.

At the start of canal construction, almost all food and materials had to be brought up from Montreal, the only supplies available locally being meat, fish, and game. These were plentiful. Salmon were caught in quantity in the North River. The Ottawa yielded a variety of species of fish, notably shad, and fishing for these small fish around the first day of June yielded enough for local residents to stock their ice-cooled larders for the full year. Small wonder that they were then called 'Carillon beef.' As settlement developed, so also did the availability of local supplies, and before construction was complete, meat was being supplied locally to the Royal Staff Corps. Not surprisingly, perhaps, a small distillery was built near Carillon in 1824, but it fell into disuse in 1828, and the building was taken over by the Royal Staff Corps when work began on the Carillon Canal. There are a few records of complaints about liquor being supplied by Daniel de Hertel from his store at Grenville, but, in so far as one can see from the records that remain, strong drink was not such a serious problem as it proved to be in other parts of the awakening land.

An early visitor had this to say about the first residents of Argenteuil County: 'Honest dealing, and a desire to observe the Golden Rule of doing as they would that others should do to them, is a prevalent trait. Hospitality is a quality found in every household. Into whatever family the stranger enters, he is welcome at the board'[24] Almost all the settlers in the vicinity of the military canals were Scottish. It is not surprising, therefore, to find that the first resident minister in the canal area was the Reverend Mr Mair of the Church of Scotland. Occasional visits from Methodist circuit riders were recorded from the closing years of the eighteenth century. There had been an Anglican priest resident at St Andrews from 1805 and a Presbyterian minister from 1818.[25] The 'Stone Hall' was erected at Cushing in 1830 by the Methodists, a well constructed masonry building which still survives, now as a private residence. It was used by the members of the Church of Scotland until they erected their own church in 1836, later (1861) named St Mungo's, also at Cushing. The land for it had been purchased from William Clark, who had taken his discharge from the Royal Staff Corps. Great was the rejoicing when the little church was dedicated. The church still stands, is in good repair and in regular use, although now as part of the United Church of Canada. In its records are still to be seen the names of men of the Royal Staff Corps.[26] It is a moving experience to worship in the lovely little building and to realize that its history goes back to the completion of the Ottawa River canals.

They were still the military canals. Even today, one can sense the alarm with which Captain Bolton in Bytown advised the military secretary at Quebec on 6 July 1838 that he had received advice by the last steamboat to the effect that a 'party of 40 men are (roving around) the country, determined to destroy some of the locks if possible.'[27] The report was a reflection of the unrest surrounding the uprising of 1837, in response to which some of the local settlers joined the volunteer regiments then quickly raised. The alarm proved to be unfounded, however, so the little canals continued in their peaceful service, traffic steadily increasing despite all difficulties.

There were other concerns, such as that addressed to the military secretary to the governor on 9 July 1840 by George Moffatt from Kingston about the serious interference with trade caused by the failure of the middle lock gates of Carillon locks in the preceding spring, with no spare gates on hand for replacing them.[28] According to Moffat, the cessation of traffic through the canals for three weeks had caused losses estimated at £20,000, owing to the hold-up of goods at Kingston, including 145,000 barrels of wheat flour, ashes, and provisions. Reply to this was furnished on 20 July by Lieutenant-Colonel Oldfield, the commanding Royal Engineer in Canada, in a spirited defence of his men.[29] Lauding the zeal of his officers, he explains that the Ottawa River canals have been closed for only twenty-eight and half days in the preceding six navigation seasons – 'a perfect refutation to the infamies which the querulous complaints of various parties would draw.' And he concludes, with great respect, to assure the military secretary of the continuation of his close attention to the operation of the canals and to 'the commercial interests of these Provinces.'

The dichotomy in the purpose of the canals must have been of increasing concern to the officers in Canada responsible for their maintenance and operation. Defence was certainly not forgotten. In commenting upon the closure of the canals in the spring of 1841, for example, the Ordnance Office in Montreal reported to the military secretary that 'the troops can march from Carillon to Grenville with no delay' should the need arise.[30] Problems of maintenance, however, increased with increasing use of the canals, especially with the growing use of steamboats. The effect of these new-fangled steamers on the canal works is indicated by the collapse of part of the banks at the upper lock on the Carillon Canal in the winter of 1844.[31] The ordnance officers advised the military secretary on 15 March 1844 that arrangements for the necessary repair work had been made, the contract stipulating that the work had to be completed by 1 May with a penalty of £10 per day for any delay after that date, an interesting and very early example of the penalty clause that is a frequent feature of modern construction contracts.[32]

This emphasis on speed clearly indicates the steadily growing use of the canals for civilian purposes. Defence requirements were reflected in discussions that took place in 1845 about the provision of a new ordnance vessel for use on the canals.[33] The governor approved this allowance in October 1845, but clearly nothing was done about it in 1846. For in January 1847 the commanding Royal Engineer, now Colonel W.C.E. Holloway, noted that no very small boat, as had been recommended by the ordnance officers, would be suitable, but that a vessel larger than one equipped with a thirty horsepower engine would not be able to use the upper three locks on the Grenville Canal until they were enlarged.[34] The problem of the small locks was still there! Colonel Holloway suggested that the government steamer *Union* could still be used, since what was wanted was a vessel to tow barges and carry passengers. Difficulties in operating even small steamers had been experienced in 1846. The ordnance officers had advised the military secretary in September of that year about the serious situation at the Ste Anne lock where 'at the lower entrance to the Lock there was ... only two feet of water ... and in the upper entrance the small steamer to which resort must be had struck the bottom three times.' They proceeded to ask if the governor would ask the provincial government what it intended to do about it.[35]

Small wonder that there were difficulties in operation, but, despite the now obvious value of the canals as a commercial waterway, the Ordnance Department continued to operate them as well as possible. The lockmasters had been drawn, generally, from the ranks of the sergeants discharged from the Royal Staff Corps. The records make clear that uniforms had been provided, a note of alarm being sounded in a communication of July 1854 about the non-arrival of requested supplies of caps, jackets, and trousers.[36] As the years advanced, the military men gradually retired from these positions, and it became necessary to advertise for new recruits. Happily, the wording of one of the advertisements has been retained in the records. After explaining what the position was, the notice (of July 1856) stated that 'The party should be able to read and write legibly and possess knowledge of the first four rules of Arithmetic with sufficient general information upon accounts to keep a simple debtor and credit account. He should be perfectly steady (and of) sober habits ... and active physically ... his usefulness principally resting upon activity and integrity.'[37]

Later that summer, the storekeeper on the Carillon Canal had to advise the ordnance officers in Montreal that there had been a deficiency in the supply of water down the little feeder canal from the North River, with the result that the operation of the Carillon Canal had been interfered with and trade had been seriously impeded.[38] This would be expected if the water level in the upper section of the canal were lower than normal because of insufficient water supply after lockages had drained some water out. Again, the plea was made to bring this serious matter to the attention of the provincial government. The development of settlement along the canal also was raising new problems, one of these being the matter of a wall between the canal property at Grenville and the graveyard of St Matthew's Anglican church there which had now been built, the church that may be seen today by visitors to Grenville.[39] And a sure indication that times were changing is a reference in one letter from the military secretary to 'The Ordnance Storekeeper on the Canal having again called attention [to lack of funds] by telegraph received this morning.'[40] This new means of communication was at first accepted with some reservations, as is shown by the fact that letters were still written by hand and copied by hand, confirming what the telegraph had advised. The service was provided by the International Telegraph Company, whose office on St Francis Xavier Street in Montreal was 'connecting with all the Principal Cities and Towns in Canada and the United States.' But even the company had some reservations about its service, since, on the old printed form still in the records, there appears the statement: 'Company not responsible for the inaccuracies of operators.'

Times were changing indeed. British authorities continued to be concerned about the defence of British North America, a position at first strongly supported by the Duke of Wellington from his retirement. More reports on the Canadian situation were ordered, notable studies being prepared by Captain Boxer, RN, and Colonel W.C.E. Holloway, R.E. (jointly), and almost the same time (1846) by Captain Frederick Warden, RN. Their recommendations naturally included urgent pleas for the improvement of the small locks on the Grenville Canal and the strengthening of canal defences, since conflict with the United States was still deemed to be a possibility. In the light of these reports, the duke wrote to Mr Gladstone (now secretary for the colonies and war) strongly urging the completion of the works that he had long ago initiated. In a letter of 29 April 1846, he said that 'No defence of Canada can be undertaken unless this water communication be completed.'[41]

A new British government took office in 1846, headed by Lord John Russell. Under his administration and those of Lord Derby (1852) and Lord Aberdeen (1852–5) economy was the watchword, affecting all public expenditures including even those for defence. Reduction of overseas garrisons, especially those in Canada, was progressively enforced. The number of regular British troops in Canada was reduced from 8,000 to 6,000 in 1847 and still further to about 5,000 in 1852; further reduction to a mere 3,000 was then under discussion. In 1849 the position of commander of the forces in British North America was abolished, again in the interest of economy, and the command was divided into two, Canada and Nova Scotia. Measures of economy were not confined to Great Britain. Despite strong urgings from the British government, the legislatures of Nova Scotia and of the Canadas refused to take any action about improving their own somewhat ineffectual militia, even in the face of the reduction of the British garrisons. And such expenditures as were approved in London did not include anything for the long-recommended improvement of the Grenville Canal.[42]

The feelings of the officers in charge of the canals as these developments took place can be well imagined. Once the first St Lawrence canals were opened in 1851, they could see the commercial uses of the Rideau and Ottawa River canals steadily declining. The canals had to be kept open and maintained in fit state for such traffic as remained. Their feelings were reflected in a masterly report sent to the inspector-general of fortifications by the commanding Royal Engineer in Canada, writing from Montreal on 12 August 1846 after he had discussed the matter with the governor, now Lord Cathcart. Clearly writing with great restraint, Colonel Ord commented, in part, that

the disputes, lawsuits, and consequent expenses, which the Ordnance have had to encounter are, and apparently will be, almost endless, that the obloquy to which the Department is exposed by the adverse strictures of a party ... in consequence of the great extent of the ordnance lands uncultivated, occasions this Branch of the Imperial Government to be held in much unpopularity, notwithstanding the vast sums of money which have been spent for the benefit of the Province, that the surplus Revenue derived from the Canals is small if indeed the balance be not on the losing side, when the whole of the expenditure for maintenance and repairs be taken into account, therefore taking all these, and other such like difficulties and circumstances which might with great truth be urged under examination he [Governor Cathcart] thought that the Ordnance would be very great gainers in every point of view, if under strict legal provisions and careful clauses the Department were to let or lease to some one or more of the leading Forwarding Companies, or to parties of due competence, the whole line of the Military Rideau and Ottawa Canals for a limited term probably for two at first, or for three years at furtherst, in like manner as is customary with the Highways on land, taking in this case, of course, sufficient care that proper Military and Civil Officers of the Department be named, or associated with other Trustees as a Committee for vigilantly superintending the fulfilment of the condition of the leases, the punctual payment of the Rents, and the perfect repair of the work.[43]

This remarkable suggestion indicates the appreciation by the Royal Engineer officers of the inability and unwillingness of the province of Canada to assume responsibility for the operation of the military canals while, at the same time, making clear that 'something had to be done.'

At the end of January 1847 Lord Cathcart was succeeded as governor by Lord Elgin, who served until the end of 1854. Before he had been in office two months, Earl Grey requested that he set up a commission of officers to inquire into the future of the ordnance canals in Canada, the commission to report to the commander-in-chief and then to Lord Elgin, whose comments were requested. The commission, consisting of four officers headed by the commanding Royal Engineer in Canada, made its report on 28 February 1849. The coincidence of this study with that of Captain Warden on necessary defence works for British North America and also with the steadily mounting pressure for economy on the part of the British government will show readers what a confused time this was. This confusion helps explain the inaction that followed this further study and also the exchangae of papers about the military canals, a full outline of which would make tedious reading and be of little significance now, since nothing was done until 1853.

There is clear indication in the records that, although the British government was now anxious to relieve itself of the expense and responsibility for the military canals in Canada, and this despite the strong urgings of defence authorities that the canals were vital to the protection of British North

America, it was the reluctance of the government of the United Province of Canada to take over the canals that was responsible for what was, for a time, a stalemate. The government in London pursued its measures of economy, the total roster of British troops in Canada being less than 1,900 by 1854. On the other hand, the legislature had finally accepted responsibility for an improved militia, and the necessary enabling legislation was passed in June 1855, and preparations were set a foot to raise an 'active militia' numbering up to 5,000. This activity in the mid-1850s gives some indication of the changing roles of the two governments, even more dramatically shown by the lords of Her Majesty's Treasury, who finally took action about the military canals, as shown by the minute they approved on 25 February 1853. This is so important a document that it deserves to be quoted in full:

Write Mr Merivale and request that he will call the attention of the Duke of Newcastle to the correspondence which has passed in former years in reference to the expense of maintaining the Rideau and Ottawa Canals and that he will state to His Grace that my Lords are of the opinion that this Country ought no longer to be subjected to this charge and that steps should be taken for the transfer of these Canals to the Provincial Government, but that in order to allow time for making the necessary arrangements for this purpose my Lords have authorized provision to be made in the Ordnance Estimate for the cost of the Establishment and of the ordinary repairs for six months ending on the 30th September next.

Also state that my Lords have authorized the Master General and Board to instruct their Officers in Canada to place the Officers of the Provincial Government in possession of the Toll-Houses and works of these Canals whenever they shall receive directions to that effect from the Governor General through the usual channel of the Lt General Commanding the Forces in Canada and that their Lordships will be ready to entertain the question of the transfer of the extensive and valuable Ordnance Estate on the sides of the Rideau Canal when the time shall arrive for considering the Subject in connection with similar arrangements in other parts of Canada.[44]

The transfer was finally authorized, but still the provincial government was reluctant to accept this munificent gift, although it did accept the suggestion that it should be responsible for maintenance and management of the military canals after 1 October 1853.[45] Not until 30 May 1855 was the necessary act approved by the legislature authorizing the transfer. The requisite order in council was not issued until 25 January 1856 and was ratified by the provincial legislature on 19 June of that year. Only on 3 March 1857 were the Rideau and Ottawa River canals finally placed under the jurisdiction of the commissioners of public works of the united province. Before that date, the government had received a report on the state of the Ottawa River canals by one of the prominent Canadian civil engineers of the time, so they knew exactly what they were taking over. The report of Walter Shanly will form a fitting starting point for our final consideration of the civilian era of the Ottawa River canals which will be found in chapter 8.

No record has yet been traced of any ceremony held to mark the momentous transfer of the canals, an important event indeed in the history of Canada. There are only passing references to the new responsibility in the annual reports of the commissioners of public works for the mid-1850s. Today, this omission is somewhat surprising, but at the time the transfer was probably regarded as an inevitable step, one agreed to reluctantly by the government of the United Province of Canada. The government and people of the province had other things to think about. The burning in 1849 of the parliament buildings in Montreal (where, incidentally, many military records were stored, including many of those of the early history of the military canals) was symbolic of the widespread political unrest. The provincial capital had alternated since that event between Quebec City and Toronto, and this cumbersome procedure in itself was enough to perpetuate the strong feelings reflected in the Montreal riot. Then in 1854 a new Conservative government was elected, led by a young lawyer from Kingston, John A. Macdonald, who would come to dominate Canadian political life for most of the next four decades. And there were the first stirrings of what would finally result in the confederation of some of the colonies of British North America into the Dominion of Canada, to be launched on its career as a new nation of the world on 1 July 1867.

Small wonder, then, that the transfer of the ordnance lands, the Rideau Canal and the Ottawa River canals from the British government to the government of the province of Canada caused so little stir. Officers of the Royal Engineers must have welcomed the move, as will be evident from some of the quotations already given. There were many administrative details to be supervised, notably the transfer of the stores which had proved such a burden to successive commanding officers. There is in the records that remain a lengthy list of the stores at Ottawa, dated 27 September 1856 and carrying the inevitable four signatures, submitted to the military secretary to the governor.[46] The only way in which the items can be conveniently summarized is to say that the list contains 'everything under the sun.'

Transfer of papers and records was not such a simple matter to deal with. Colonel Ord, commanding Royal Engineer in Canada, had to report to the military secretary in January 1857 that he would

not be justified in resigning the Office Books and other documents (very many of which are wholly or partially confidential communications of the British Government) into the hands of any party whatsoever without special orders to do so; since to me it is far more probable, that to some minds it might occur that political malversions were to be discussed in the Mass within the course of the last half century, worthy of being published for amusement or reform, than that the mass should ever be sent to any other quarter of the globe than this.

I have the honour to be, Sir,
     Your most Obedient Humble servant[47]

The somewhat involved wording of this message suggests that Colonel Ord was deeply worried by the request for the records which he had received, but all was quickly smoothed over when the military secretary was able to send to him a copy of a response from the assistant provincial secretary with which was enclosed a letter from William Coffin, the ordnance land agent, written from Toronto on 9 February 1857.[48] He apologized for giving the Royal Engineers the wrong impression about the papers and records required; all he wanted were engineering papers (to assist in the operation of the canals). And he concludes with a flattering reference to 'those noble Works which reflect so much honor on the Department over which Colonel Ord presides.' The final actions regarding the transfer were authorized in a letter from the War Office, then in Pall Mall, London, dated 4 May 1857, authorizing the respective officers in Canada to dispose of all stores – to the provincial government all items required by them, 'accoutrements and camp equipage' to the military headquarters in Kingston, books and papers to Montreal, with all other items to be sold on the spot.[49]

Such was the end of the British Army's long connection with the Ordnance Canals of Canada, and in particular with the Ottawa River canals. Recalling the peaceful decades of the nineteenth century, the reader will naturally assume that this marks the end of the association of the Ottawa River canals with the defence of British North America. It is true that this part of the century saw no fighting, but there were repeated alarms and rumours of war. And in the strange way in which history seems so often to develop, one such alarm was raised in 1856, just as the canals were to be handed over to civilian control. Relations between Great Britain and the United States of America had again deteriorated to such an extent that 5,000

British troops were hurriedly sent out to Canada, with all necessary arms, and the position of commander-in-chief in North America was revived, Major-General Sir William Eyre being appointed to this post. Transportation again was seen to be vital to defence measures, one of the experts (who had been in Canada) advising British statesmen of the time that not only was the Canadian militia unprepared and ill equipped, but also that the canals were unsafe and incapable of passing useful warships!

The panic was gradually dissipated, but the troops remained. Then in 1861 the *Trent* affair erupted, an international incident that brought the two great nations almost to the brink of war. The greatest steamship in the world, the *Great Eastern*, was dispatched to Quebec with 2,000 additional troops, as one way of impressing the United States. More troops were sent out during the winter of 1861–2, until there was a total of 18,582 of all British Army ranks in Canada. John A. Macdonald assumed the position of minister of militia affairs. Happily this alarm was also stilled, and hostilities did not break out. But it is not surprising to find British authorities again extremely worried about the state of defences in Canada. As always, transportation matters loomed large in the series of inquiries that were then set on foot, some of the most important studies of the defence of Canada ever undertaken by British authorities.

8

The Ottawa River canals under Canada:
1856–1962

The Ottawa River canals were but a small part of the completely canalized Ottawa River, so zealously considered in all British studies of the defence of British North America to give access to the upper Great Lakes wholly within Canadian territory. (The full story of this project is given in appendix D.) But they were the only canals on the Ottawa that were ever built, despite all the hopes and dreams for the Georgian Bay Ship Canal throughout a full century. A timber lock was built in the Culbute Channel, north of Pembroke, in 1876, but it was abandoned in 1888 after little use; previously, in 1854 a start was made at excavation for a canal around Chat Falls, but work was abandoned in 1856. Both abortive works were what can only be called 'political engineering.' After the three small canals had been transferred by the British government to the government of the United Province of Canada, they remained under direct Canadian control just over a century. They finally disappeared under the rising water in the reservoir created by the new hydroelectric power dam at Carillon, constructed by Hydro-Québec between 1959 and 1963. Throughout this long period of service, the canals were used for peaceful commercial purposes, but they still continued to be a vital element in British defence planning. Their history while under Canadian control is, therefore, still a part of their contribution to the defence of British North America, and then of Canada, even though to a very minor and steadily decreasing degree. Their century of peaceful operation must be summarized, therefore, in order to complete the record of their long service to Canada, as measures for defence and as waterways of commerce.

The provincial government naturally needed to know just what they were taking over from the imperial authorities. On 22 July 1856, therefore, the commissioners of public works requested a famous engineer of the time,

Walter Shanly, to carry out a survey of the Ottawa Waterway starting with a detailed survey of the Ottawa River canals. This he did, his full report on the little canals appearing as appendix C to the report of the commissioners for 1856.[1] (He had men at work on the river within three weeks of the date of his instructions and so had his report on the canals completed that same summer.)

Shanly's report is almost wholly factual, all necessary dimensions being given with precision. The Carillon locks were found to be thirty-two feet six inches wide and 128 feet long, designed for five feet six inches of water over the sills. But 'the dimensions of the cuttings are very variable, being from 18 to 40 feet wide on bottom, with irregular slopes; the surface widths vary from 50 to 90 feet; the extreme depth of cuttings is 22 feet; the average all over about 10 feet; the whole in rock. The canal is designed for a minimum depth of water of 5½ feet, but not more than five feet can safely be counted upon for purposes of navigation.' Shanly comments on the unusual arrangement of locking up and then down in using the Carillon Canal, necessitatng the feeder from the North River, and states that this arrangement 'will have to be done away with, and the canal fed from the main river, whenever an enlarged system of navigation may come to be adopted for the Ottawa.' He found the masonry of the locks in poor shape generally, 'some of them indeed in an almost ruinous condition. Nos. 1 and 2 at the foot of the Carillon Canal, especially, are in a dilapidated state ... and are, in fact, not safe.' He also found that the two dams on the North River were in 'a miserably inefficient state of repair, consisting of little more than heaps of bare stone thrown in indiscriminately ... calling for constant renewal' (every spring) and being thus responsible for the inadequate supply of water in the upper part of the canal.

Above the upper Carillon locks was a stretch of still water 3.65 miles long, 'reported to have deep water throughout.' Shanly deferred taking 'the soundings until the ice shall offer facilities for doing so with accuracy.' The 'Chute aux Blondeau' Canal he found to have an average width of about thirty-seven feet, all in rock, 'with almost perpendicular sides,' the single lock having a lift of three feet ten inches and overall dimensions the same as those of the Carillon Canal. Mean depth of excavation was twenty-eight feet, another reminder of the great expenditure of human effort required to make these rock cuts. Deep water navigation for one mile led to the foot of the Grenville Canal, which was 5.78 miles long, its locks having a total lift of forty-six feet.

Walter Shanly was clearly puzzled by what he found when he measured up the Grenville locks, since, in his otherwise factual report, he allows himself to say that the seven locks 'present a singular medley in point of dimensions. The four lower locks were, I presume, intended to be on length from sill to sill, 129 ft 1 in., and in width between quoins 32 ft 6 in. But from imperfections of construction the actual lengths vary between 131 ft 8 in. & 129 ft 1 in., and the width between 32 ft 3 in. & 32 ft 6 in.' Naturally he was concerned by what he found when he came to survey the upper three locks:

in their dimensions they differ entirely from those already enumerated and to a certain extent even from one another. Their measurements are as follows:

Lock No. 9	106 ft 8 in.	long	(by)	19 ft 5 in.	wide
Lock No. 10	107 ft 3 in.	"	"	19 ft 4 in.	"
Lock No. 11	108 ft 6 in.	"	"	19 ft 3½ in.	"

it will be seen that the capacity of all three works is practically controlled by Lock No. 11, and consequently the size of vessels capable of navigating the Lower Ottawa, limited to about 100 feet in length by 19 feet in width.

He proceeded to give the detailed and varied dimensions of the Grenville Canal prisms between the locks and concluded by explaining that 'the excavations are wholly in rock, and the bottom level is so irregular that not much more than 5 feet can be counted on as the maximum draft of vessels that could be floated through the cuttings.'

Shanly summarized what he saw as the essential repairs – almost complete reconstruction of the three Carillon locks (estimated to cost £3,000), minor repairs to the other eight locks (£3,200), reconstruction of the North River dams (£300), and removal of some shoals and bars at canal entrances (£265). His estimate of the total expenditure necessary to put the Ottawa River canals into serviceable shape was therefore £6,765. He suggests that this work should be done in the next two years, clearly anticipating that if these repairs were carried out, the little canals could serve until major reconstruction was carried out. 'To treat of the best means of carrying out such an improvement will belong more properly to my future report on the general result of the "Ottawa Survey" and need not therefore be more particularly noticed here.' Shanly was clearly a realist, but even he must have felt frustrated as he witnessed the expenditure of only the minimum possible funds for essential repairs to all three canals prior to the final decision in 1871 to rebuild, fifteen years after his report was written. As if in direct response to Shanly's stress upon the need for immediate repairs to the canal, the commissioners of public works said in their 1857 report: 'any serious outlay being manifestly imprudent, until a final decision can become to, as to the scale upon which the continuous navigation of the Ottawa should be effected.' That reference to 'continuous navigation' is probably a reflection of the then current interest in building the Georgian Bay Ship Canal.

In this same year (1857) one of the first major works on the Ottawa River for assisting the passage of cribs of large timbers down rapids was undertaken at Carillon. This was the construction of a rock-filled-crib dam across the river just above the downstream entrance lock to the canal. It was 3,000 feet long, eight feet high, and the dam was eighteen feet wide at its base; sluiceways were provided for passing timbers. The little structure was completed in 1859 at a cost of £26,563 – a modest improvement. Since there was a normal drop of ten feet in the Carillon rapids, the dam still left some swift water upstream and so did not interfere with the operation of the canals. Its efficacy is indicated by the fact that it was replaced by a higher dam only twelve years later; as we shall shortly see, this second dam had considerable influence on canal operation.

The three canals therefore continued their service to the valley through the 1860s, but little changed from the state they were in when ceded in 1857 by the British government to the province of Canada. Through traffic to the Great Lakes was now using the St Lawrence route, but local trade up and down the Ottawa River was steadily increasing. As may be seen from appendix C, well over 3,000 vessels were using the canals each season, in both directions, in the later years of the decade. Tonnages reveal the pattern of trade, upstream volumes being only about 15,000 tons per year but downstream tonnage exceeding 200,000, proof indeed that the sawmills of Ottawa and Hawkesbury (mainly those of the Hamiltons) were now in full swing. Sawn lumber was conveyed to the expanding markets of Montreal and the northeastern United States in barges, dimensioned to fit into those three small Grenville locks, and hauled by tugs. The number of passengers is at first surprising, until it is recalled that the river was the only convenient transportation route for the better part of each year. Railways started their service up the valley only in the latter part of the nineteenth century; through highways were a development of the twentieth century.

Although some small steamships did sail right through the Ottawa-Rideau route, utilizing the canals, prior to mid-century, the slow passage through the locks and the limitations upon the beam of all vessels imposed by those three small locks at Grenville combined to point to the need for a more efficient solution for passenger traffic up and down the Ottawa. The first steamship in this service equipped to carry passengers was the *Oldfield*, outfitted in a very simple way for this purpose during the winter of 1840–1. It started a regular daily service from Lachine to Carillon in 1842. The

Albion was similarly equipped for daily trips between Grenville and Bytown (Ottawa after 1855). Connection between the two services was made by horse-drawn vehicles rather than by way of the canal, in view of the unavoidably slow transit through the eleven locks. This was the beginning of the development of two fleets of fine Ottawa River steamships – almost all much too large to pass through those three locks – one fleet above Grenville, the other below Carillon.

Canoes were still regularly using the Ottawa and the canals until the 1860s, since even the tedious passage through the locks was greatly to be preferred to the arduous and dangerous journey up or down the rapids. The most famous of all canoe travellers was Sir George Simpson, governor of the Hudson's Bay Company from 1821 until his death in 1860. He recounts, in the one book that he wrote, how

At the foot of the Long Sault, a succession of rapids of about twelve miles in length, we breakfasted [after his usual very early start]. Soon afterwards, we reached the Lock of Carillon, the first of a series of artificial works, erected by the Government to avoid the rapids in questions; passing through the whole, without delay or expense, as part and parcel of Colonel Oldfield's suite. In the lake above Grenville, into which these works conducted us, we met a steamer gliding so gently and silently along, that she might almost be supposed to have gone astray on these once secluded waters.[2]

Frustrating in its brevity (as are almost all other accounts by early travellers up and down the Ottawa), Sir George Simpson's simple words at least indicate the convenience that the canals had introduced into what was, for over 200 years, the main traffic on the Ottawa.

It is not surprising to find that Simpson was one of a group of local men who formed a company to put on a sound footing the staging business between the two ends of the Ottawa River canals. But this improved service was soon superseded by a railway line linking Grenville with Carillon, one of the most remarkable railways ever built in Canada, happily known to several generations of Ottawa Valley residents as the 'Portage Railway' or, more popularly, as the GOP Railway – 'Get out and Push.' A railway up the lower part of the Ottawa Valley had been proposed as early as 1840, but it was not until 1854 that the Carillon and Grenville Railway was constructed. It was the first section completed of a grandiose scheme called the 'Great Montreal and Ottawa Valley Trunk Line' but it was also the only section ever to be built, because the gold bullion to pay for the continuation of construction was lost at sea. The twelve-and-a-half-mile line was constructed to

Passengers transferring from the train of the Portage Railway at Carillon station to the S.S. *Duchess of York* for the sail to Lachine or Montreal, about 1900; this is the only known photograph of this operation.

the 'provincial gauge' of five feet six inches and was never converted to standard gauge, since it was completely isolated from all other railway lines. It was in regular service until 1910 and so was for many years the only 'broad gauge railway' in North America.[3]

It started at the Carillon wharf and finished at the water's edge at Grenville. Its locomotive, facing upstream, would be waiting with its two or three small cars at the Carillon wharf when the morning steamer from Lachine arrived. Passengers and their baggage were transferred to the little train and conveyed to Grenville in about twenty minutes, in contrast with the better part of a day had they sailed through the three canals. At Grenville transfer was made to the waiting Ottawa steamer, whose downstream passengers were waiting to take the little train back to Carillon where they boarded the waiting steamer for the remainder of their journey down to Lachine (or to Montreal, if they stayed on the steamer and shot the Lachine Rapids). The railway continued to be used into the early 1920s for special excursions but was then abandoned. All trace of it quickly disappeared, most unfortunately, since here was one railway that should have been preserved. A branch of Canadian National Railways used part of the old route for its right of way, until it was closed and removed in 1980.

Although carrying a steadily increasing volume of freight, most of it in barges, the canals were therefore bypassed by almost all passengers for the last half of the century and until all passenger traffic on the Ottawa ceased after the First World War. But passengers would still see the canals, although few of the records made by travellers up and down the Ottawa by the steamship service ever mention the canals or the railway. Anthony Trollope, for example, who travelled up the Ottawa from Montreal in 1860, merely records in the book chronicling his visit to North America in 1861-2

This boat conveyance from Montreal to Ottawa is not all that could be wished in convenience, for it is allied too closely with railway travelling. Those who use it leave Montreal by a railway; after nine miles, they are changed into a steamboat. Then they encounter another railway, and at last reach Ottawa in a second steamboat. But the river is seen, and a better idea of the country is obtained than can be had solely from the railway cars. The scenery is by no means grand, nor is it strikingly picturesque; but it is in its way interesting. For a long portion of the river the old primeval forests come down close to the water's edge, and in the fall of the year the brilliant colouring is very lovely.[4]

The most distinguished traveller of these years was His Royal Highness, Edward, Prince of Wales, a youth of nineteen in 1860. He was one of the first royal visitors to Canada; his large entourage was headed by the Duke of Newcastle. In the course of a crowded itinerary, he opened the great Victoria Bridge carrying the Grand Trunk Railway (now CNR) across the St Lawrence at Montreal, and then he travelled up the Ottawa River in order to lay the foundation stone for the new parliament buildings. He left Montreal early on the morning of 31 August 1860, travelling by rail to Ste Anne de Bellevue. Here he boarded a new steamer, named *Prince of Wales* in his honour, and sailed on it to Carillon. He was received by a great assembly (estimated at 5,000) including two troops of cavalry. Addresses were given, and three distinguished local citizens were presented to the prince before he boarded the little portage train for the journey to Grenville. Here were another loyal display and more presentations, but eventually he boarded the *Phoenix* for the journey to Ottawa. The climax of his river journey was a greeting by about 1,000 lumbermen, all in similar gay costumes, paddling in 150 canoes, who met the steamer two miles below Ottawa and escorted it to its wharf.[5]

The parliament buidlings so royally inaugurated in 1860 were planned to serve the legislature of the United Province of Canada. When completed, they did house the last session of that legislature (in 1865) but continued to

serve the new nation of Canada from the opening of the first dominion parliament. The east and west blocks are still in use today, but the present centre block was built after the First World War to replace the original central
building which burned to the ground in 1916, apart only from the parliamentary library. The early 1860s were, therefore, times of great political
activity, times of change indeed. Ottawa had been declared the capital of
the province of Canada by Queen Victoria on 31 December 1857. The construction of the parliament buildings followed, the small permanent staff of
the Legislative Assembly gradually moving from Quebec to Ottawa. The
governor-general, Lord Monck, took up his residence in the new capital for
a brief period in 1866, following his return from leave in England. And during these crucial years there took place the complex discussions, formalized
in Charlottetown, Quebec City, and then London, which led to the passage
by the British parliament of the British North America Act, establishing the
new Dominion of Canada on 1 July 1867.

Small wonder, then, that such a mundane matter as the repair or rebuilding of the Ottawa River canals had to await the termination of this political
upheaval. It is interesting to reflect, today, that all the many journeys up
and down the river, between Ottawa and Montreal, by those actively
engaged in these vital political discussions, were by steamship and the Portage Railway. These travellers, in particular, would have no time to spare
for a leisurely sail through the three canals, but they would doubtless hear
much about the iniquity of the narrow width of those three upper locks of
the Grenville Canal. Correspondingly, all the members of the new parliament of Canada from Quebec and the maritime provinces would also make
the same Ottawa River journey on their way to attend the first session of the
first parliament of Canada. It convened on 6 November 1867 and sat until
22 May 1868.

No official stenographic record of the proceedings of parliament was kept
during its first few years, but, fortunately, newspaper correspondents were
there and did note what transpired. Under the direction of the librarian of
parliament, these unofficial records have been skilfully blended with what
official records do exist, so that one can read today what appears to be
'Hansard for 1867-8.'[6] In it one finds that little more than a month after the
opening of parliament, a petition was presented from 'Mr. Currier and
others praying that certain obstructions to the navigation of the River
Ottawa might be removed and for the improvement of the Grenville and
Carillon Canal.' (Use of the singular suggests unfamiliarity with the Ottawa
River canals, possibly on the part of the reporter.) The petition was read
and received by the House of Commons. And about one month before the

House adjourned, on 15 April 1868, 'Hon. Mr Holton, in the absence of Hon. Mr Dorion, moved an address for the plans, specifications, etc., relating to the Carillon and Grenville Canal.' This motion was carried, and so the reconstruction of the Ottawa River canals and the rebuilding of those three upper locks on the Grenville Canal might possibly begin at last.

These first references in the parliament of Canada to the rebuilding of the Ottawa River canals are brief in the extreme, but, in great contrast, almost four columns of this early 'Hansard' are taken up with a record of the pointed discussion on 13 May 1868 of a motion by Mr Abbott (MP for Argenteuil County and a future prime minister) praying the governor-general to close the Grenville and Carillon canals to traffic on Sundays! Earnest and serious were the arguments in favour of the motion, one member averring that 'By observing the Sabbath the country would undoubtedly be more prosperous, for they could not expect the Blessing of God while violating deliberately and continually His express commands.' On the other hand, the Honourable Mr Dorion 'thought that if the barges on the canal were stopped on Sundays, the employees, instead of going to church, would procure liquor, and the scenes of tippling and disorder that would occur, in consequence would be deplorable.' The Honourable Mr J.S. Macdonald told of a lady he knew who had appealed to him for the Sabbath closing of the canals. Lock gates near her home had been damaged and could not be replaced until a Monday. The pandemonium created by the crews of the barges thus held up over the weekend by the damaged lock had included even the stealing of her geese and turkeys. Mr Macdonald related that the next time he saw her, she said that she would like the observation of the Sabbath on the canals 'to commence at the next lock. (Laughter).' Despite such arguments, the motion was passed by the House, and so for some years there was no Sunday traffic on the Ottawa River canals.

The second session of the new parliament lasted from 15 April to 22 June 1869. Short though it was, it included some consideration of navigation on the Ottawa. In response to another petition, on 8 June the House appointed a select committee of twenty-eight of its own members to study the matter, as requested. Chairman of the committee was Alonzo Wright, son of Philemon Wright, the pioneer settler at the Chaudière, the member for Ottawa County (Quebec). One of the members was Walter Shanly, the civil engineer who had made the first survey of the Ottawa, from whose report on the Ottawa River canals we have quoted; he later became a confidant and engineering adviser to Sir John A. Macdonald whom he already knew. 'Hansard' records that Mr Wright presented the first report of the committee to the House on 18 June, another example of swift committee work. Reading of the report was dispensed with in the House, presumably because it was to be available in printed form. As such it has fortunately been preserved in the journals of the House of Commons.[7]

According to the printed report it is the committee's 'Second and Final Report' but how two such publications could have been prepared in ten days it is a little difficult to imagine. Possibly Mr Wright had presented a brief oral statement to the House which was not recorded. The report consists of only two printed pages; it deals entirely with the proposed 'Ottawa and French Rivers Navigation Project,' the name 'Georgian Bay Ship Canal' not yet having been adopted. The reports of Messrs Shanly and Clarke (see p. 251) are succinctly summarized, the project being warmly commended as a potential benefit to settlement and to commerce, while 'from a defensive or military point of view, the advantages of such means of communication with the Lakes, if, unfortunately, they should ever require to be tested, need hardly be remarked upon.' The report concludes with a plea that 'this most important National question may soon engage the attention of Parliament.'

This wish was granted during the third session, which extended only from 15 February to 12 May 1870. On 28 March there took place an interesting and well-informed discussion, the record of which fills twenty-four columns of 'Hansard.' It was as a result of this debate that the government agreed to establish a royal commission covering the subject of inland water navigation in Canada. It was an able commission, and in many respects its report marks the most important milestone in the history of Canada's canals.[8] It should be said again that the production of this 205-page printed document between 16 November 1870 and 24 February 1871 is still a remarkable feat, but Samuel Keefer was the secretary, a notable civil engineer. Hugh Allan of Montreal was the chairman, a man whose name will always be associated with that of Sir John A. Macdonald; C.S. (later Sir Casimir) Gzowski (also a civil engineer) was another member, as was D.D. Calvin, prominent lumberman of Wolfe Island and Kingston. The other members were P. Garneau, A. Jardine, and G. Laidlaw, the latter being the author of the ultra-conservative minority report, which urged no enlargement of any canals!

The report itself takes up only fifty-seven pages, an abstract of the evidence presented comprising eighty-two pages, the remaining sixty-six pages being factual appendices. A useful historical sketch of the then existing and proposed canals prefaces the concise recommendations. All the canals are divided into four classes, with the exception of the Rideau Canal. This was in such good shape that no change in it was proposed. The Ottawa River canals were placed in the first class, with the highest priority given for their reconstruction and enlargement. Basic dimensions of all new locks were suggested as 270 feet long, forty-five feet wide, with a depth of twelve feet of water (fourteen feet also being mentioned). The commission regarded the St Lawrence route most favourably and even accorded the small Murray Canal (across the isthmus linking Prince Edward County with the mainland of Ontario) a second-class rating. The visionary proposal for a canal linking the Richelieu River with the St Lawrence at Caughnawaga got into the third class. But the proposed Georgian Bay Ship Canal got the lowest rating of all.

The main recommendations of this royal commission, unlike those of so many commissions of more recent years, were implemented by the government of the day. This action was naturally aided by the availability of money from the loan from the imperial government (to assist the fledgling dominion to 'get on its feet'), and the timing of the report was especially fortunate. Construction of the intercolonial railway was proceeding satisfactorily under the expert guidance of Sandford Fleming. Talk of the transcontinental railway to the Pacific coast was in the air. Sandford Fleming, having been called upon to make the necessary survey, did not make his preliminary personal journey to the coast until the summer of 1872. Work on the survey did not start until the summer of 1873. 'Railway mania' had not yet gripped the country. Inland navigation on the waterways of Canada was still a matter of major national importance. And the government of John A. Macdonald was still firmly in power in its fourth session when the report of the royal commission was presented to the House of Commons on 27 March 1871.

The report was debated two days later, in relation to a vote on $624,000 for canal reconstruction. The debate was brief and not at all acrimonious, the record taking up only four columns of 'Hansard'; the motion was readily passed. The commissioners of public works had been replaced (late in 1867) by the new Department of Public Works, with the very able John Page as chief engineer. The department was ready for what was certainly the country's greatest co-ordinated engineering project up to that time – the rebuilding of all the St Lawrence canals, the Welland Canal, and the Ottawa River canals (but not, unfortunately, the Chambly Canal on the Richelieu River, which even today operates with its original tiny locks, approximately 120 feet by twenty-three feet wide. A projected Caughnawaga Canal, which would have made it redundant, was never built). The work was necessarily spread over a period of more than a decade, but, even so, it remains an outstanding achievement, especially when it is recalled that all the rebuilding had to be carried out without interfering with normal operations of the canals.

Wisely, as can now be seen, the fourteen-foot depth was adopted for all the St Lawrence canals and the third Welland Canal, with the recommended overall lock size of 275 feet by forty-five feet. The St Lawrence canals with the new Welland Canal, when thus reconstructed, formed the '14 foot canals' which served Canada so well for three-quarters of a century until the building of the St Lawrence Seaway, opened in 1959. For the lock at Ste Anne-de-Bellevue and the Ottawa River canals a judicious compromise of dimensions was adopted. The Ottawa River would have its own traffic, but some of the traffic through the canals would be travelling also into and through the Rideau Canal, with its locks 134 feet by thirty-three feet and only five feet of water over the sills. Colonel By's insistence in 1827 upon these larger dimensions for the Rideau locks could be seen, even in the 1870s, to have been a far-sighted and wise judgment, despite all the opposition he had had to face. For the Ottawa River canals' rebuilding, locks measuring 200 feet by forty-five feet were therefore adopted, with a depth of nine feet of water over the sills. This was the size to which all the locks were rebuilt. And when the time came for the canals to be superseded by the great lift lock in the Carillon hydroelectric dam, the same overall dimensions for its lock chamber were used.

So urgent and well recognized was the need for rebuilding the three upper locks on the Grenville Canal – at last, it must be said again – that the government had not waited for the report of the royal commission before starting on this long-deferred work. In the course of the debate in the House of Commons in March 1870 (which led to the royal commission's establishment), the Honourable Mr H.L. Langevin, the minister of public works, said that 'In the improvement of the Ottawa the first thing would be to improve the Grenville Canal. It was the intention of the Government to place in the estimates an appropriation for the purpose of increasing the size of the canal.'[9] It had been a long wait for this promise of real action, more than forty years since the need for the reconstruction of the three locks had been clearly recognized. During the debate on the report of the royal commission, on 29 March 1871, the same minister said that 'the House was aware that the locks of the Grenville Canal were in course of enlargement so as to allow two boats to be in the lock at once,'[10] adding that the work already started could easily be co-ordinated with the general rebuilding recommended by the commission. The minister's statement about two boats being in a lock at the same time suggests a slight misreading of his notes or, possibly, slightly garbled reporting.

The minister might have been thinking of the Carillon Canal, since one of the first actions of the new Department of Public Works, as reported in its first annual report (for 1868), was the award of a small contract for increasing the depth in the prism of the main section of the Carillon Canal and the provision of extra passing places. Although this project involved only excavation work, it was not completed until 1869. In the department's second annual report, it is stated that it was proposed to enlarge the three small locks at Grenville and to build a more substantial dam across the Ottawa River at Carillon to raise the water level above that at the upstream Carillon lock. The department's estimate of cost for enlarging the three Grenville locks to a length of 180 feet, a width of forty feet and a depth over sills of six feet was $278,000. A contract for the work was finally awarded in October 1870, the sum of $125,000 having been voted in that year to provide for a start with the contract.

Unfortunately some confusion appears to have arisen over the initial award, made to William Kingsford on 10 October; but the contract was cancelled on 21 October. The original set of tenders must have been used again, since on 29 October a new contract was awarded to James Goodwin, who proceeded to carry out the work. He started work on 8 November, clearly intending to prosecute the job while canal navigation was suspended for the winter. The 1871 report recorded disappointment that Goodwin had only 250 men at work instead of the 500 expected, and no work had been done on the necessary cofferdams. These manpower figures are an interesting reflection upon construction methods of those days, since little mechanical equipment was yet available to supplement human effort. Then the report of the royal commission and consequent parliamentary authority for the rebuilding of all the Ottawa River canals revitalized the situation.

Although reconstruction work involving all three canals thereafter proceeded almost simultaneously, it will be convenient to consider the rebuilding operations for each one separately. The first step on the Grenville Canal was to extend James Goodwin's contract to include the new size of lock in the rebuilding of the three upstream locks for which his original contract had been awarded. A small contract was also awarded to James Fleck of Ottawa for the ironwork for the new lock gates. This fact is of interest not only because it introduces a name still well and favourably known in the Ottawa of today, a century later, but also as an indication of the start of light manufacturing in Ottawa, soon after it had been disparagingly described as no more than 'an Arctic lumber village.'

The next major step was the award of a contract for the reconstruction of the four downstream locks (built, it may be recalled, as two flights of two locks). Both contracts included not only the locks but the necessary deepening and widening of the respective sections of the canal prism in order to provide the same depth of water as flowed over the sills of the new locks, and to facilitate the passage of the larger vessels that would be accommodated in the new locks. This second contract was not awarded until 1879, the successful tenderers being Messrs Heney, Nicholson, Steward and Strachan. Many years later, Mr Steward said that he was the contractor for the 'Grece's Point locks' under the firm name of Brecken and Company. His memory was correct, since in November 1881 the government had to take the work out of the hands of the original contractors, awarding a new contract to Brecken and Company in February 1882. The design upon which this second contract was based called for only two new locks, in place of the original four, a desirable economy in construction that would add convenience to passage through the reconstructed canal by reducing the time necessary for lockage.

The strange delay in awarding this second contract for the rebuilding of the Grenville Canal will be understood better if the political history of these years is recalled. In the fall of 1873 the government of Sir John A. Macdonald resigned as a result of the 'Pacific Scandal.' It was replaced, after the general election that followed, by the Liberal administration of Alexander Mackenzie. During the five years he led the government of Canada, Mackenzie served as his own minister of public works in order to keep firm control of this sensitive department and to keep a tight rein on all expenditures. Times were hard also, so it is not too surprising that only after Sir John A. Macdonald had been returned to office late in 1878 did the completion of the reconstruction of the Grenville Canal win governmental approval. The fact that the Honourable Mr J.J. Abbott (of St Andrews) was minister of public works may have helped.

Another factor in the delay was railway building! So active had this become, and so involved was the government of Canada, not only in the Canadian Pacific Railway but also in the many smaller lines started in those busy years, that in 1879 parliament approved the formation of a new Department of Railways and Canals. Responsibility for railways and canals was therefore transferred from the Department of Public Works to the new department on 20 May 1879. Although the necessary staff transfers were also made, John Page, for example, continuing as chief engineer of Canals, the administrative rearrangements necessarily involved interference with projected works. but all the necessary contracts had been awarded before the end of 1879, and there was clearly pressure upon contractors to get their jobs finished as expeditiously as possible.

This was before the advent of the professional organization of engineers

Lock No. 5 (Stonefield) on the Grenville Canal, looking upstream, the original lock (now disused) on the right, the 'new' lock, built 'in the dry,' on the left, in September 1909

in Canada and well before the start of what may be called engineering journalism in this country. The Canadian Society of Civil Engineers was founded only in 1887, and the first issue of the *Canadian Engineer* did not appear until 1896. There is not available, therefore, any technical account of the rebuilding of the Ottawa River canals. This lack is unfortunate, since the building of five new masonry locks and deepening a six-mile long canal, without interfering with normal canal operations, would be a considerable undertaking even today. One hundred years ago, it represented a major achievement for the two contractors concerned. The following summary account of the essential features of the reconstruction has been compiled after a study of all available official documents, aided by personal knowledge of the Grenville Canal before it disappeared beneath the rising waters of the river in 1963.

An ingenious but very simple arrangement was adopted for the building of four of the five new locks. The original locks were left just as they were and were operated normally during the construction period. Entirely new locks, to the new dimensions, were built immediately adjacent to the old locks, on the river side of the canal. Through the use of simple cofferdams at each end of each of the four new locks, these fine masonry structures were built 'in the dry,' with consequent great convenience. When they were finished, the cofferdams were removed; the necessary small amount of excavation to bring the canal prism to each end of each lock was carried out; and then the new locks were placed in service. The old locks were left in place but rendered inactive, and some of the lock chambers were filled in. At old locks Nos 2 and 3 (below Grenville and at Stonefield) the old locks served as spillways for any excess water flowing down the canal. The dual lock structures at these two locations must often have puzzled visitors of this century who did not know the history of the canal.

The locks were all renumbered soon after the reconstruction. The use of the two sets of numbers is confusing, but unavoidable, since the new numbers were those used for the next ninety years and therefore appear in all official references to the Ottawa River canals, whereas the old numbers were those quite naturally used by the Royal Staff Corps during the original building of the canals, when work started at the Grenville end. The two sets of numbers are presented in table 2.

Table 2 provides a reminder of the bold expedient for the time of making two pairs of the locks on the Grenville Canal into combined flight locks in the original construction. The entrance locks on the Rideau Canal at Bytown may have encouraged Henry Du Vernet and the officers of the Royal Staff Corps to adopt this feature of design. By the 1880s canal-building was so advanced that there was now no problem of providing a lift of 16.7 feet in the new Lock No. 4 (and 13.2 feet in Lock No. 3), so that two of the original seven locks on the Grenville Canal were eliminated. The procedure followed for building these two new locks was the same as that used for the (old) Locks Nos 2 and 3, but the old locks were not left exposed but were covered completely by a rebuilding of the north bank of the canal from the new No. 4 Lock to the downstream entrance. Overflow weirs leading directly to the river eliminated the need for old locks as spillways. Only in the case of the upstream entrance does this general pattern of rebuilding seem to have been different, quite possibly because the small village of Grenville had already started to grow up along both sides of the entrance to the canal. The records suggest that the entrance was blocked by a cofferdam, and the new lock was then built 'in the dry' on the same site as the original lock during winter months when it was possible to close off the canal.

TABLE 2
The numbering of locks on the Ottawa River canals

Canal	Original		As rebuilt		
	Order of building	Official number	Official number	Lift (ft)	
	1	11	7	2.5	D
	2	10	6	4.0	O
	3	9	5	6.6	W
Grenville	4 } 5 }	8 } 7 }	4	6.7	N S
	6 } 7 }	6 } 5 }	3	13.2	T R E
Chute À Blondeau	8	4	–	–	A M
	9 (up)	3			
Carillon	10 } down 11 }	2	2	3.5	
		1	1	10.5	↓

Winter work must have been involved in the deepening and widening of the canal prism under both contracts. All the necessary excavation was in rock, and underwater rock excavation is a sophisticated operation even today, with the most modern of equipment available. Once traffic through the old Grenville Canal had stopped in the late fall, it would have been an easy matter to drain the whole canal dry, by keeping the upstream guard lock closed or closing the entrance by the cofferdam just noted, leaving all other lock gates open. (A similar procedure is now carried out each winter on the Rideau Canal at Ottawa, but for quite a different reason – to ensure an annual change of water, the famous 'skating rink' being on the frozen surface of the pool that remains after draining.) Excavation had still to be done manually after the laborious drilling of holes in the rock by hand, followed by primitive blasting. Safety precautions were elementary, and nasty accidents due to premature explosions and flying rocks were recorded.

James Goodwin seems to have made good progress with his large contract, despite his slow start. He had carved on a stone built into the wall of lock No. 6 the date *1874*, followed by *Hon. Alexander Mackenzie, Premier and Minister of Public Works; John C. Sippell, Engineer; James Goodwin, Contractor*. All his work seems to have been finished by 1879. After the change of contractors in the winter of 1881–2, work on the two lower locks at Grece's Point seems to have gone well. One lock was ready in the summer of 1882 and the other one late in that same year, although they were not fully operational until the 1884 navigation season because of delays in completing the deepening of the adjacent channels. But the 'new' canal, in its entirety, was in use from 1884 onwards.

During the work of reconstruction a number of reminders of the Royal Staff Corps came to light. In the walls of the original Locks Nos 2 and 3 (two of the smaller ones) dressed stones were found built into the lock walls bearing inscriptions, that in the third lock reading

No. III
Royal Staff Corps
1827

Boundary stones were found marking the limits of lands acquired for the building of the canals. Those on the Grenville Canal had the usual broad arrow mark, the number of the stone in Arabic numerals and 'B.O.' for the Board of Ordnance, while those for the Chute à Blondeau Canal had 'W.R.' for William Rex, 'O' for Ordnance, and the number of the stone in Roman figures. Some of these stones were retrieved before the canals were flooded in 1963. And as a reminder of the unknown human background to the building of the canals, during the work at Grece's Point, the skeleton of a man was unearthed, with a rusty knife blade embedded in his bones, from the fill behind the masonry.

The Chute à Blondeau Canal had been in only partial use since the building of the rock-filled crib dam across the river at Carillon in 1857. This had raised the river level at the small canal to such an extent that, although the lock was still used by vessels coming upstream, all downstream vessels were able to sail directly from the exit from the Grenville Canal to the upstream entrance to the Carillon Canal. There was still swift water in the vicinity of the canal, but the rapids had been drowned out so that it could be readily navigated going downstream. It was, therefore, a logical extension of this development, which had been welcomed by those responsible for log-driving on the river, to construct a higher and more permanent dam at Carillon, raising the water level in the river so that the Chute à Blondeau Canal

Typical view on the Grenville Canal in June 1904 near its western (upstream) end, as it was in use until 1962; the bridge carries the track of Canadian National Railways (formerly Canadian Northern Railway) to its bridge across the Ottawa River (see photo on page 106).

Upstream (western) entrance to the 'new' Carillon Canal, looking westward up the Ottawa River, showing one of the guiding lights for aid to navigation, in September 1909

would no longer be necessary, since the slight rapid would be 'drowned out.'

This was done, as a part of the new works at Carillon, and so the Chute à Blondeau Canal was not reconstructed. It was abandoned after the new Carillon Dam was finished at the end of 1881, the simple gates on the dam being first closed on 9 November of that year. Thereafter all river traffic, both upstream and downstream, sailed directly between the Carillon and Grenville canals. In due course, the lock gates and fittings were removed from the little central canal. Only the masonry lock walls and the almost vertical sides of the rock cut remained. These could still be seen until 1962, although the surrounds were much overgrown with bush.

It will be recalled that, in his report of 1856, Walter Shanly had strongly urged that the old layout of the Carillon Canal (involving locking up at both ends) should be abandoned when the time came for the canals to be reconstructed. His advice was not forgotten when engineers of the Department of Public Works prepared plans for the rebuilding of the Carillon Canal shortly after the royal commission had presented its report in February 1871. It was decided to abandon the old canal completely and to construct an entirely new 'normal' canal with just two locks, one at each end, each of them to have the new dimensions of 200 feet by forty-five feet, the downstream lock with a lift of 10.5 feet and the upstream lock with a lift of 3.5 feet, these figures being for normal river levels. Because of the inland routing of the original canal, it proved possible to locate the new canal between the old one and the river. And by combining the building of the canal with the construction of the new crib dam across the river, it was possible to have smooth water at the upper end of the new canal, even though it was about one mile downstream of the upstream entrance to the old canal. The new canal was therefore only 0.76 miles long between the two locks and 0.94 miles between the two entrances, a reduction in length of well over a mile.

Even in the early 1960s it was still possible to admire this eminently sensible layout of the new works, extremely simple in essence, as are many sound designs. The overall plan had the further advantage that all the new works could be carried out without interfering with the older work, the original canal could continue to serve until the new one was ready. Work in the river would even be aided to a degree by the existence of the 1857 dam. Tenders were therefore called for the combined dam and canal, since it would clearly be economical if the two jobs were carried out in concert. The contract was awarded to the firm of R.R. Cooke and Company of Belleville in the spring of 1873. For some reason, not evident from the remaining

records, the work was discontinued in the spring of 1877. In the following
year, the department took over the uncompleted works, settled the outstanding payments due to the Cooke Company, and advertised for new
tenders for finishing the job.

The firm of F.B. McNamee of Montreal was the low bidder, but, in view
of the poor state of the national economy, the government decided not to go
ahead with the work. McNamee therefore withdrew its bid. Cooke asked to
be reinstated as contractors and offered to withdraw all its claims for
damages against the government. This was agreed to provided that Cooke
would work in partnership with McNamee. This unusual arrangement was
also agreed to. McNamee finished the Carillon Dam, and Cooke finished
the new canal. Some delay was experienced when it was found that the location of the downstream lock had to be moved ten feet because of poor foundation conditions but the work proceeded smoothly; the dam was finished
in the fall of 1881, and the canal was in full use from 27 May 1882. The old
canal was abandoned in August of that same year, but the old locks were
left in place and filled in, as were those on the Grenville Canal.

There remains the lock at Ste Anne-de-Bellevue to be considered, since it,
too, had to be reconstructed to the larger dimensions if it were not be
another bottleneck. Here there was fortunately enough room for the building of a new, larger lock, parallel and close to the original lock, but inshore
from it. This situation greatly facilitated construction, because the new lock
could be built 'in the dry,' protected by cofferdams at each end. The contract for the work was awarded to the firm of Baskerville, O'Connor and
Cassidy of Montreal; it carried on steadily until the work was complete.
Stone for the locks was obtained from the Île Bizarre quarry in Hull, and the
work at the site started in mid-summer 1880. All the masonry was complete
by the end of 1881, but the new approach channels had yet to be dredged.
The new lock was first used in August 1882 while the last channel improvements were being carried out by the firm of E.E. Gilbert and Sons.
The original lock was later filled in, but its outline can clearly be seen today,
close to the attractive enclosure around the 'new' lock – now almost a century old! The site is an attractive one with a splendid view upstream of the
Lake of Two Mountains and busy railway and highway bridges almost
overhead, with the splendidly conserved Simon Fraser House just a stone's
throw away, where simple, pleasant meals are available throughout the
summer.

It would be agreeable to be able to record that there was a grand and
glorious opening of the completely reconstructed Ottawa River navigation
– the lock at Ste Anne and Ottawa River canals – to mark this significant

event in the history of transportation in eastern Canada. No such celebration, however, appears to have been held. The railway era was just beginning. The Canadian Pacific Railway Company had been formed. William Cornelius Van Horne had taken up his position as general manager on the first day of January 1882. The great task of linking through the mountains of the west the two sections of the transcontinental railway already completed was well advanced and was already the centre of public attention. It was certainly the dominant interest of Sir John A. Macdonald and his colleagues in the government. In the Ottawa Valley, the Brockville and Ottawa Railway had reached Sand Point, on Chats Lake, as early as 1865 and was already drawing some of the lumber trade down the St Lawrence. The Bytown and Prescott Railway had provided another link with the St Lawrence and the main line of the Grand Trunk Railway, from Montreal to Toronto, as early as 1855. These were no more than small branch lines, but in 1883, just as the reconstructed canals were approaching completion, J.R. Booth of Ottawa completed the building of his own railway, the Canada Atlantic Railway, to transport his lumber from Ottawa down to Coteau Junction, and across the St Lawrence to the United States. It was a major railway, later to become part of Canadian National Railways. The coincidence of its completion with that of the reconstruction of the Ottawa River canals is another of the ironic twists marking their chequered history.

Although there was no celebration to mark the end of rebuilding, there is a report which states that 'Local legend has it that Princess Louise and the Marquis of Lorne opened the Carillon Canal, also that the barge on which they were standing broke loose from its moorings at one end and swung around the pier with the heavy current, so that they had to be rescued from the craft'[11] – but that is all! Every preceding Vice-Regal couple had had to use the Ottawa River route when visiting or coming to or from Ottawa. Lady Dufferin has left a brief reference to her final journey down the river in 1878. But the Marquis of Lorne and Princess Louise were probably the last representatives of the queen to use the river for official journeys, since no sooner was the Canada Atlantic Railway opened for its lumber business than a passenger service was added with a through train between Ottawa and Montreal.

Those were busy days in the growing Canada. Even with the availability of the two Canadian Pacific Railway lines between Ottawa and Montreal, in addition to the Canada Atlantic, traffic on the river and canals decreased only slowly until after the turn of the century, while passenger traffic held its own until well into the present century. Travellers of those days clearly enjoyed the pleasure of sailing in the vessels of the two fleets established to

Downstream (eastern) entrance to the 'new' Carillon Canal, in September 1914, looking upstream and showing on the far left the white water of the Ottawa coming over the crib dam; the guide well on the left can be seen also in the photo on page 207.

Typical barge transport on the Ottawa River canals, in this case, of sand and gravel

provide the Ottawa to Montreal service, with the portage railway serving as the connecting link around the canals, until just before the outbreak of the First World War. Talks with older people who used this service in its final years leave no doubt that it was a very civilized way of travelling, far different from today's rushed trips by automobile, with their hair-raising escapes from the uncontrolled speeders on 'The Racetrack,' otherwise known as Ontario Highway 417.

The passenger service on the river was provided by the same company from the year 1864 – when it changed its name to the Ottawa River Navigation Company and Captain R.W. Shepherd, its president, bought the little Portage Railway – until 1907, when it was sold to the Central Railway of Canada. Captain H.W. Shepherd, one of the legendary figures of the Ottawa River succeeded his brother as senior captain of the Ottawa service. This fine gentleman died at the age of eighty-five in 1910, just as the passenger service on the Ottawa was coming to an end, his life spanning the full cycle of the coming and going of the 'white ships of the Ottawa.'

This was the company's daily schedule at the turn of the century:

Ottawa	lv.	7:30 a.m.	ar.	6.35 p.m.
Grenville	ar.	12:50 p.m.	lv.	1:05 p.m.
	lv.	1:05 p.m.	ar.	12:55 p.m.
Carillon	ar.	1.40 p.m.	lv.	12:30 p.m.
	lv.	1:45 p.m.	ar.	12:25 p.m.
Lachine	ar.	5:25 p.m.	lv.	8:20 a.m.
	lv.	5:35 p.m.	ar.	8:18 a.m.
Montreal	ar.	6:30 p.m.	lv.	8:00 a.m.

Travelling downstream to Montreal, passengers could stay on the streamer while it shot the Lachine Rapids, then delivered them to a wharf in Montreal harbour, the vessel then returning up the Lachine Canal for its start the next morning, when passengers would board it off a train that had brought them from Bonaventure Station. This procedure explains the difference between the last two times in the schedule. The single fare was $2.50 first class and $1.75 second class, and first class return fare was only $4.00. And meals, excellent by all accounts, were 50 cents. But those days have gone forever.

The Ottawa River canals were involved only indirectly with this delightful service, even though all passengers would see them en route. The canals did, however, convey all the freight that moved up and down the Ottawa, apart only from the large timbers which were still being rafted slowly down the river sixty miles from the great white pine forests of the upper part of the valley to the head of the Long Sault. Here they were split up into separate cribs each of which was piloted down the rapids by the expert rivermen who formed a unique team of pilots. Below the Carillon Dam the cribs were reassembled into rafts for their further slow sail across the lake of Two Mountains.

Shipments of sawn lumber continued downriver long after the rafting of the big timbers started to decline. The regular pattern was for the Ottawa barges to be loaded up at the huge lumber yards that existed on both sides of the Ottawa immediately below the Chaudière. Sawn lumber was shipped similarly from Calumet. Sturdy tugs would then haul strings of barges the sixty miles down to Grenville. Here the tugs would relinquish their loads and return upstream to Ottawa hauling empty barges. The loaded barges would be hauled through the Grenville Canal by horses walking along the well-kept towpath by the north side of the canal, the horses stabled at Grenville and at Grece's Point. Between the canals the barges would be hauled by one of the tugs kept there throughout the season for that purpose. Then followed the transit of the Carillon Canal, haulage again by horses but this time along a towpath on the south side of the canal; these horses were stabled at Carillon. Finally came the haulage of the barges, again by tugs, across the Lake of Two Mountains, through the lock at Ste Anne and so to delivery in Montreal.

The best tabular statement that it has been possible to prepare, showing traffic through the Ottawa River canals throughout their history is presented as appendix C. Gaps in the records now available make gaps in the table unavoidable. In some of the older compilations, for example, traffic on the canals is combined with that through the lock at Ste Anne, traffic through the latter being shown as that also going through the canals. Unfortunately, this discrepancy distorts the picture badly, since an increasing volume of sand and gravel was excavated in the northern part of the lake in Oka Bay and hauled down in barges to Montreal, through the Ste Anne lock, for use as concrete aggregate and other building material in Montreal. These shipments continued until relatively recent years, when environmental concerns put an end to the business. The overall pattern, however, can be gauged from the table, despite all its imperfections – great activity until the turn of the century and then a gradual but inexorable decrease. Not only sawn lumber was conveyed in barges, but other types of freight were also, all hauled by tugs. In addition, the river hosted an assortment of 'steam barges,' as they may be called, special craft designed to fit into the canal locks but fit only for navigation on the relatively secluded waters of the Ottawa. There were also some standard steamboats which regularly

The tug *Gaëtan* used for hauling barges between the Grenville and Carillon canals, in the upper lock of the 'new' Carillon Canal, October 1922

M.V. *Ottawalite*, on its first downstream trip from Ottawa to Montreal, approaching the upper lock of the Grenville Canal in June 1930

traversed the canals, for many years one of these being the *Dagmar* of the Ottawa River Navigation Company. This vessel left Montreal on Tuesdays and Fridays and was known as one of the 'market boats,' since it docked at every stopping point on the way to Ottawa after its first call at Carillon.

A number of companies were active in the freight services on the Ottawa, as were, naturally, some sturdy independents. The last company to be in business was the Ottawa Transportation Company, which gave up its charter in 1941. In its final years, shipments of oil up to Ottawa kept the Company active, oil being delivered to large storage tanks at the Richmond Landing, just below the Chaudière. Some oil companies then built their own fleets of specially designed tankers for the Ottawa service, and for some years these kept up a limited but regular service between Montreal and Ottawa. They, too, were superseded in 1953, when the first oil pipeline reached Ottawa; since then there has been no regular freight traffic on the river. One of the special tankers, built for Imperial Oil Company, was equipped with a British-built triple-expansion marine engine. By a happy turn of the wheel of fortune, this fine piece of engineering has been preserved, not on the banks of the Ottawa but at the Marine Museum in Toronto. It is almost the only relic of the many fine vessels that provided this century-old river service between Ottawa and Montreal to which the Ottawa River canals contributed so much.

The two canals changed little throughout their long period of service and were always well maintained. The lockmasters and their staff had an unusually keen loyalty to the canals and to their department. This continued to be the Department of Railways and Canals until 1935, when it was united with other units in the government of Canada to form the Department of Transport, whose first minister was the Honourable Mr C.D. Howe. By this time, traffic through the canals had dropped to a total of only 700 transits each way during the season. Of these about 125 were pleasure craft, the vanguard of what would become in the 1960s almost the sole traffic up and down the Ottawa. The nadir came in 1961 when a mere 212 vessels (112 up and 100 down) used the canals, all but six being pleasure craft, the others being the service vessels of the department. By 1961, however, the demise of the Ottawa River canals was at hand.

The energy available from the Long Sault and the Carillon Rapids had long been under scrutiny by those interested in power development. An early grant of 'rights' for the development of power at Carillon, in 1908, had been one of the complications in the complex story of the Georgian Bay Ship Canal. When Ontario and Quebec made an agreement for the development of the energy available from all the rapids of the Ottawa River, the

The last traffic on the Ottawa River canals, in 1959 – pleasure craft in the downstream lock of the 'new' Carillon Canal

Carillon site was allocated to Quebec. Because more power was needed for the expanding industries of that province, the decision was reached in the late 1950s that the power at Carillon should be developed. Inevitably, this decision would mean the end of the canals, but from the start of planning of the great dam and power house that now span the river, replacement of the locks was an integral part of the project.

This had to be since, in the remarkable order-in-council through which the government of Canada eventually ceded to the two provinces its rights, it is stated that 'Nothing shall be deemed to authorize the construction of any work ... on the Ottawa River otherwise than in accord with the provisions of the Navigable Waters Protection Act.' Not only had there to be provided a new navigation facility, but the Ottawa River canals had to be kept in operation until the new facility was ready for use. Through masterly planning of construction operations by Hydro-Québec – owners of the plant – their consulting engineers, and contractors, this was done.

The beginning of the end! Cofferdam built by Hydro-Québec across the southern half of the Ottawa River at Carillon in 1959 within which foundations for half of their great dam would be constructed, the other half of the great river being then correspondingly controlled; the 'new' Carillon Canal may be seen on the right, the lower lock in the foreground, and the upper lock adjacent to the end of the crib dam; the abandoned entrance to the 'old' canal may be discerned immediately below the lower lock, surrounded by trees.

Work started in 1959. The river was 'controlled' by the construction of a massive cofferdam, extending halfway across the river from the Ontario side and enclosing an area large enough for the foundations of the spillway part of the main dam to be constructed on the bedrock beneath the river, now exposed to view after the area had been pumped out and after it had been cleaned and prepared. This process completed, the cofferdam was removed and the other half of the river treated in the same way, so that the foundations for the power house end of the great structure could be set in place. With the foundations constructed from one bank to the other, the flow of the river over the partially built works could be controlled by skilful scheduling of the remaining construction operations.

The line chosen for the axis of the dam was just upstream of the downstream entrance to the Carillon Canal and so downstream of the old Carillon Dam. Accordingly, it was possible to keep the Ottawa River canals in operation throughout most of the construction period, even though the traffic they carried in the 1961 and 1962 seasons was limited. Work proceeded all around the two canals. All trees and surrounding bush in the area eventually to be flooded had to be cut down and cleared away. Parts of the highway between Carillon and Grenville had to be relocated. All building within the flooded limits had to be demolished (some being used for research purposes in the course of demolition by controlled blasting). Some were old, some new; some were in good condition, others poor. All were carefully studied and recorded by devoted members of the Historical Society of Argenteuil County. A summary of their findings, prepared by Dr G.R. Rigby and Miss Helen H. Lambart, happily was published.[12]

Gradually the great structure took on its final form. Main roads on both the Quebec and Ontario sides of the river being some distance from the site, few Canadians, other than those who lived nearby and those who worked on it, saw this splendid example of Canadian construction at its best. Having witnessed many large construction jobs in various countries, the writer can say without qualification that he has never seen a better-laid-out and managed project. The clean lines of the finished dam and power house are in keeping with the efficiency of their construction. Today, the elegantly simple power house is a third of a mile long. It contains fourteen generating units, each producing 60,000 hp when operating under full head of sixty feet. It is, therefore, by far the largest water-power plant on the Ottawa River, with its total potential output of 840,000 hp. It is what is known as a 'run-of-the-river plant,' normally using the entire flow of the Ottawa for power generation; when necessary, it can meet peak demands for short periods during the winter by taking extra water from the reservoir.

All the power generated is fed into the Hydro-Québec system, the necessary transmission lines leaving the outdoor substation at the northern end. The water not used in the power house is passed over the 785-foot-long spillway. This is equipped with twelve electrically operated roller-type gates, each thirty-two feet wide and fifty-six feet high. The openings they normally close being capable of carrying the greatest possible spring flood on the Ottawa. On the Ontario side, a thirty-foot-high dyke extends half a mile upstream to prevent water from flooding valuable river-bank land. A similar earth dam extends for three miles along the Quebec bank, to the outskirts of Cushing, and this dyke carries a portion of the relocated highway.[13]

And navigation? Adjacent to the north end of the power house is the most modern ship lock in Canada. It has a single lock chamber, with the same dimensions as the masonry locks, 200 feet long by forty-five feet wide, with fourteen feet of water available over the sills. But the full lift of sixty feet is made in the single lock, and vessels are raised or lowered the full distance in twenty minutes. Two radial gates are used to close the upstream entrance, but the lower entrance is closed by a massive steel gate measuring forty-five feet wide and sixty-seven feet high, operating like a guillotine. It weighs 180 tons and is operated in its movements up and down by a forty hp electrical motor. It was first used on 15 November 1962 by M.V. *Salvar*,and since then, has served as the equivalent of the Ottawa River canals, lifting and lowering an ever increasing number of pleasure craft, service vessels (now of the Canadian Coast Guard), and occasional barges carrying special loads, such as structural steel fabrications that are too large for transport by road or rail.

And the canals? There was a flurry of activity during the 1962 open season when everything that could be dismantled was. The canals were therefore stripped down to bare essentials. Hydro-Québec was ready. The northern end of the dam and the necessary concrete work for the new lock on both sides of the old canal channel had already been constructed. The canal, in effect, went through the last remaining gap in the half-mile-long structure. Once the canal was closed, filling of this gap began. Construction of the new lock chamber was completed. The big gate and other lock machinery were assembled and installed, so that by the end of November 1962 the new lock was ready for use. Throughout this period, the river level had been no higher than just above the crest level of the main spillway. All the gates had been installed and tested individually, but the water level above the dam was still not much higher than that which had existed above the old Carillon Dam since 1882.

When all was ready, and after both banks of the river had been checked all the way up to Ottawa and Hull, the sluice gates were first lowered in February 1962, leaving only a necessary minimum flow of water still running over one spillway. The water level above the dam began to rise, at first rapidly but then gradually more slowly as the effect of the rising water was felt further and further upstream. The swift water of the Long Sault was finally stilled as the water level rose inexorably. When the level of the new 'lake' (for that is what it now looks like) reached the level of the river at Grenville, it was within two or three feet of its final level, and this was reached in October 1963. By then, the finished turbines in the power house were able to generate power at almost full head, to supply electricity to the

Hydro-Québec system. But the Ottawa River canals had disappeared beneath the rising waters, in all probability never to be seen again by anyone now living. They had served Canada well, in peace, just as they had been a vital part of the defence of British North America in days long ago.

9

Epilogue: The canals today

What can be seen of the Ottawa River canals today? Despite the disappearance of the three canals beneath the impounded waters of the river, there are fortunately a few features that remain, one or two virtually unchanged since they were constructed more than a century and a half ago. As the conclusion to this review of the history of the canals, therefore, the reader is invited to take an imaginary tour around the canal area as it is today. It is hoped that some may be moved to pay an actual visit to the area; with this possibility in mind, directions for travel will be included.

The village of Carillon, Quebec, must be the starting point from whichever direction the traveller may come. Two routes are available for the fifty-mile drive from Montreal. One may come by Quebec Highway No. 344 from St Eustache, along the north shore of the Lake of Two Mountains, passing through Oka and St Andrews. Alternatively, one may take the old road along the south shore of the lake, after passing through Dorion and Vaudreuil, and cross either by the ferry between Como and Oka or, by going further along Highway 342 as far as Pointe Fortune, by the ferry crossing from there to Carillon. Travellers from Ottawa, with a longer drive of about seventy miles, can follow either of the two main roads to Montreal as far as the turn-off to Pointe Fortune, close to the interprovincial boundary, turning down to this old village where the ferry to Carillon will probably be waiting.

Crossing by this ferry from Pointe Fortune to Carillon gives all travellers a fine view of the new Carillon Dam and Power House but those interested in the old canals will look rather at the stone building just to the right of the ferry landing and the larger stone building set among the trees up the hill. The latter is Bellevue, the house built in 1827 by Deputy Commissary-General Forbes (p. 131). Its entrance will be seen by those coming by road

The completed Carillon hydroelectric installation, the main spillway on the left, the power house in the centre, the lift lock on the far right, and the earth dam on which the main road is now located immediately behind the right end of the power house; the west end of Pointe Fortune is in the lower right.

from Montreal soon after they have traversed the wide gracious main street of St Andrews, where they may possibly notice the plaque commemorating the first paper-making plant in Canada, founded here in 1803.

The appropriate and quite delightful starting point for this canal visit is the fine masonry building immediately adjacent to the ferry landing at Carillon. This is the storehouse built by the Royal Staff Corps in 1829 (p. 132). It has been wonderfully well preserved in its original condition and is now the museum of the Historical Society of Argenteuil County. Soon after the canals were completed, during the uprising of 1837, the building was used as a barracks for 108 officers and men. In subsequent years it was used for a variety of purposes, finally coming into the possession of Mr Felix Hungerbuhler, who in 1938 generously donated it to the society. With the assistance of the government of Canada, it was restored and adapted for its service as a museum. Now appreciated by thousands of visitors annually, it is open every afternoon from May until the end of October.[1]

The front doorway itself is clearly from an earlier age, and all the interior woodwork and stairs are as originally built. It requires little imagination, therefore, to picture the building as it was when in use in its earliest days, especially when we examine the beautiful and well-preserved nineteenth-century ladies' costumes and early military uniforms. Somewhat naturally, the museum contains few mementoes of the building of the canals but its collection covers all main features of the development of the canals throughout the last century. Of special interest to canal-lovers will be the models of Ottawa river steamboats and the interesting exhibit featuring the Portage Railway. The Abbott Room contains many memorials of Sir John J.C. Abbott, a native of St Andrews and the first Canadian-born prime minister of Canada. And the old kitchen, its open fireplace, crane, and built-in oven, are vivid reminders of the 'domestic economy' of an early day. It can be seen from even this brief note that a full afternoon would not be enough to study the museum exhibits fully, and this without even glancing into its valuable library. But we must leave the building and its treasures, remembering as we pass through its doorway that Henry Du Vernet and his men erected this gracious building and used it well.

As we leave the museum, we can look down the Ottawa River towards the Lake of Two Mountains. Up these waters sailed the fine white steamers of an earlier day. They berthed at a wharf just beyond the modern parking lot for the museum and here, too, was the starting point of the Portage Railway. It crossed the line of the present road close to the corner of the building. If we look across the road, we can just make out the levelled area on which the track was built. From aerial photographs we can trace its route all the way to Grenville, but, since the track has long since been removed, there are only one or two other places where the old right of way can still be distinguished on the ground.

As we walk along the road through the village, it is a delight to see the attractive masonry building that still remains. We pass a pleasing little memorial to Dollard des Ormeaux and his companions, who perished nearby in their valiant fight to the death in 1660 against Indians intent on invading Montreal. As the great power house and dam come into full view, on the right can be seen the bronze plaque and cairn erected by the Historic Sites and Monuments Board of Canada to memorialize the Ottawa River canals, unveiled in 1933. In view of the splendid job that Parks Canada is now doing (since 1972) in preserving and interpreting this beautiful and historic area, we may be sure that the error on the plaques will be corrected.

Before we go up to the lock and power house, we must turn to the left and walk across a lawn toward the isolated masonry building that can soon be seen to stand on a point of land. This is the only one of the original lock-keepers' houses remaining, a fine example of the utilitarian architecture of those days, well preserved down the years. On the right as we approach the buildings are the river and the wide channel that can be seen leading to the new navigation lock, but on the left is the greatest surprise of the whole canal area. Here are the remains of the two *original* locks of the first Carillon Canal, the locks that lifted vessels to the main part of the canal that was above the level of the upstream lock, built by contract under Henry Du Vernet in 1830–3. Although superseded in 1882 by the second Carillon Canal (p. 190), and although all other parts of the original canal soon disappeared, the two old locks happily were left untouched throughout the century. They are not in good condition today, but now that they are under care, the old masonry will long remain as the only visible reminder of the valiant work of the Royal Staff Corps when all around was virgin forest.

This is a spot where it is tempting to linger, a place to stir the imagination of all who know the history of the Ottawa River canals. Some day, it is greatly to be hoped, a fitting memorial to Henry Du Vernet and his men will here be established. The canals were the first 'public work' of any size to be constructed in Canada, if one considers the starting date of 1819 as the significant year. Only a few very small isolated locks had been built before that year and it was not until 1822 that the first Lachine Canal was started and 1824 the first Welland Canal. This quiet and secluded spot on the Ottawa River was recognized and properly marked, therefore, as the place where modern Canadian civil engineering really began, civil as distinct from military engineering. On a windy day in September 1984 a small plaque was here unveiled by the presidents of the Institution of Civil Engineers (U.K.), the American Society of Civil Engineers (U.S.), and the Canadian Society for Civil Engineering.

But there are other things to see! As we walk away from this historic point of land towards the navigation lock, a close look at the concrete wall on the river side of the approach channel will reveal one short section of masonry, skilfully incorporated into the mass concrete. This is part of the

The approach channel to the new lift lock, the wall on the far side of the channel being, in part, that seen in the photo on page 193

masonry wall of the first lock of the second Carillon Canal, of 1882, imaginatively preserved and utilized in this way by design engineers of Hydro-Québec when the new lock was built. The actual size of this new facility is dwarfed by the majestic power house building and the dam beyond, but it will be better appreciated when viewed from the top. Here the lift of sixty feet and the great steel gate necessary to achieve it are truly impressive. If we are fortunate enough to see a vessel locked either up or down, the twenty minutes that it will spend in the lock provide perhaps the most striking of all contrasts between this fine modern piece of engineering and the tedious progress involving many hours through the old canals that it replaces – the original canals with their eleven locks, and the rebuilt canals of a century ago with their seven improved locks – all three works performing the same function of passing vessels up and down the sixty-foot fall in the Ottawa River as it used to be.

Back to the road and automobile, with a brief visit to the power house for those interested (a superb example of modern Canadian water-power engineering, but not really a part of this story), we start on our journey upstream by leaving the village of Carillon along one of the relocated sections

The new lift lock with its downstream guillotine gate in the open position to permit egress of the vessel from the lock; with its lift of sixty feet, this one lock replaces the three original Ottawa River canals.

of Highway 344. It sweeps grandly around the elevated land at this end of the power house and dam, a final turn to the right leading to a long, straight stretch of road right along the shore of the 'lake' into which the dam has here transformed the river. If we stop just after rounding this corner and look down to the right, a small, straight ditch is to be seen, almost at right angles to the road. It is hard to believe that this is the 'feeder canal' that brought water from the North River to supply the upper section of the original Carillon Canal, must to the chagrin of the local inhabitants, but so it is! One can walk along it, with some difficulty, as far as the North River and possibly make out the location of the Portage Railway crossing.

Back at the road, a glance will show that the new highway is located along the top of an embankment. It is rather more than an ordinary embankment, however, since it is really an extension of the Carillon Dam, protecting all the lower land that can be seen on the right from being flooded by the waters of the new 'lake.' The structure over which we ride for the next two miles is, therefore, an earth dam, specially designed for its dual purpose and for the varying water levels in the lake. When river flow is low in late summer, the lake level may drop when there is an extended demand for full power from the station and will then rise again when demand decreases and the normal river flow can replenish the extra water that has been used. When the water level is very low, a few remains of the earlier landscape can be seen protruding from the water, but it is next to impossible to associate them with the second (1882) Carillon Canal, whose line parallels the new road.

As the end of the long, straight stretch is reached, the remains of a railway line can be clearly seen on the right, running roughly parallel with the road. This was a branch of Canadian National Railways which started at a junction from the Montford subdivision of CNR at Grenmont and terminated at Grenville. Prior to 1962 the line carried on across the Ottawa River to Hawkesbury and points south. The bridge that carried it over the Ottawa consisted of twelve through truss spans supported on concrete piers. So little traffic did it carry in its final years that, when the necessity for raising it arose owing to the construction of the Carillon Dam and the pending rise in the level of the river at Hawkesbury, it was decided to demolish the bridge rather than rebuild it. There was very limited freight traffic to Grenville until 1980; the last passenger service (to Grenville from Montreal on Friday evenings and back from Grenville on Monday mornings) operated in 1977. The writer travelled to Grenville in the locomotive of one of the last of the Friday trains not just for its railway interest but because the last six miles into Grenville, from a point just west of Cushing station, used the right of way of the Portage Railway. This line provided the closest modern equivalent to travelling on the old broad gauge line.[2]

A transition to the original 'canal road' (Highway 344) is made at the end of the long, straight stretch just as we pass one of the pleasant areas (this one for camping) developed in association with the Carillon Dam as the Dollard des Ormeaux Park. The old road is narrow and winding, and so careful driving is essential, especially as houses and other buildings now stand on both sides of the road for several miles. They form part of the modest development along the line of the old canals. Although the majority of the structures were built in this century, the occasional older stone building can still be seen. The most interesting of these is the Stone House, a fine, two-storey, masonry building on the north (right) side of the road. Built in 1830, while the canals were still under construction, it served first as a Methodist meeting place. Renovated in 1936, it is now used as a private residence. Another fine masonry building now serves as a splendid 'country store' and is well worth visiting; just ask for Mrs Elliot's.

As the pleasant drive along this winding rural road continues, the village of Chute à Blondeau can be seen across the Ottawa, its name a reminder of the third of the original Ottawa River canals, which was, however, located on this side of the river, and of the ferry service that used to link Cushing with the other bank. On the river side of the road the square masonry tower of St Mungo's church is soon discernible. Here a stop must be made, if only to admire the spacious churchyard and the trim lines of this first church of the canal, the 'canal cathedral' as it might have been called had it not been established by the Church of Scotland, later the Presbyterian Church of Canada, and now part of the United Church of Canada. The congregation was organized in 1833 and the church structure erected in 1836 on land purchased from a former member of the Royal Staff Corps. It is entirely probable that the craftsmen who built the fine masonry walls and tower had previously worked on the locks of the canals, so recently completed when the church was built. If arrangements can be made, the interior of the historic church should be examined and admired, since it is a fine example, on a small scale, of a typical Church of Scotland church of the early nineteenth century, there being only one other in eastern Canada, at Williamstown. The interior has an austere beauty all its own, with a high pulpit for use on special occasions and the gallery extending around three sides of the church. Services are still held every Sunday, although the small congregation does not now warrant the regular use of the gallery. The privilege of worshipping in this old building, the use of which spans the whole period of the history of the Ottawa River canals, is a unique and moving experience.[3]

The next surprise along the road is a sign bearing the legend 'Greece's Point,' a reminder of the problems caused by Mr Grece's claims of long ago. The point, encompassing the downstream entrance to the Grenville Canal, was a singularly lovely spot, but all that can now be seen is the smooth water of the impounded Ottawa. Stonefield follows, the name clearly explained by the glacial boulders still to be seen in the fields around. Short sections of relocated highway can readily be distinguished, if only by their straight courses in contrast with the winding route followed by the original road. The approach to Grenville, after some fine open views across the river, is along the original meandering road; we cross the CNR track that led to the bridge, now demolished, just as the final speed reduction sign is passed. The terminal point for the last CNR passenger service was just to the right of the main road at the crossing, a Y-arrangement of track enabling locomotives to run around to the other ends of their trains. A short spur line, not visible from the road, continued into the village of Grenville, as we shall shortly see, since this was still a part of the route of the Portage Railway.

We must stop before crossing the busy road connecting the Sir George Perley Bridge from Hawkesbury with the main north shore highway (48). Proceeding to the west, still on Highway 344, another attractive masonry church is approached on the left as the village of Grenville begins. A halt should be made here and the interior of the church visited if possible; it is a place of rare beauty. St Matthew's Anglican Church was built in 1832, before the canals were finished. Its grounds abut on the Grenville Canal, but by the time it was built, the work of the Royal Staff Corps was centred on the Carillon Canal.[4] In the Church is a memorial tablet to Lieutenant George Hopper, who died in September 1833, the only memorial in the canal area to any member of the Royal Staff Corps.

Proceeding into the village we pass the remains of a venerable masonry building (it was a hotel) at a right-hand bend in the road. We should take the next turn to the left and continue out to the river. Here railway tracks will be seen again, just as similar tracks could have been seen here a century ago, although without the surrounding modern industrial scene. For this was the upstream terminus of the Portage Railway. Here the steamers coming down from Ottawa would berth, exchanging their passengers for those bound upstream for Ottawa, who had come up from Grenville on the little train. So much has changed here that it is difficult to imagine the daily social gatherings at this 'clearing in the woods,' during the brief stopover of the daily steamer, or the special occasions when distinguished visitors, such as HRH the Prince of Wales in 1860, were appropriately greeted.

The upper (guard) lock of the Grenville Canal, now without its gates, but otherwise as rebuilt in the 1870s; the water level is approximately that behind the Carillon Dam; the view is taken looking upstream with some of the attractive houses of the village of Grenville in the background.

Returning to the main road and retracing our route to the bend in the road, a sharp turn here to the right brings us to one of the few equivalents of an English 'village green' to be found in eastern Canada. A pleasant place, this open space is the more notable, since along its southern side runs the upstream end of the Grenville Canal with the 1878 guard lock still in place, although now with its gates removed and crossed by a fixed timber bridge. The rise in the river level caused by the Carillon Dam has given a water level here that is little different from the normal high water level of the Ottawa each spring prior to 1963, and so the canal walls and lock appear quite natural, apart only from the missing lock gates and the absence of the equipment normally found around a lift lock in service. This is the upper guard lock of the canal, as built in the 1870s to replace the first little lock which was the real bottleneck of the original Ottawa River canals. As we admire the fine century-old masonry of the lock and adjacent walls, we may well remember the many people who worried about the urgent necessity for rebuilding this first of all the locks on the original canals. The peaceful setting of today encourages such meditation about the years that have gone.

If the bridge across the lock is crossed and a sharp turn made to the right, we can drive almost to the end of the long neck of land that forms the south bank of the approach channel to the lock. Automobiles should be parked and the final few yards travelled on foot, so that the full beauty of the scene may be enjoyed. The soundness of Henry Du Vernet's decision to place here the entrance to the canal can be appreciated even today; it was even more evident before 1963, when the swift water at the head of the Long Sault could be seen on the left.

But technical matters will soon fade into the background as the eye ranges the beauty of the smooth water of the river and the forest-clad Precambrian hills beyond. This scene has not changed since long before the canals were built. This is the view that Henry Du Vernet would have delighted in as he took an evening stroll from his first simple camp in the woods nearby. Let this tribute to his work then end with the picture, so easy to imagine, of this fine man standing on this selfsame spot on a warm summer evening in 1820, enjoying just as we do the quiet beauty of the scene and dreaming of the challenge that lay ahead for him – the building of the Ottawa River canals, the first public work of this land, then so vitally necessary for the defence of British North America.

APPENDICES

The Royal Staff Corps in Canada

John T. Hancock* and Robert F. Legget

The Royal Staff Corps is one of the least-known regiments of the British Army. This low profile is understandable to a degree, since the regiment existed only between 1800 and 1839, after which its records disappeared; its total establishment never exceeded about 500 officers and men. Despite its relatively short existence, it carried out notable work in all parts of the (then) British empire. A number of eminent military leaders received their first training in the Staff Corps. It was a most distinguished although small part of the British Army in the first third of the last century.

Lieutenant-Colonel Henry Du Vernet was the senior officer of the Staff Corps to serve in Canada, having the further distinction of being the longest-serving officer in the history of the corps. His name is still well known in Canada, although the Du Vernets in Canada today are descendants of his brother Francis, who was also an officer in the Staff Corps. Officers of the corps who achieved distinction in other parts of the world included men such as Lieutenant-Colonel W. Nicolay, who became governor of Mauritius (where the corps had served). Captain Westmacott (a brother of an officer who served and died in Canada) became governor of South Australia. Lieutenant D'Urban became governor of the Cape Colony and Lieutenant Napier a general and the commander-in-chief in India. Lieutenant Freel served with the British Army in England, eventually becoming the quartermaster-general. These few names are testimony to the high standing of the men who served as officers in the Staff Corps, about whom one would like to know more.

* Major, Royal Engineers (rtd), now librarian, Royal School of Military Engineering, Chatham, England

Despite the *loss* of the regimental records, a little is known about some of the works these soldiers carried out in addition to their military duties, since they were also a combat regiment. In Great Britain, they constructed the Royal Military Canal with efficiency. In Australia and the West Indies they constructed fortifications some of which are still to be seen. They served also in Egypt, where they won their first battle honours. And in Canada, as this volume shows, the corps built the Grenville Canal and designed and supervised the construction of the two smaller Ottawa River canals. It seems desirable, therefore, that there should be included in this book a brief history of this quite remarkable regiment together with a summary of its service in Canada before, and after, its fifteen years of work on the Ottawa River canals.

A BRIEF HISTORY OF THE STAFF CORPS

The only history of the corps to be published so far is a paper by J.T. Hancock[1] of which the following is a summary only. At the end of the eighteenth century, the British Army existed in two parts. The infantry and cavalry were under the commander-in-chief, at the Horse Guards. The Royal Artillery and the Engineer Department were under the master-general of the ordnance, who was then a member of the British cabinet. The Corps of Royal Engineers consisted of commissioned officers only, and the Royal Military Artificers, consisting of non-commissioned officers and privates, worked under them. When an expeditionary force was required, it was customary for the master-general of the ordnance to supply a small detachment of Royal Engineers and Royal Military Artificers to accompany the force.

In 1799 the commander-in-chief was Frederick, Duke of York, a prince of the royal house. In that year he formed a force for the expedition to the Helder, with a total strength of 12,000 men. The master-general proposed to supply the normal small engineer detachment of one sergeant, two corporals, and thirty-five artificers. Since the role of the engineers in combat operations had increased considerably since the start of the Napoleonic Wars, the Duke of York did not regard this contribution as adequate. He therefore extended the powers of the quartermaster-general (under his direct command) who proceeded to form a military Company of Pioneers for the expedition. This company served well in the Helder campaign. A warrant was issued on 15 January 1800, as a result, for raising a corps of pioneers which was to be known as the Staff Corps.

Initially, the new corps was to be commanded by a major, to have a small regimental headquarters, and to consist of four companies each commanded by a captain, the total authorized strength being 423 rank and file with twenty-two officers. By the end of the year 1800 almost the full establishment had been recruited. (For comparison, the establishment for the Royal Military Artificers was 975 of all ranks). Headquarters for the new corps was to be at Chatham, then merely a station of the Engineer Department, which had its early headquarters at Woolwich. The Staff Corps had little time to get organized, since early in 1800 one of the new companies was sent to work at Dover, and in May of the same year another company formed part of Abercrombie's expedition to the Mediterranean and Egypt, there winning the corps' first battle honours.

The major engineering achievement of the corps in England came early in its short career. This was the building between 1805 and 1807 of the Royal Military Canal linking Sheerness with Rye on the south coast of England, one of the military defence works carried out at that time under threat of invasion by Napoleon. This was regarded as a virtual certainty in the first few years of the century. There was general agreement that the landing place would probably be on the long stretch of low-lying coast on either side of Dungeness which is backed by the great Romney Marsh.

Martello Towers were therefore built along this part of the coast, but Lieutenant-Colonel John Brown (then an assistant quartermaster-general but appointed in May 1802 as the commandant of the Staff Corps) suggested, in a report made in September 1804, that as a second line of defence a canal should be excavated around the north side of the Marsh, between Hythe and Rye. It would be sixty feet wide at the top and forty feet at the bottom, with a depth of nine feet of water – in effect a vast moat upon which defence weapons could be floated on barges; a road along the north bank would provide access for the military.

Further and more detailed reports were submitted to the commander-in-chief on 18 September of the same year and were given approval by the prime minister six days later, such was the fear of invasion. Experienced contractors were engaged, as was the famous John Rennie as consulting engineer. Work started in October, but initial progress was so poor that the contractors failed and were removed from the job; John Rennie resigned in a huff; and the execution of the entire project was placed in the capable hands of Lieutenant-Colonel Brown and the Staff Corps.[2]

Working with his men of the new corps, Brown had the entire nineteen-mile length of the canal excavated by the summer of 1807; the control lock at Iden was built in that year; and a three-mile extension from Rye to Cliff End was also finished at the same time under the direction of Lieutenant-Colonel William Nicolay (who has already been mentioned). The whole job was completed at less than the estimated cost and in less than the scheduled time, tribute indeed to the new corps and its commandant. Excavation was relatively easy, all in soil (unlike the rock excavation on the Grenville Canal), but the two jobs – in Canada and in England – were comparable, both a credit to the Royal Staff Corps.

By November 1807, however, fear of invasion started to dissipate, so the Royal Military Canal was never used, fortunately, for its intended purpose. It did serve for almost a century for the handling of a small freight traffic on barges. It is still there today, now used only for pleasure sailing. The barracks building of the Royal Staff Corps may also still be seen at Hythe, the corps having moved its headquarters there in 1805. After the disbandment of the Staff Corps, the building was used by the army's school of musketry. Even before the move to Hythe, the Staff Corps had instituted field engineer training at Chatham, eight years before the Royal School of Military Engineering was established at Chatham, the headquarters of the Corps of Royal Engineers having been moved there in 1812.

After 1813 the Royal Staff Corps had a rival organization with a training program similar to their own, since in that year the Royal Military Artificers were reconstituted as the Royal Sappers and Miners with military operations now included in their training. The Peace of Amiens (1802) had led to a reduction in the strength of all army units, and so the company establishment of the Staff Corps was reduced to fifty-three; it varied from that figure up to sixty-four for the rest of the corps' existence. With the renewal of fighting in 1803, however, the number of companies was increased to eight, so that the total establishment remained virtually unchanged. Strangely, no record has yet been found of authorization for the prefix 'Royal' in the name of the regiment, but it was certainly in use by 1804.

Even before the completion of the Royal Military Canal, companies of the corps had been sent to Ireland, Jersey, and Guernsey. Three companies took part in the retreat to Corunna under Sir John Moore in the early part of the Peninsular War. They were later joined by a fourth, all serving later under the Duke of Wellington, returning to England in 1814. In that same year one company sailed for New Orleans and two companies left for Canada. Before their work in this country is described, it may be noted that other companies served later in St Helena (while Napoleon was there), Gibraltar, the Leeward Islands, and Mauritius. A new company was raised in 1823 to go to Ceylon, expenses of this company being paid for by the colony. Yet another was formed two years later for service in New South Wales. These locations amply demonstrate the widespread distribution of Britain's armed forces.

From the year 1818 onwards, there were repeated suggestions that the Royal Staff Corps should be abolished, but its founder, the Duke of York, was still alive. It may be rather more than coincidence, therefore, that the first actual moves in this direction were taken only in 1829, two years after the duke had died. A gradual reduction in establishment was then ordered. Only ten officers remained on strength in the United Kingdom by the end of 1831. Soon after the only men remaining on strength were those constituting the maintenance staff for the Royal Military Canal. In 1839, however, the Board of Ordnance took over complete responsibility for the canal, and the last remaining RSC officer completed the handing-over of duties late in that year. The Royal Staff Corps then disappeared, as did its regimental records. The Corps of Royal Engineers assumed all its duties, becoming the corps as it is known today in 1856, when the officer corps was amalgamated with the Royal Sappers and Miners to form one combined unit.

THE ROYAL STAFF CORPS IN CANADA

It can be seen from this summary history of the corps that it was in keeping with the way in which this small regiment was used in the British Army for two companies to have been sent to British North America in 1814. They embarked at Portsmouth on 6 October 1814 and apparently sailed first to Cork, in Ireland, where they waited ashore for a vessel to take them across the Atlantic. It was a long wait, since available records suggest that they did not embark on the *Stag*, a small transport, until 12 January 1815. They must have had a rough crossing, because they eventually put into Bermuda. For some reason, possibly overcrowding on the *Stag*, Major Long, Captain Westmacott, and Lieutenant Lloyd, with one sergeant and six privates, landed at Bermuda, continued their voyage in another vessel named the *Atlas*. The *Stag* continued its journey on 1 April, arriving in Halifax on Saturday 6 May. The *Atlas* did not leave Bermuda until 16 April but reached Halifax one day ahead of the *Stag*.

Unfortunately, the *Stag* (which was only of 320 tons burden) ran into trouble as it approached Halifax harbour and ran aground on the Thrumpcap shoal.[3] Its rudder was knocked off, and it sprang a leak before drifting into Herring Cove, where it went hard aground. All members of the detachment managed to get safely ashore. Here they were mustered, and then they marched into the small town of Halifax on the Saturday evening. The full detachment consisted of Major Andrew Long, Captains F.W. Mann and J. Westmacott, Lieutenants Hill, Lloyd, Harris, and F. Du Vernet, with Ensigns Dillon, Fraser, and Cleather, one sergeant-major, six sergeants, two buglers, and 113 privates (first, second, and third class).

The little town in which the detachment was to spend its next year had been founded in 1749 as a military and naval outpost in opposition to the great French fortress at Louisbourg on Cape Breton Island. Settlement in its hinterland had proceeded slowly, but by the year 1815 the province of Nova Scotia was well established as a part of British North America. Halifax was its capital, even though its population was only about 10,000. Population of the whole province did not exceed 60,000, scattered in tiny settlements around the rocky coasts with access, generally, only from the sea.

In Halifax, the first magistrate had just been appointed. Government House, residence of the governor, had been first used by Sir John Wentworth (an outstanding governor) in 1807, even though it was not then finished. The Province House, today Canada's oldest governmental building, was under construction, being first used by the small legislature in 1819. Streets were dirty and still dangerous at night, since street lighting had not yet been installed. The road linking the two military barracks was then known as Knock Him Down Street![4] Dominating the little town, developed along the broad channel leading into its magnificent harbour, was the hill now widely known as the Citadel. Work on fortifying it had started, not to be finished until 1859, and it was to assist in this building work that the two companies of the Staff Corps had been brought over from England.[5]

While the Staff Corps companies were stationed at Halifax, the town was served by two newspapers – the *Nova Scotian Royal Gazette* and the *Acadian Recorder*. Complete files of these papers have been studied to glean any information about the activity of the men of the corps in their first engagement in British North America, since military records detail only, and in brief, the work at the Citadel. Singularly little was found because, as was the custom of the time, both papers were filled with small advertisements with but little editorial matter and even less news, this being based almost entirely on reports from newspapers in London and Paris! One issue of the *Royal Gazette* contains this plaintive note: 'We have nothing of importance to present to our readers this day; the Halifax packet brought Cork papers only.[6] What would we not give for some items of local news, then regarded as so unimportant!

Both papers did report the arrival of the *Stag* but neither mentioned the departure of the Royal Staff Corps detachment one year later. The *Gazette* reported the list of subscribers from the garrison to the fund then raised for the benefit of the slain and severely wounded in the British Army 'in the late engagement of the French at Waterloo.' Major Long gave £5, the two Captains £2-10-0 each, the subaltern officers a total of £10, and the non-commissioned officers and men the sum of £12-17-0.[7] The *Gazette* alone reported that, on 2 February 1816, William Weberstadt was fined £5 for receiving a shirt from a private of the Royal Staff Corps for which he paid 2/6d, 'which fine (after the expenses were deducted) was paid into the hand of Rev. George Wright for the benefit of the Poor.'[8]

The only appreciable attention paid by both papers to the Royal Staff Corps was to a most unfortunate affair, the murder of Captain Westmacott. The governor issued a proclamation in early May 1816 in which it was stated that 'about three o'clock in the morning of Wednesday, the 17th day of April last, two persons having the appearance, and part of the dress, of soldiers, armed, and with stolen goods in their possession, assaulted Captain John Westmacott, of the Royal Staff Corps, and wounded him mortally, of which wounds he died on the 4th instant ... He was on horseback, and alone ... they dragged him from his horse, and with a sword struck him the deadly blow, and departed ... He succeeded in gaining the King's Wharf Guard ... but languished in extreme pain.'[9] A reward of £100 was offered for apprehension of the murderers. Two privates in the 64th Regiment were later charged with the murder. Captain Westmacott's body was buried in Halifax, with full military honours, on Wednesday 8 May 1816.

Captain Westmacott was a member of a noted British family. He had intended to be an architect and won the annual gold medal given by the Royal Academy for the best architectural design; he then became a pupil of Mr James Wyatt. But he gave up this career in order to join the army, in which he served, under Wellington, in the Peninsular War. He was wounded three times, once very severely before Badajos, and never really recovered from the effects. He was a gifted linguist and had developed unusual skill in freehand sketching. One of his brothers, Richard, was a noted sculptor, and a Royal Academician; in 1816 he was engaged on memorial monuments to those who fell during the battle of Waterloo. He is thought to have sculpted a memorial to his brother.[10]

The loss of this fine officer must have cast a pall on the officers and men of the Royal Staff Corps in Halifax, so that they probably welcomed the news that they were to be transferred to Lower Canada (Quebec) for work on the small canals in the Soulanges section of the River St Lawrence. The entire detachment, with the exception of one officer who was on leave, embarked at Halifax on the vessel *Eliza* on 20 May 1816 and sailed for Quebec, where they arrived on 10 June. The long voyage around Cape Breton and into the Gulf of St Lawrence was typical of the slow journeys of the time, when sailing vessels were the only available transport, there being still no road connection between Quebec and the Maritimes. Five officers, one sergeant-major, five sergeants, one bugler, and 115 privates made the journey, going on to Montreal, where they arrived in mid-July.

The one officer on leave was Lieutenant Francis Du Vernet, brother of Lieutenant-Colonel Henry Du Vernet. He left a special legacy to Canada and so warrants brief mention. He was born on 19 November 1793, the fourth son and fifth child of Lieutenant-Colonel Abraham Du Vernet, RA, and his wife. Following his brother's example, he was commissioned as an ensign in the Royal Staff Corps on 28 June 1809, but as 'Frederick'; the name was later corrected in the records of the corps. He worked in Halifax until 27 April 1816, when he went on leave, returning to duty on 27 August of the same year, when he joined the detachment then at work on the Soulanges (or Haldimand) canals. During this period, he married Eliza Jane Parker, the only sister of Judge Neville Parker of Saint John, New Brunswick. The imprecision is due to the fact that all marriage and birth records for the two oldest churches in Saint John were lost in a disastrous fire in 1839. But the first child of the young couple was born in 1817. Francis returned to England in November 1819 and was later sent to Ceylon, one of the last overseas postings of the Royal Staff Corps. His wife must have accompanied him, because two of their children were born in Ceylon. Mrs Du Vernet presumably returned to her home in Saint John separately from her husband, since he was lost at sea in 1833 in the vessel bringing him back to Saint John. He had transferred to the Ceylon Rifle Regiment (as a captain) when the Royal Staff Corps was disbanded and had been promoted to major before he left Ceylon. Mrs Du Vernet apparently remained in Saint John. All the Du Vernets in Canada today are their descendants; many have given distinguished service to Canada, one an archbishop in the Anglican Church of Canada.[11]

There had been a period of transition in the office of governor-general of British North America (p. 61). Sir George Prevost had sailed for England on 3 April 1815; General Sir Gordon Drummond served as administrator for just over a year, and then he, too, returned to England on 21 May 1816; he was followed by John Wilson, who served as administrator for just two months. The office of commander-in-chief was then filled by Sir John Sherbrooke, who arrived in Quebec from Halifax on 12 July 1816, having served there as governor of Nova Scotia. He therefore knew the Royal Staff Corps and their work and so had arranged for their transfer to Lower Canada. At Quebec there were small detachments of the Royal Engineers and the Royal Sappers and Miners but additional help was needed for the improvement of the small St Lawrence canals.

Map 2 on p. 27 shows that the Ottawa River joins the River St Lawrence at the west end of the Island of Montreal to form Lake St Louis. Entering from the west, the St Lawrence descends from Lake St Francis through a drop of almost 100 feet, followed by a splendid series of rapids, the last one of which can still be seen today from the junction of the two rivers. This stretch of fast water has long been known as the Soulanges section of the St Lawrence, and the various canals constructed to circumvent the rapids have been known generally as the Soulanges (or Haldimand) canal(s) until they were succeeded by the Beauharnois canal(s) on the south shore, the modern one now serving as part of the St Lawrence Seaway.

The first Soulanges canals were constructed under the direction of Royal Engineers commanded by Captain Twiss, starting in 1779, to the instructions of the governor, Sir Frederick Haldimand. A canal 900 feet long and seven feet wide with three small wooden locks was first built at Coteau du Lac; it was probably the first canal with locks to be built in North America.[12] It was completed in 1783. A smaller canal with one lock was built downstream at Split Rock in 1782 and 1783, and a cut 120 feet long with no lock at Trou-du-Moulin. The last of these small canals to be built was at Rapide à la Faucille near Cascades Point. All were small affairs, the depth of water over lock sills being only about two feet. Little was then known of the hazards of winter ice on such structures and maintenance was minimal, but they did serve to improve navigation up the St Lawrence for canoes and bateaux.

That they were not well maintained was demonstrated in a report prepared in 1800 by Colonel Gother Mann of the Royal Engineers, who recommended a program of rehabilitation, only part of which was carried out. Locks at Coteau du Lac and Split Rock were partially rebuilt in 1804, and the two small works at the downstream end were replaced by a canal half a mile long with six small locks. The urgent transfer of troops and supplies from Montreal to Kingston during the War of 1812 again drew attention to the inadequacy of the small canals. The commissary-general urged their improvement in a memorandum that he sent to Sir George Prevost. Once the war was over, attention could again be directed to such civil works. It was to undertake the necessary improvement to all three canals that the two companies of the Royal Staff Corps were transferred from Halifax. By 1817, the width of all the canals had been doubled and the depth over sills increased to three feet six inches to accommodate large vessels, such as Durham boats, now using the St Lawrence.

The two companies reached the Cedars area in June 1816, moving to the Cascades Canal in August and then to the canal at Coteau du Lac in February 1817. They spent the next eighteen months stationed in the Soulanges area before their headquarters was moved to Lachine (adjacent to Montreal) in September 1818. In August 1819 they were summoned to Grenville, by order of the new commander-in-chief, the Duke of Richmond, to start work on the Grenville Canal. The two companies had then spent more than four years in Canada. There had been some desertions, a few deaths, and some replacements, but the men still remaining must have been pleased when they were relieved by Captain Henry Du Vernet and his two new companies. They returned to England in November 1819.

The work of the new companies of the Staff Corps on the Ottawa River canals has been described in some detail in this book. They spent the summers stationed at Grenville and the winters in barracks in Montreal until 1829 after which they remained at Grenville, or Chatham, until the works were substantially complete. Many then stayed in Canada as settlers (see appendix B), but eventually the last group (apart only from Du Vernet and his small support staff) returned to England on the troopship *Orestes* in August 1832. Lieutenant-Colonel Du Vernet and his few companions followed in November 1833, as related in the text.

It has recently been discovered that yet another company of the Royal Staff Corps served in Canada. The Citadel of Halifax has already been mentioned. It was one of the most extensive and elaborate of the early fortifications built for the defence of British North America. The government of Canada has embarked upon a major restoration of this significant fortress. In the historical research carried out as background for this work, it was found that the Royal Staff Corps supplied one more company to assist in the original construction of the Citadel.[13] The company arrived in Halifax just as disbandment of the corps was starting – on 9 June 1829 – so that their service was probably the last major overseas work to be undertaken by the Royal Staff Corps.

Captain Piers was in command until July 1831 when he was promoted to major, relinquishing his command to Captain Jackson who was in charge until the company sailed back to England on 9 November 1833. Because of the change in the status of the corps, the company was made directly responsible to the Ordnance Department in Halifax, which had therefore to pay for their services. Although this annual charge never exceeded £2,600, none the less it figured in a somewhat unusual letter written in August 1833 by the newly appointed chief Royal Engineer at Halifax, Lieutenant-Colonel Rice Jones. He wrote:

I ... conceive the employment of the Royal Staff Corps in Nova Scotia is not advantageous to the Engineer Department there in consequence of the amount charged to the Estimates for the Citadel for the expenses of the Company being more than the value of the labour that can be obtained from them, particularly now when, as the only part of the Corps remaining abroad, the non-commissioned officers and men must naturally be looking with eagerness to their discharge, and the organisation of the Corps itself precluding their being stimulated to exertion by the working pay other bodies receive for the work they perform.[14]

There is drama behind those simple words. All available records of the way in which the men of the Staff Corps carried out their duties suggest that the real reason for the request, which the letter conveys, was the second matter raised and not the first. The regiment had been officially disbanded and did not appear in the Army List. The company had been away from England more than four years. It would have been only natural, therefore, for them to want to return home if only to find out what lay ahead for them. An appeal to the newly arrived chief Royal Engineer would therefore have been a natural course to follow. And the latter part of Colonel Rice Jones's letter is strangely reminiscent of the corresponding appeal made by Lieutenant-Colonel John By on behalf of the men of the Royal Staff Corps on 30 June 1829 (see p. 102).

So ended the contributions made to the development of early Canada by this now-forgotten but distinguished little regiment. They had built the Ottawa River canals, reconstructed the Soulanges canals, and assisted with the building of the Citadel in Halifax as the main works carried out during their employment in British North America from May 1815 to November 1833. Their strength never exceeded 200 and was generally much less. When it is recalled that they had available no modern construction equipment at all (as the description of the building of the Ottawa River canals makes clear) theirs is a really remarkable record. The Royal Staff Corps occupies, therefore, an honourable place in the history of engineering in Canada.

Records of
Royal Staff Corps personnel

The names of quite a number of the members of the Royal Staff Corps who worked on the Ottawa River canals are known through lists of men who took grants of land upon their discharge, and also from an old record book. The names, which follow, add a human dimension to the account of the building of the canals.

LAND GRANT LISTS

Annual list of Non-Commissioned Officers and Privates of the Royal Staff Corps recommended for Grants of Land on their Reduction agreeable to the authority received from the Colonial Department and Instructions from the Honourable Board of Ordnance:

1. Sergeant James Kelly
2. Sergeant James Mountstephen
3. A/Sergeant James Richards
4. Corporal John Hornby
5. Corporal Thos George
6. Private John Bainfield
7. " Richard Bird
8. " William Borden
9. " Edward Clinton
10. " George Cooze
11. " Thomas Foreman
12. " James Goodland
13. " Evan Lawrence
14. " George Masters
15. " Jonathan Moss
16. " Thomas Phillips
17. " David Reeves
18. " James Richards
19. " William Wilks
20. " Jacob Williams
21. " Edmond Williams
22. " William Williams
23. Bugler William King

24. Civilian William Blow }
25.   "   John Hockin   }   late Privates with Corps

Signed by Henry Du Vernet Lt. Col.
Royal Staff Corps Office,   Royal Staff Corps
Chatham, 24 Octr. 1831

(SOURCE: Public Archives of Canada RG 8, C Series, vol. 53, 139)

The following is a second similar list issued the following year, with the same introduction and the location (township) selected:

1. Sergeant George Evans – dead
2. do.   James Murray   Wentworth L.C.
3. Private John Brydon
4.   "   Edwd Byrne
5. Corporal Geo. Cassie   Wentworth L.C.
6. Private Willm Cox
7. Corporal John Hilliard   Wentworth L.C.
8. Private Frek. Hinty   Kilkenny L.C.
9.   do.   John Hoopell   Abercrombie L.C.
10.   do.   John Keatley   Wentworth L.C.
11.   do.   John Lee   Wentworth L.C.
12.   do.   Thos. Ludford
13. Corporal Alexr. McCammins   Kilkenny L.C.
14.   do.   John Mason   Abercrombie L.C.
15. Private Thos. Middleton   Wentworth L.C.
16.   do.   Michl. Nowlan   Wentworth L.C.
17.   do.   Willm. Palmer   Kilkenny L.C.
18.   do.   Richard Quint   Abercrombie L.C.
19. Corporal Patk. Russell
20.   do.   John Rutledge   Wentworth L.C.
21.   do.   Michl. Scully
22. Private James Snook   Wentworth L.C.
23.   do.   Thomas Stokes   Kilkenny L.C.
24.   do.   Joseph Tanner   Abercrombie L.C.
25.   do.   Willm. Tasker
26.   do.   Thomas Taylor   Wentworth L.C.

27.   do.   Joseph Thomas dead
28.   do.   John Vennard   Wentworth L.C.
29.   do.   John Whitehead   Chatham L.C.

Signed by Henry Du Vernet Lt. Col.

R. Staff Crps Office,   Royal Staff Corps
Chatham 1 Octr. 1832.

(SOURCE: Public Archives of Canada RG 8. C Series, vol. 55, 67)

WEDDINGS AND BIRTHS

A chance reference in an old duplicated pamphlet on the history of St
Mungo's Church, Cushing, to 'records of the Royal Staff Corps' led to the
discovery, by the (then) minister, the Reverend Mr W.E. Black, of an old
'exercise book' containing the following records. Mr Black kindly had the
entries in the old book photocopied, one set now being in the library of the
Royal Engineers at Chatham, England, another in the possession of the
author. The original book has been placed in the archives of the United
Church of Canada in Montreal. All entries were written in a fine copperplate hand, the headings at least being by the same writer. Blanks in the lists
that follow are blanks in the original record.

WEDDINGS

No.	Date	Location	Groom	Bride	Witnesses	Chaplain	Certified
1	28 May 1820	Grenville	Pvt Richard Caile	Charlotte Shane ×	H. Piers & R. Greene	Rev. J.O. Abbott	Lt. J. Purdy
2	1 April 1820	Montreal	Pvt P. Sayers	Margaret Pegg ×	–	Mr. Gow (?) (?) J.O. Abbott	Lt. J. Purdy
3	10 Feb. 1823	Montreal	Pvt Clifford Haskett ×	Jane Cavage ×	J. Tritter & G. Archibald	(?) J.O. Abbott	Lt. J. Purdy
4	31 Dec. 1821	Montreal	Pvt. E. Terrance ×	Catherine Dillon ×	J. Dillon & G. Archibald	(?) J.O. Abbott	Lt. J. Purdy
5	6 Nov. 1820	Montreal	Pvt John Hornsby ×	Marianne Decarie ×	–	Rev. ? Jenkins (deceased)	Lt. J. Purdy
6	8 July 1821	Grenville	Pvt William Williams	Ann Jeffice	J. Jennings ×& W. Clarke	Rev. J.O. Abbott	Lt. J. Purdy
7	26 Oct. 1823	Grenville	Sgt G. Evans	Mary McGowan	W. Clarke & E. Phillips	Rev. J.O. Abbott	Lt. J. Longmore
8	29 Aug. 1824	Grenville	Pte James Snook (Blank)	Elizabeth Aspeck ×	R. Edwards & ?	–	Lt. J. Longmore
9							
10	7 Aug. 1825	Grenville	Pvt Benjamin Dixon	Rosannah Kelly	A. Maguire & J. Hooke ×	Rev. J.O. Abbott	Lt. F.H. Robe
11	11 Aug. 1825	Montreal Christ Church	Captain F.M. Read	Christiana Gordon	Major General Gordon & F.H. Robe	J.J. Abbott	F.H. Robe Acth. Adjutant
12	20 Mar. 1826	Montreal	Pvt J. Thomas	Jane Matthews ×	J.H. Stevens & J. Goddard	J.J. Abbott	F.H. Robe
13	8 Jan. 1827	Montreal	Sgt W. Clarke	Ann Wade	A. Maguire & C. Maguire	J.J. Abbott	?
14	? April 1827	Montreal	Pvt J. Hockin	Flora McPhee ×	H. Symon & E. Stearns	J.J. Abbott	?

WEDDINGS (*concluded*)

No.	Date	Location	Groom	Bride	Witnesses	Chaplain	Certified
15	25 Sept. 1829	Greece's Pt. (Chatham)	Pvt T. Foreman ×	Jane Spink ×	C. Pagman & J. Chapman	Wm. Abbott	?
16	11 July 1830	Greece's Pt. (Chatham)	A/Sgt J. Richards	Mary McBride ×	R. Burrows & T. Tighe	Wm. Abbott	?
17	27 Feb. 1831	Chute à Blondeau (Chatham)	Pvt J. Brydon	Isabella Brookleys	D. Wright & W. Walker	Wm. Abbott	?
18	11 April 1831	Grenville	Cpl J. Mason	Mary McCue	– –	Wm. Paisley	?
19	11 April 1831	Grenville	Pvt J. Banfield	Mary Hall	– –	Wm. Paisley	?
20	20 April 1829	Montreal	Sgt J. Kilby	?	W. Barton & R. Sutherland	B.B. Stevens	?
21	10 Dec. 1831	Grenville	S. Major E.C. Correl (?)	Elizabeth Hogben	– –	J. Abbott	?

BIRTHS AND BAPTISMS

No.	Date of Birth	Date of Baptism	Name	At	Parents	Chaplain	Certified by
1	25 Sept. 1819	29 Dec. 1819	Robert*	Grenville	Sgt Wm and Elizabeth Clarke	J.J. Abbott	J.H. Purdy
2	1 Dec. 1819	8 Dec. 1822	Hugh	Chambly	Pt Richard and Charlotte Caile	T. Mignault	J.H. Purdy
3	17 Nov. 1822	24 Nov. 1822	John	Chambly	Pt Samuel and Catherine Forman	T. Mignault	J.H. Purdy
4	30 Mar. 1823	5 April 1823	Elizabeth Sophia*	Chambly	Pt Henry and Jane Cobden	E. Parke	J.H. Purdy
5	7 Jan. 1822	20 Feb. 1822	Amy Sophia	Montreal	Sgt Samuel and Marie Mason	W.O. Abbott	J.H. Purdy
6	23 Mar. 1822	1 April 1822	Elisabeth	Montreal	Pt William and Ann Williams	W.O. Abbott	J.H. Purdy
7	27 June 1823	7 July 1823	Francis	Grenville	Pvt John and Maria Hornsby	J.J. Abbott	J.H. Purdy
8	19 July 1823	24 Aug. 1823	John	Grenville	Pvt William and Mary Ann Pratt	J.J. Abbott	J.H. Purdy
9	13 June 1823	1 Sept. 1822 (?)	Philip*	Grenville	Pvt Thomas and Marina Taylor	J.J. Abbott	J.H. Purdy
10	20 July 1823	11 Aug. 1823	Ann	Grenville	Pte John and Ann Bird	J.J. Abbott	J.H. Purdy
11	25 July 1823	11 Aug. 1823	Ann	Grenville	Pte Evan and Ann Lawrence	J.J. Abbott	J.H. Purdy
12	22 Aug. 1823	7 Sept. 1823	Elizabeth	Grenville	Sgt Wm. and Elizabeth Clarke	J.J. Abbott	J.H. Purdy
13	3 June 1821	8 July 1821	William* Andrew*	Grenville	Sgt Wm. and Elizabeth Clarke	J.J. Abbott	J.H. Purdy
14	17 Aug. 1823	7 Sept. 1823	Charles	Grenville	Pte Wm. and Elizabeth Hopkins	J.J. Abbott	J.H. Purdy
15	29 Aug. 1823	7 Sept. 1823	Alicia Mount Stephen	Grenville	Sgt James and Phillipa ?	J.J. Abbott	J.H. Purdy
16	9 Dec. 1823	28 Dec. 1823	John	Montreal	Pte John and Mary Ann Hornsby	B.B. Stevens	–
17	25 Dec. 1823	11 Jan. 1824	William James	Montreal	Pte Peter and Ann Landeyou (?)	B.B. Stevens	–
18	24 Feb. 1824	2 Mar. 1824	Margaret	Montreal	Pte William and Ann Williams	B.B. Stevens	–
19	28 Feb. 1824	17 Mar. 1824	William	Montreal	Pte Jeremiah and Isabella Beadle	B.B. Stevens	–
20	18 Aug. 1824	2 Sept. 1824	William*	Grenville	Pte Thomas and Marina Taylor	J.J. Abbott	–
21	13 Sept. 1824	3 Oct. 1824	Mary Ann	Grenville	Cpl Thomas and Elizabeth Phillips	J. Abbott	–
22	28 Sept. 1824	3 Oct. 1824	George	Grenville	Sgt George and Mary Evans	J. Abbott	–
23							

BIRTHS AND BAPTISMS (continued)

No.	Date of Birth	Date of Baptism	At	Name	Parents	Chaplain	Certified by
24	3 Feb. 1825	6 Mar. 1825	Montreal	Ann Maria	Pte James and Elizabeth Snook	B.B. Stevens	Lt. F.H. Robe Actg Adjutant
25	4 Mar. 1825	1 April 1825	Montreal	Willie Thomas	Cpl Henry and Jane Cobden	B.B. Stevens	F.H. Robe
26	6 Mar. 1824	3 April 1824	Montreal	Hannah Mary*	Sgt Wm. and Elizabeth Clarke	Wm. Abbott	F.H. Robe
27	28 June 1825	7 Aug. 1825	Grenville	Henry William	Sgt John and Hannah Lang	Wm. Abbott	F.H. Robe
28	11 Aug. 1825	3 Sept. 1825	Grenville	Elizabeth Ellen	Pte Wm. and Mary Ann Pratt	Wm. Abbott	F.H. Robe
29	7 Oct. 1825	11 Oct. 1825	Grenville	Thomas	Cpl Thomas and Marina Taylor	B.B. Stevens	F.H. Robe
30	3 Dec. 1825	25 Dec. 1825	Montreal	Edward	Pte William and Elizabeth Hopkinson		
31	7 Nov. 1825	11 Dec. 1825	Montreal	Jane	Sgt James and Ann Goodland	Stevens	F.H. Robe
32	14 Feb. 1826	22 Feb. 1826	Montreal	Catherine	Sgt James and Phillippa Mountstephen	Stevens	F.H. Robe
33							
34	3 Feb. 1826	27 May 1826	Grenville	Mary	Pte William and Ann Williams		
35	9 Sept. 1825	15 July 1826	Grenville	Mary Ann Jane	Cpl James and Ann Murray		
36	16 May 1826	27 May 1826	Grenville	Dinah	Pte Benjamin and Rosanna L. Dixon		
37	9 June 1826	24 June 1826	Grenville	Edward	Pte Evan and Ann Lawrence		
38	6 Aug. 1826		Grenville	Mary Ann	Pvt Pater and Ann Landry (?)		
39	7 Dec. 1821	6 Dec. 1821	Montreal	Margaret	Pvt William and Mary Walton		
–	7 Sept. 1823	28 Dec. 1823	Grenville	Elizabeth	do. do.		
–	24 June 1825	24 July 1825	Grenville	Anne Marie	do. do.		
–	15 June 1827	8 July 1827	Grenville	William Delany	do. do.		
40			Montreal		Pte William and Elizabeth Timmins		
43	7 July 1827	27 July 1827	Grenville	Vashti*	Cpl Thomas and Marina Taylor		
44	8 July 1827	29 July 1827	Grenville	Jane	Pvt Joseph and Jane Thomas		

No.	Date of Birth	Date of Baptism	Place	Child	Parents	Officiating Minister
45	1827		Grenville		Pvt James and Elizabeth Snook	
(46)			Montreal		Pvt William and Elizabaeth Hopkinson	
(47)	28 Sept. 1828	12 Oct. 1828	Grenville	Richard	Sgt George and Mary Evans	
(48)		3 Aug. 1828	Grenville	William	Pvt David and Susan Reeves	
(49)		10 May 1828	Grenville		Pvt William and Ann Williams	
(50)			Grenville	–	Pvt Murray	
(51)	8 July 1827	31 July 1827	Grenville	James	Pvt Joseph and Jane Thomas	
(52)	20 Jan. 1828	4 Feb. 1828	Montreal	Daniel	Pvt John and Susan McLure	
(53)	7 Mar. 1828	28 Mar. 1828	Grenville	William	Pvt William and Ann Williams	B.B. Stevens
(54)	9 Mar. 1828	17 Mar. 1828	Greece's Pt.	Ann	Pts William and Ann Williams	
(55)	28 Oct. 1828	11 Nov. 1828	Grenville	Catherine	Sgt James and Ann Murray	
(56)	25 Feb. 1831	6 Mar. 1831	Grenville	Richard	Sgt George and Mary Evans	B.B. Stevens
(57)	26 Aug. 1830	21 Sept. 1830	Grenville	Henry	Sgt George and Mary Evans	
(58)	30 Mar. 1829	23 April 1829	Montreal	Phillippa	Sgt James and Philippa Mountstephen	
(59)	12 April 1829	11 May 1829	Greece's Pt.	Harriott	Sgt James and Nancy Kilby	
(60)	7 May 1829	4 June 1829	Grenville	James Wm. Mortre	Pvt Samuel and Mary Hewson	
(61)	2 July 1829	15 July 1829	Greece's Pt.	William	Pvt David and Susan Reeves	
(62)	3 July 1829	2 Aug. 1829	Greece's Pt.	Selina	Pvt John and Hannah Keatly	
(63)	2 May 1829	12 May 1829	Grenville	Mary	Pvt Even and Eliza Lawrence	
(64)	? Aug. 1829	15 Sept. 1829	Grenville	Elizabeth	Pvt James and Eliza Snook	
(65)	6 Feb. 1830	4 Mar. 1830	Greece's Pt.	Jane	Pvt Peter and Ann Bryce	
(67)	30 Mar. 1830	7 May 1830	Greece's Pt.	Julia Ann	Pvt Peter and Ann Lenderjohn (?)	
(68)	19 Sept. 1829	20 Oct. 1829	Grenville	Charles	Cpl John and Mary Ann Hornby	
(69)	17 July 1830	1 Aug. 1830	Chatham	William	Pte John and Joanna Hurley	
(70)	? Sept. 1830	26 Sept. 1830	Grenville	Elizabeth	Pvt Thomas and Elizabeth Phillips	
	20 Oct. 1830	7 Nov. 1830	Greece's Pt.	William	Cpl John and Eliza Rutledge	
	6 June 1830	10 Feb. 1831	Belle Vue	Maria Ellen Jesopp	Deputy Commissary-General Charles John and Sophia Margaret Forbes	Revd. Paisley, Wm. Abbott (Acting Chaplain)

BIRTHS AND BAPTISMS (concluded)

No.	Date of Birth	Date of Baptism	Name	Parents	At	Chaplain	Certified by
	27 Feb. 1831	6 Mar. 1831	Henry	Sgt George and Mary Evans	Grenville	Wm. Abbott	(a/c)
(71)	6 Mar. 1831	15 May 1831	William	Pvt Thomas and Phoebe Lindford	Greece's Pt.	Wm. Abbott	(a/c)
	18 April 1831	15 May 1831	Sarah	Pvt Thomas and Jane Foreman	Greece's Pt.	Wm. Abbott	(a/c)
(72)	8 June 1831	19 June 1831	Mary Ann	Pvt John and Susanna McClure	Grenville	Wm. Abbott	(a/c)
	8 June 1831	19 June 1831	Emma	Pvt James and Elizabeth Snook	Grenville	Wm. Abbott	(a/c)
(73)	20 May 1831	26 June 1831	William	Cpl John and Mary Ann Hornby	Greece's Pt.	Wm. Abbott	(a/c)
	12 Aug. 1831	21 Aug. 1831	Benjamin George	Pvt George and Eliza Wesley	Greece's Pt.	Wm. Abbott	(a/c)
(74)	20 Sept. 1831	5 Oct. 1831	Martha Elvin	Bugler Wm. and Mary King	Grenville	Wm. Abbott	(a/c)
	13 Aug. 1831	13 Nov. 1831	Elizabeth	Pvt James and Elizabeth Barber (?)	Grenville	Wm. Abbott	(a/c)
(75)	6 Nov. 1831	20 Nov. 1831	Robert	Pvt John and Janet Hoppel (?)	Grenville	J. Abbott (officiating minister)	
(76)	28 Oct. 1829	13 Dec. 1829	Eliza Jane Piercy	Lt Richard and Annabelle Hayne	Greece's Pt. Chatham	Wm. Abbott	
	4 May 1832	26 Aug. 1832	Annabelle Gertrude Gardener	Lt Richard and Annabelle Hayne	St. Andrews	Wm. Abbott	

NOTES TO TABLES OF WEDDINGS, BIRTHS, AND BAPTISMS

1 Each entry in the old book is entered on a separate sheet, in general, but where several baptisms in a family had been celebrated but not entered at the time, they are combined on the one page. This will explain the few entries that are not in chronological order.
2 A few marks – 'x' – have been indicated, as accurately as possible, in the records of marriages, but some of the original marks are difficult to decipher. They seem to indicate that the person in question could not write.
3 The Reverend J.J. Abbott came from England with his younger brother William O. Abbott, later ordained as the Reverend William Abbott. The older brother was appointed Rector of St Andrew's in 1818 and from there served the Royal Staff Corps by coming to Grenville to take services from 1820 on. His first son was born in March 1821 and, as Sir J.J.C. Abbott, became prime minister of Canada in 1891. The younger brother appears to have taken over the services at Grenville after 1834, although the Reverend J.J. Abbott was officially the Incumbent of St Matthew's Church from 1831 to 1846.

Traffic on the Ottawa River canals

The Ottawa River canals were in unbroken use throughout every summer season from 1834 to 1962. It would be pleasing to be able to present a complete record of the traffic that passed through them, but this can be done with certainty only from 1873 onwards. In the tables that follow statistics have been restricted for convenience to the total number of vessels transiting the canals and the total tonnage of freight that they carried. The number of vessels would be approximately equally divided in upstream and downstream directions, but for most years, up to about the turn of the century, all but a very small percentage (usually less than 1 per cent) would be downward-bound freight. It consisted largely of sawn lumber for most of this period. After the turn of the century, the quantity of lumber shipped down to Montreal started to decrease, while upward-bound freight began to increase, being general cargoes for the young settlements growing up along the banks of the Ottawa. Gradually this business was captured first by the railways and eventually by road transport. It is significant that, despite these competing forms of transport, the old canals still carried almost 200,000 tons of freight each year until 1961, although this figure was well below that of the peak year of 1882 when 790,400 tons were transported.

It has so far proved impossible to locate (with one exception) traffic statistics for the years 1834 to 1850, so that the effect of the opening of the St Lawrence canals in 1851 cannot be determined; but traffic through the Ottawa River canals must have been significantly decreased. This lack of information is not surprising; even in 1865 William Kingsford, CE, when writing his book, *The Canadian Canals*, had this to say (p. 120):

For my part I could find nothing to guide me, although I looked through them [all the public documents then available] with fair industry. The first Trade and

Navigation Returns are those of 1849, and they are far from the full and satisfactory Returns of the following years. In 1850 the present system was inaugurated, each year being continued with more or less improvement. It is not therefore possible to go back earlier than this date.

But he missed one isolated record which may be found on page 330 of volume C. 60 in the great series of canal record books in the Public Archives of Canada:

1845

Traffic through 11 locks of the Ottawa River Canals	
Steam boats	354
Barges	903
Cabin passengers	484
Merchandise	19,381 [tons, presumably]
Iron and Fish	4,715 (Free)

The mention of steamboats and barges only, as the vessels using the canals, is an interesting indication of the speed with which the character of shipping on the Ottawa River had changed. This shift was anticipated in a report sent to the 'respective Officers' at ordnance headquarters by the ordnance clerk at Carillon, on 14 June 1841 (vol. C 59, 360) in which it is explained: 'steamers upon the principle of the screw propellor, as well as others were about to navigate the whole route, carrying burdens the same as a barge ... steamers [are] now passing to and fro, constructed for passengers only and towing boats as well as being towed by horses themselves.'

Since Kingsford's book was really a piece of special pleading on behalf of the St Lawrence route to the Great Lakes rather than the Georgian Bay Ship Canal route (see appendix D), it is not surprising that his treatment of statistics for the Ottawa River canals is sketchy, to say the least. He provides a small table in which he gives tonnage figures for the Ottawa and Rideau Canal (singular), with figures from 1858 only. But on page 128 he tabulates tonnages for traffic through the 'Saint Anne's Lock,' which is probably a true reflection of the tonnages through the Ottawa River canals, since there was then little development around the shores of the Lake of Two Mountains. The total tonnages as recorded by Kingsford are presented in table C1. (In 1857, ownership and operation of the canals was passed from the British Board of Ordnance to the commissioners of public works of the United Province of Canada, but the table shows that this transfer had little effect on traffic.)

The figures in table C1 for the number of vessels are not given by Kingsford but come from the annual reports of the commissioners of public works. They contain much relevant information such as the traffic in cribs of large timbers down the Ottawa River. These cribs did not go through the canals but were taken through the adjoining rapids by intrepid rivermen. In 1854, for example, 13,935 cribs were taken down the rapids, those containing 294,457 'pieces,' or large timbers, going down to Quebec for shipment to Europe.

From the sessional papers of the province of Canada and, after 1867, of the dominion of Canada, the tonnage record can be continued as table C2. The fragmentary figures for the number of vessels again are found in the Public Works reports. They are significant in that, with an operating summer season of approximately 180 days, they show an average daily traffic of about forty transits of the canals which must, even in those early years, have presented a busy sight.

As one of its many splendid services, the Dominion Bureau of Statistics (now Statistics Canada) gathered together the many scattered records of traffic on all Canadian canals, publishing them as *Summary of Canal Statistics 1848–1936* in 1937. For the Ottawa River canals, therefore, the record is complete from 1873. These figures are presented in table C3.

TABLE C1				TABLE C2		
Year	Tonnage	Number of vessels		Year	Tonnage	Number of vessels
1850	59,830			1864	47,410	
1851	105,933			1865	239,530	
1852	99,054			1866	282,501	
1853	137,159			1867	343,139	
1854	120,069			1868	373,583	6,244
1855	126,361	2,874		1869	376,162	6,898
1856	169,401	2,565		1870	483,346	7,356
1857	148,845	2,849		1871	358,962	
1858	154,444	2,922		1872	100,865	
1859	88,696	3,245				
1860	204,574	3,695				
1861	199,097	3,650				
1862	228,096	3,650				
1863	240,370	5,041				

TABLE C3

Year	Tonnage	Vessels	Year	Tonnage	Vessels
1873	518,473	5,097	1918	167,170	1,488
1874	559,988	5,410	1919	218,438	1,790
1875	497,494	4,801	1920	233,329	1,551
1876	514,481	4,974	1921	171,769	1,807
1877	487,651	4,446	1922	213,227	2,197
1878	454,793	3,734	1923	233,092	2,428
1879	486,722	4,058	1924	205,534	2,313
1880	644,549	5,202	1925	214,940	2,246
1881	698,260	4,907	1926	321,456	2,573
1882	790,400	4,735	1927	455,759	3,210
1883	743,274	4,134	1928	487,786	3,872
1884	673,760	3,558	1929	537,037	3,615
1885	763,236	3,572	1930	540,933	3,258
1886	745,335	4,224	1931	492,919	3,135
1887	683,047	3,346	1932	253,523	1,360
1888	693,249	3,174	1933	253,764	1,448
1889	694,771	3,266	1934	273,121	1,679
1890	651,355	2,829	1935	289,526	1,802
1891	585,041	2,464	1936	261,493	1,742
1892	647,011	2,667	1937	349,078	1,735
1893	581,521	2,448	1938	299,693	1,219
1894	562,010	2,197	1939	301,671	1,266
1895	541,220	2,195	1940	317,412	1,360
1896	502,046	2,073	1941	309,509	932
1897	562,370	2,198	1942	289,970	534
1898	549,986	2,401	1943	240,496	558
1899	520,105	2,653	1944	272,211	593
1900	389,145	2,114	1945	258,172	760
1901	445,862	1,821	1946	261,295	604
1902	444,682	1,906	1947	254,827	249
1903	436,473	2,094	1948	263,343	294
1904	335,993	1,805	1949	282,330	316
1905	390,771	2,152	1950	294,604	343
1906	397,415	2,207	1951	277,171	365
1907	336,850	2,034	1952	201,151	426
1908	258,527	1,882	1953	243,032	434
1909	336,939	2,181	1954	190,810	533
1910	385,261	2,601	1955	206,525	596
1911	320,071	2,413	1956	283,500	600
1912	392,350	3,059	1957	356,640	691
1913	365,438	2,938	1958	189,980	735
1914	335,132	2,472	1959	327,643	866
1915	272,370	2,040	1960	278,200	241
1916	237,651	1,987	1961	196,977	212
1917	214,835	1,696	1962	300	254

At the end of the year 1962, the Ottawa River canals were flooded by the rising waters impounded by the Carillon hydroelectric dam of Hydro-Québec; they had served Canada well for almost 130 years. It is of some interest to note that great political events (such as Confederation in 1867) and engineering operations (such as the rebuilding of the canals between 1870 and 1880) are not reflected in the records of traffic through the canals. Only the Great Depression starting in 1931–2 is indicated by a sudden drop in traffic.

CARILLON LIFT LOCK

As the Ottawa River canals finished their service, the single lift lock incorporated in the Carillon Dam began its equivalent service. This record may then well be completed by table C4, a listing of the vessel transits through the great lock, almost all pleasure boats but including the regular start- and end-of-season passages of the vessels of the Canadian Coast Guard in their servicing of the Ottawa River. Occasional freight shipments also use the lock, the main traffic of this commercial variety having been the lockage of over thirty bargeloads of structural steel from the plant of the Dominion Bridge Company at Lachine, en route to the Hunt Club Road Bridge across the Rideau River in Ottawa. (Figures for the Carillon lock traffic have been kindly supplied by the Socio-Economic Information Division of the Socio-Economic Branch of Parks Canada, part of the Department of the Environment, courtesy of D.J. Gormley.)

TABLE C4

Year	Vessels	Year	Vessels
1963	1,431	1976	2,055
1964	1,309	1977	2,376
1965	1,098	1978	2,542
1966	1,375	1979	2,638
1967	2,085	1980	2,441
1968	1,636	1981	2,643
1969	1,689	1982	2,689
1970	1,642	1983	2,858
1971	1,610	1984	3,647
1972	1,924	1985	3,386
1973	2,071	1986	3,800
1974	1,847	1987	4,578
1975	1,740		

The Georgian Bay Ship Canal

On 16 March 1829 Lieutenant-Colonel John By wrote from the Royal Engineer's office at Bytown to Colonel Durnford, his commanding officer at Quebec, the following letter:

Sir, I have the honour of transmitting for the Information of His excellency Sir James Kempt a report by Mr Shirreff on the advantages that would accrue to the country by forming a water communication from the Ottawa to Lake Huron; and as I believe a canal could be executed of sufficient size to pass steam boats for the sum of £800,000. I have enclosed a sketch showing the route of the proposed Canal and request you will also have the kindness to lay it before his Excellency. I have the honour to be, Sir, Your most obedient Humble Servant, John By, Lt. Col., Royal Engineers, commdg. Rideau Canal.[1]

This was the formal beginning of what was to be a dream for many people for the next century, a project that came close to implementation in 1911, only to fall into the background of national planning after Sir Wilfrid Laurier was beaten in the general election of that year. It still has its proponents almost a century and a half later. If a ship canal had been constructed from the Ottawa River to Lake Huron, the entire economy of eastern North America would have been affected. That it has not yet been built makes that 'if' one of the great question marks in the history of Canada.

It is significant that this first civilian proposal for the canalization of the upper Ottawa was submitted to the governor by a senior army officer. This conjunction of civilian and military interest in the great project that came to be called the Georgian Bay Ship Canal continued until the end of the nineteenth century. It was, therefore, the second part of the interrelation of the

Ottawa River with the defence of British North America. Initial studies were strictly military in character and purpose. Civilian interest gradually took the lead, but as late as 1894 civilian promoters of the project still regarded its importance as a defence measure to be their 'trump card.' The active history of this abortive project spans almost a full century, so that even a summary of its defence aspects must be an encapsulation.

The main features of the Ottawa River watershed have already been described (p. 22) and map 6 shows the essential features of the Georgian Bay Ship Canal. Quite the most remarkable feature of the Ottawa River is the fact that, if one leaves the main stream as it turns north at Mattawa and proceeds up the small Mattawa River, there is only a short portage from its headwaters in Trout Lake over to a small stream that flows into Lake Nipissing. This lake is drained by the French River which flows into Georgian Bay on Lake Huron. Here, therefore, was the most direct and so the shortest route between Montreal and the upper Great Lakes, a route known through the centuries to the Indians and shown by them to Champlain on his two journeys up the Ottawa in 1613 and 1615. He described it in his travel volumes. It quickly became the accepted route to the west and was so used by the early explorers, the first missionary priests, and then by the fur traders – French, Scottish and English. For over 200 years, it was truly the gateway to the northern part of the North American continent. Only after the amalgamation of the Hudson's Bay Company and the North West Company in 1821 did its canoe traffic begin to decline. The later development of canals along the St Lawrence finally diverted all through traffic away from the Ottawa.

Use of the waterway was not easy, because there were many portages around the successive rapids. But portage paths were steadily improved, and expert voyageurs developed an intimate knowledge of the route. Stops were made only to camp overnight, and they were always short. Captain Landman of the Royal Engineers, with a picked crew of voyageurs, once made the downstream journey from Sault Ste Marie to Montreal, for example, in seven days of intrepid travelling. It is not surprising, therefore, that nothing was known about the country on either side of the route until settlement began. The Ottawa waterway was traversed just as quickly as possible on journeys finishing in the mid-west of the United States, the west of Canada or, eventually, the Mackenzie River watershed and ultimately the Arctic. What is surprising is that the early planners of the military defences of British North America seem to have been ignorant of this well-travelled route, as shown by the explorations that were ordered by young engineer officers seeking a direct route between Montreal and the new naval base at Penetanguishine.

This base was established in 1814, when naval occasions on the Great Lakes were prominent in military planning, following the War of 1812. A glance at a map will show why such efforts were made to find a route to the base from Montreal, so that the little post could be supplied and manned without the risk of travel up the St Lawrence, in exactly the same way as the Ottawa-Rideau route provided this alternative route to the fortress of Kingston. The Duke of Wellington, in his memorandum of 1 March 1819 to Lord Bathurst, urged the necessity of a canal or railway to Lake Simcoe by way of the Black River and the Rideau River, two streams at least 100 miles apart, indicative of the little that was then known of the country between the Ottawa River and Lakes Ontario and Huron. But surveys were ordered, and so, as early as 1819 a first exploration along this proposed military route was made by Lieutenant Catty, RE. With an Indian guide he left Lake Simcoe by ascending the Talbot River, then portaging to Balsam Lake, to the Gull Lake chain, then to the York River, which he followed to the Madawaska and so to the Ottawa. No record of any map that he made has been found but there does exist a sketch map by J.G. Chewett showing what is thought to have been Catty's route and also those routes followed by Lieutenant Briscoe in 1826 and 1827 and by Lieutenant Walpole in 1827, all searching for a convenient through route to the Ottawa but finding none.

These later journeys were undertaken as a direct result of the report of the commission headed by Sir James Carmichael Smyth. The officer commanding the Royal Engineers in the Canadas wrote from Quebec on 27 July 1825 that 'His Grace the Master General attaching much value to the practicability of a communication between the Ottawa and Lake Simcoe, it will be necessary that the journey performed by Lieut. Catty in 1819 should again be undertaken and the Officer employed upon it instructed not to hurry himself but to give himself sufficient time to make every observation which may hereafter be of use to the service.' Lieutenant Henry Briscoe was given this interesting assignment. Accompanied by Ensign Durnford, he left Holland Landing on 6 September 1826 and reached Fort Coulonge on the Ottawa on 2 October. His report, dated from Kingston on 16 October, is the first written account of the now well-known Muskoka-Algonquin Park area.[2]

Both Lieutenant Briscoe and Lieutenant Walpole carried out an additional survey in 1827 in still further search for a through waterway. Each reported on his difficulties, Lieutenant Walpole's report concluding with these words: 'that though (this route) comprises a large quantity of navigable water (it) possesses some obstacles that could only be overcome by more than ordinary degree of labour and expense. It may be added that the Country through which we passed unusually bore a most barren and cheerless aspect.'³ The details of the various routes followed through the remarkable lake country that is now so well known by summer canoe travellers need not be detailed. All who have been into Algonquin Park can well imagine the innumerable variations possible for travel from west to east through this area, still wild today.

The contrast between the sober judgment of Walpole and the wildly enthusiastic reports of Charles Shirreff and his son is typical of the conflicting ideas about the canalization of the upper Ottawa that persisted throughout the century. Shirreff was a native of Leith, Scotland, who first settled at Port Hope in 1817. He received a grant of land of 3,000 acres around the great Chats Falls (the first rapids above the Chaudière) and moved up to make his new home there in the winter of 1818–19. With his home on the banks of the Ottawa, it was natural that he should have become enthusiastic about its possibilities as a transportation route. His 1829 report of thirteen pages was entitled 'observations on the advantages of a Canal from the Ottawa to Lake Huron with information collected respecting its practicability.' It is a curious document, especially in this statement which is the only quotation that need be made: 'The route of the Hudson Bay Company by Lake Nipissing besides being circuitous is impeded by numerous falls and rapids, particularly in the upper part of the Ottawa.'⁴ Clearly he was influenced by the reports he had heard, probably at second hand, of the early military surveys for the route to Penetanguishine; it is doubtful if Charles Shirreff had ever travelled the route that he advocated so warmly.

There is no record now available of John By's having taken any further action in support of his letter of 16 March 1829, most fortunately, since his off-the-cuff estimate of cost could have proved embarrassing. Later in 1829, however, Charles Shirreff's son, Alexander, did make a journey up the Ottawa, seeking a new way into the lake country south of the Ottawa. After much searching, he used a portage over to the Petawawa River by turning off from the Ottawa at Deux Rivières, far past the Lac des Allumettes mentioned in his father's report. Thence he travelled to Cedar Lake by way of (another) Trout Lake and finally down the Muskoka River to Penetanguishine. He made the return journey by using the Opeongo and Madawaska rivers. The report that he made on his journey was published in Quebec City two years later and was used by later surveyors of this route, but his estimate of the quality of the land through which he travelled as potential farm land was most inaccurate. His father petitioned Sir John Colborne in March 1830, invoking the name of Colonel By, for the sum of £106-18-6, as the cost of his son's journey, but this expense was not granted.⁵

Disappointed at the lack of action, Charles Shirreff left his home at Chats Falls in 1835 and was appointed the first government collector of timber dues at Bytown. There he must have transmitted his enthusiasm for the Ottawa canal scheme (although now using the full Ottawa waterway) to other residents of the little town, particularly William Stewart, another early Scottish settler. Stewart supported the idea from 1830 until his death in 1856: his enthusiasm was transmitted to his son, McLeod Stewart, who became probably the most active of all the proponents of the Georgian Bay canal scheme, as will shortly be seen. Meetings were held, notably one in June 1841 at Kirk's Hotel in Bytown; petitions for support were addressed to successive governors, an especially persuasive one being that submitted to Lord Durham; but all to no avail. Attention then turned to the possibility of forming a joint stock company in the United Kingdom, along the lines of the Canada Company, with the idea of promoting settlement along the Ottawa, but this proposal also failed to win favour.

The government of Upper Canada by the year 1835 was looking for new areas for settlement. The inevitable influence of Toronto led to lands north of the provincial capital being given first consideration. The government therefore obtained the services of two British officers, Lieutenant Carthew, RN, and Lieutenant Baddely, RE, and commissioned them to survey the coast of Georgian Bay and to study the river flowing into it. Since Baddely was a competent geologist who was interested in natural history, and as he had a copy of Alexander Shirreff's report of 1829, he was able to make a shrewd assessment of the land through which he travelled. He almost reached the limit of Algonquin Park, his observations completely disproving Shirreff's suggestions about good farm land being found in the Ottawa-Huron tract. He also pointed out that the area could be penetrated much better by way of the Ottawa River and Rice Lake than by the approaches already attempted.

The 1830s was a decade of what can only be described as 'waterway fever' in Canada and elsewhere. Thus it is not surprising to find the government of Upper Canada, already involved with the Welland Canal and seeing the construction of the Rideau Canal completed, with work in progress along the St Lawrence, turning its attention to the long-studied connection between the Ottawa River and Lake Huron. A commission was appointed in 1836 with Baddely, now a captain, as one of its members, to study this and other northern possibilities. The commission appointed three men to carry out the necessary surveys. David Taylor was sent to study the lakes and rivers of the Temagami region, a scenic area but one outside the region in which we are interested. William Hawkins, who had accompanied Baddely in his trip as a surveyor and who was now the deputy provincial surveyor, was directed to study the French River-Mattawa route and also the possibility of the Magnetawan-Petawawa route. David Thompson was directed to try the Muskoka-Madawaska route. His is a name that will be familiar to many readers; it was, indeed, the same David Thompson who had made history with his journeys through the mountains of the west. Although he was now sixty-six years old, the start of this Muskoka journey must have been almost a holiday for him.

William Hawkins submitted a report on his surveys. He makes quite clear his opinion as to the unsuitability of the Magnetawan-Petawawa route, showing that the rise to the height of land from Lake Huron was 340 feet. He is in no doubt as to the foolishness of contemplating the building of a canal along this route. It was his report that led to the abandonment of any idea of using the Huron route, so strongly urged by Charles Shirreff, and the selection of what is, today, the 'obvious' route, using the Mattawa and French rivers with their linkage through Lake Nipissing. David Thomson does not appear to have prepared an official report, but being the geographer that he was, he did leave four beautifully drawn maps which are still preserved.[7] These included the first accurate maps of what is now well known as the Muskoka region. He did keep a diary, which shows what a very difficult time he had at the end of his journey because of the lateness of the season. During his study of the Muskrat Lake route, he records that it snowed for most of the day on 16 November. Temperatures fell to 3°F and his men (not unnaturally) became disgruntled; ice formed on the river but it was not strong enough to bear them. Eventually they proceeded on land from Portage du Fort to Bytown, which they reached on 18 December. The route he followed was through Lake of Bays, the Muskoka River to Oxtongue Lake, and then through to the Madawaska River by a route that is today one of the most popular for modern summer canoeists, with a final 'side-trip' to study the Muskrat Lake route. All travellers of today who dip their paddles into the still waters of the lakes in Algonquin Park and the region around may remember that these same waters, when still unexplored, were paddled well over a century and a half ago by young officers of the Corps of Royal Engineers with their Indian guides and some years later by one of the very greatest of all Canadian explorers. These reports marked the end of such surveys of the Huron route, and all future discussions related only to the canalization of the Ottawa, Mattawa, and French rivers.

Another of the Duke of Wellington's justly famous memoranda on the defence of Canada was prepared in January 1842 for Lord Stanley. General

Sir George Murray, who knew Canada from his service as lieutenant-governor of Upper Canada in 1814–15, was now master-general of the ordnance, and he was soon adding his voice in support of needed attention to the defences of Canada. His report of 26 May 1845 to his minister followed the receipt of the initial report of an inspection of the defences by Colonel Holloway, RE, and Captain Boxer, RN, the first of a notable series of on-the-ground studies by joint navy and army teams.[8] Captain Warden, RN, was the next officer to be sent to Canada (in 1845) with instructions that included a requirement for a study of the size and defences of the canals. His report, submitted early in 1846, again stressed the vital character of the canals in the defence system and urged the necessary reconstruction of the Ottawa River canals as well as attention to the Georgian Bay Canal. So alarmed had the British government become at this time that an important conference (to which the Duke of Wellington was not invited) was held in London on 3 March 1846. The defence of British North America as a whole was reviewed, canals receiving due consideration, but economies took precedence at the meeting. Even the reconstruction of 'those three Grenville locks' was again postponed, and no action was taken about the upper Ottawa.

It will now be abundantly clear that the civilian and military interests in the Georgian Bay Ship Canal proposal were inextricably mixed. In Canada, civilian interests appealed to government for action, in the interests of settlement and commerce – any government, that of Upper Canada, later of the United Province of Canada, or that of Great Britain. In London, those with responsibility for defence planning were anxious to see the upper Ottawa developed, but Treasury authorities could not be persuaded about the need for the vast expenditure that would be involved. The British Ordnance Department was anxious to rid itself of the responsibility for maintaining and operating the military canals that had been built, culminating in the legal transfer of 1857. Army authorities, however, continued to see the need for direct access to the upper Great Lakes. Commerce was developing rapidly by mid-century, and the opening of the St Lawrence canals, finally in 1856, directed public attention to the growing traffic in freight from the Great Lakes, much of it diverted to the Erie Canal in the United States.

Civilian interest in the Georgian Bay scheme was renewed; it had never actually lapsed, McLeod Stewart and others continuing their advocacy. Mr Stewart, who was the member of the legislature for Bytown, presented a resolution favouring the project, for example, to a committee of the whole House of Assembly on 26 July 1847. The great civilian argument in favour of the scheme was that it would give a wholly Canadian route from the

Great Lakes to the sea. Possibly of more importance was the saving in sailing distance. Here are the distances given in the form in which they appear in the greatest of all reports on the project: 'Fort William to Montreal / By the Georgian Bay Ship Canal 934 miles; By the St Lawrence-Lakes route 1,216 miles,' a saving of 282 miles. If the total distance from the Lakehead to Liverpool, England, is reckoned by way of the canal and then by way of the Erie Canal and New York, a saving for the all-Canadian route of 806 miles will be found. Even in days when speed was not worshipped as it is today, this saving in the distance to be sailed between the Great Lakes and Montreal was a feature easily understood and appreciated by all who were willing to think about the future of the colony.

Sir Richard Scott relates[9] that in 1851 or 1852 a group of interested Bytown citizens decided to invite members of the government of the United Province of Canada to a banquet, in order to discuss with them the 'Ottawa and Georgian Bay Canal.' The dinner was held under canvas in the vicinity of Wood's Hotel, west of the Uppertown Market, the prime mover being John Egan, MLA, a famous political figure of the Ottawa Valley. It must have been quite a dinner; for it resulted in the vote of $50,000 in the government's next estimates for circumventing the obstruction between Lac Deschenes and Chats Lakes, the fifty-foot drop in the Chats Falls. The commissioners of public works were instructed to prepare plans. Never was a more political canal devised. It provided magnificent material for the hustings, loud claims as to what the canal was to do for the valley being drowned out (as far as one can now tell) by the vituperation showered upon Mr John A. Macdonald, as he then was, for this profligate waste of public money – which, one must admit, it certainly was. A canal just under three miles long was planned to be excavated throughout in solid rock. Six locks were found to be necessary. The site was on the northern bank of the river, the downstream entrance in what is now known as Pontiac Bay.

The first contract was awarded for channel excavation on 19 June 1854 to the firm of A.P. MacDonald and P. Schramm, and work started in August of that year. The firm did manage to excavate a few hundred feet of the downstream end of the canals and to do some work at the lock sites, but with increasing difficulty because of the hardness of the rock. This was not surprising in view of the equipment then available and the fact that the excavation was in the toughest type of igneous rock of the Precambrian shield. Work finally stopped in November 1856, and the arguments about payment, already well under way, continued with increasing vigour. The whole story is too pathetic an example of 'political engineering' to dwell on in any detail, but the final settlement was about $373,000. The total cost, by the time all the work was stopped, amounted to $482,950.81. When it is added that the works included the opening up of a quarry in Torbolton Township, on the *south* side of the river, with the construction of a wharf from which the cut stone for the locks could be ferried across to the other rocky shore, it will be realized how far politics penetrated this piece of engineering design. The great rock cut may still be seen by the inquiring wanderer, and the start of the quarry may still be found in the woods.

Whether the presence at the dinner of Sir Francis Hincks and the Honourable Mr John Young, his minister of public works, was related in any way to the commission given shortly after this abortive start to Walter Shanly cannot now be determined. In 1856 this great civil engineer was requested by the Department of Public Works to study the possibility of canalizing the Ottawa River in connection with the detailed examination he was also to make of the Ottawa River canals. Shanly's energetic approach to his assignments is shown by the fact that, after getting his instructions on 22 July 1856 he had a party of surveyors at work on the Ottawa by mid-August. He examined the whole route himself, as might be imagined, and gave his overall impression in these words: 'I voyaged the whole of the above mentioned portion of the route, some 260 miles, by canoe ... and I reached the end of my journey strongly impressed with the conviction that nature has thus marked out a pathway in the desert that the Genius of Commerce will, at no far off day, render subservient to its ends; the navigable connection of the Great Lakes with "La Grande Rivière du Nord," I look upon as inevitable.'[10] Assuming a navigable depth for his locks and channels of twelve feet, Shanly estimated that the total cost would be $24 million.

This estimate probably caused dismay, since in 1859 another civil engineer, T.C. Clarke, was put in charge of another Ottawa River survey and the work was done all over again. Clarke's estimate for a canal that would accommodate vessels of 1,000 tons burthen, with locks 250 feet long, forty-five feet wide, and twelve feet of water over their sills, was only $12,057,680. The difference between the two figures is readily explained when the respective plans for the canalization are examined. Clarke did not hesitate to show dams raising the water level at each rapid to give, in effect, a series of pools between locks. Shanly, on the other hand, preferred to rely more on channels excavated in the rock to circumvent rapid water.

The Montreal Board of Trade tried to reconcile the two figures, attempting to persuade Shanly to reduce his estimate but he would do so only by reducing the controlling dimensions that he had used. It was natural, therefore, that Clarke's estimate is the one that usually figures in the discussions of the project that were to continue for the next fifty years. His report was reprinted forty years later, when he was a consulting engineer in New York, with a supplementary report he had then prepared for the Montreal, Ottawa and Georgian Bay Canal Company of Ottawa (to be mentioned shortly), generally confirming his earlier figures and noting that 'it does not now seem possible, except at prohibitive cost, to deepen the Ottawa navigation to 20 feet, and fortunately it is not necessary.'[11] The only revision he then suggested was to enlarge the locks to 300 feet by forty-five feet with fourteen feet over the sills.

One feature of Clarke's report, as it was also of Shanly's report, is the tribute paid to the early work of that great man, Sir William Logan. 'I cannot conclude this report,' says Clarke (and Shanly used similar words),

without expressing how much we have been indebted to the labours of the Geological Survey, and its accomplished director, Sir William Logan. Their plans of the French River, Lake Nipissing, and the Mattawa, were so complete, and after a close test, proved so accurate, that they left nothing further to be desired towards a general map of that section of the waters. Had they not been in existence, this report could not have been made without another season's field work.

This tribute will not be surprising to those who know something of the life and work of this first director of the Geological Survey of Canada, the same survey that has continued its important work until the present day.

No sooner were these reports published than the arguments started. They were to continue throughout the remainder of the century with steadily increasing vehemence. Typical of the more mature comments on the Upper Ottawa project that were made is this extract from the writings in 1865 of another civil engineer, William Kingsford:

In Western Canada, with our canals neglected, we can only recognize in the project a continuance of the policy which we desire to reverse. The Ottawa route will not enlarge the commercial relations of the Province as a whole and is injurious to the west. It can be regarded in no other light than as a local improvement, and must give way to the adoption of the true provincial policy of making the Saint Lawrence navigable for ocean going vessels.[12]

These were prophetic words, but at the time they simply fuelled the fires of controversy which worthy citizens of Ottawa, in particular, were to keep alight for many years to come. It would be of little interest to attempt even to summarize the arguments pro and con, because no action was taken to implement the grand overall plan until 1894. Nor need the plans of either

Walter Shanly or T.C. Clarke be described in any detail, since they were to be superseded in the first decade of the new century by an entirely new proposal. But many of those who travelled so pleasantly on the several stretches of the Ottawa during these years of controversy must sometimes have allowed their imaginations free rein as they pictured steamers being locked into the next stretch of the river through non-existent locks, on their way up to the Great Lakes or down to Montreal.

Defence interest in the development of the upper Ottawa was, as usual, running parallel to these civilian concerns. Further alarms of possible conflict with the United States were raised at the time of the *Trent* affair, prior to which reinforcements for the British forces in Canada had been sent out to Quebec in no less a vessel than the famous masterpiece of Brunel, the *Great Eastern*. More inquiries on the spot were made, notably by Sir John Burgoyne in February 1862, followed by yet another investigation by Burgoyne's deputy, Lieutenant-Colonel W.F.D. Jervois, who reported in 1864. Even though the Ottawa and Rideau canals had been transferred to the provincial government, they continued to figure significantly in these reports. Jervois left Canada for England just one week before the conference of delegates met in Quebec City to consider the federation of British North America; a second report he made was addressed directly to the Canadian ministers, in answer to queries they had raised. Some idea of the feelings that were already being generated by these continued reviews of necessary defence works is given by this extract from a letter written to a Colonel Gray in New Brunswick by the young John A. Macdonald on 27 March 1865, just before he embarked for England to attend the fateful conference which would result in the formation of the new dominion: 'The indiscreet publication of Co. Jervois' Report in England has at present caused a panic in western Canada, as it shows the defencelessness of most of our provinces unless protected by permanent works ... Fancy the British Empire, for the purpose of defending Canada and the British flag from an impending war, voting £200,000 in all to be expended at £50,000 a year. Any war with the United States must occur within two years.'

It was a significant coincidence that in this same year (1865) yet another naval-military investigation was made of the Ottawa but this time by an admiral, Sir James Hope, and a general, Sir John Michel. And they voyaged the entire length of the Ottawa waterway. The journey of these two distinguished men – the one, the commander-in-chief at Halifax of British naval forces in the North Atlantic, the other, the commander-in-chief of British military forces in North America – must have been one of the most remarkable of all such adventures. Because of its highly confidential character, however, it is still little known. Sir George Simpson, the great governor of the Hudson's Bay Company, had died five years before, but one can imagine the pleasure he would have had in making the necessary arrangements, since the company was naturally approached about providing the necessary craft and crews. The request was forwarded to the London headquarters of the Honourable Company by Edward Hopkins, now in charge of the Lachine-Montreal operations, and he was asked to accompany the party himself, in view of the special nature of the journey. He met the official group at Little Current on Lake Huron and accompanied them as far as Fort William on Lac des Allumettes, leaving them there to make the remainder of the journey to Montreal with the picked crew he had provided while he went back upstream in order to inspect the company's post on Lake Temiskaming.

Lieutenant-Colonel Millington Synge, a distinguished member of the Corps of Royal Engineers, was in all probability responsible for alerting Sir John Michel to the military significance of the Ottawa route, with special reference to the possibility of extending its canalization all the way to Lake Huron. The only known records of the journey are contained in the reports made by Sir John Michel to HRH the Duke of Cambridge, then the commander-in-chief of the British Army. These documents are now in the Royal Archives at Windsor Castle. It is a privilege to be able to give the following brief quotations from two of Sir John's letters by gracious permission of Her Majesty the Queen. Writing from Toronto on 22 August 1865, Sir John explained that

The Inland defence of Canada is as much naval as Military, and I deferred my tour until the arrival of the Commander-in-Chief, Sir James Hope, at Quebec, in order that we might together see the country. We have just finished the civilized part of our tour, and we are going to start from the French River and Nipissing Lake, leaving civilization, postal communication, etc. for almost twelve days. I consider this portion of the tour of vital importance both in a military and naval point of view.[13]

Sir John was able to report to the commander-in-chief on the successful completion of their journey in a letter written from Montreal on 12 September, just three weeks later. After explaining that, accompanied by Admiral Sir James Hope and 'one or two engineers,' they had proceeded up the French River, across Lake Nipissing, and then down the Mattawa and Ottawa rivers, he goes on to say:

We proceeded in native Bark Canoes, which I procured from the Hudson Bay Company, taking with us one of their principal factors. For the 1st 150 to 200 miles, we did not see a living soul. All was one wild solitude. The rivers were broad and deep, interspersed with rapids, and occasionally fine falls: whilst the banks were rocky and covered with pine trees. Shooting the rapids, with the water surging and eddying round us was very enjoyable, and there was quite sufficient risk to make it exciting. The system (when striking a rock, on one's rapid descent, and thus injuring the Canoe bottom), of having the canoe on shore ten minutes afterwards and of having her bottom plastered with bark, and cemented with gum, was to be quite a new feature in dockyard work: more especially as in half an hour, the canoe was again afloat, as sound as ever.

That delightful expression 'dockyard work' must surely have come from the admiral!

The letters from which these extracts come were the personal reports of Sir John Michel to his chief. His official report was entitled 'The Reports on the Ottawa and French River Navigation Projects' and it was accompanied by a special memorandum on 'Our Military Position in Canada' – documents that are thus mentioned to indicate the importance which was still attached, in 1865, to defence measures against the Americans. So keenly did General Michel feel about the matters that he had studied with such care that, in his second letter to the Duke of Cambridge, he said that from the report His Royal Highness would see 'the reasons that have made me so enthusiastic on the subject of the French River project: reasons of so imperial a nature, that I shall deem it my duty with the Governor General's concurrence to urge the same with all the arguments and weight that lies in my power.' When it is recalled that this military exploration of the Ottawa Waterway was made less than two years before Confederation, its significance will be at once apparent.

In the spring of the year following, on 19 March 1866, Lieutenant-Colonel Millington Synge delivered a paper to the Royal United Services Institution (later published in their journal) on 'The Lakes and Canals of Canada.' It makes interesting reading today, containing even such an unusual suggestion as the establishment of a limited liability company for the purpose of draining Lake Erie. The following extract, however, is a good indication of British military thinking about the Georgian Bay project at the time of Confederation:

Of these (proposals) the last (the Georgian Bay Ship Canal) deserves an unqualified and unreserved preference on general considerations. It ought, indeed, to form the base and foundation of all others ... it affords a cheap and peaceful solution of the difficulties attending the defence of Canada. If the country is to remain British, it is, therefore, a work of the first imperial interest (and) it ought to be highly esteemed by the Canadians for its commercial value.[14]

Once again, defence and civilian interests were linked.

Colonel Millington Synge waxed even more eloquent as he proceeded to describe the military significance of the Georgian Bay Canal project – and this, it is to be recalled, in 1866:

Its general characteristic from end to end is that of a chasm in a granitic formation [crystalline gneiss], and on the French River more especially, in long straight lines, where a few guns in position could defend the necessary works and destroy any fleet that might attempt to enter ... [and as he neared the close of his lecture] ... I will only add that His Excellency the Commander of the Forces, Administrator of the Government and, I believe, Admiral of the North American Station, whom I had the honour of being invited to accompany over the route, are as favourable to its construction, and earnest for it ... as I can possibly be.

The complex negotiations leading eventually to the passage of the British North America Act by the British parliament, and so to the formation of the new dominion of Canada, demanded so much attention that even views such as those just quoted were put aside until the new government of Canada was well settled into its monumental task of building the new nation. Quite naturally, it was not long before the whole question of waterways forced itself upon official attention. It is sometimes thought that the device of appointing royal commissions to inquire into particularly difficult public question is one that has developed within comparatively recent years. But as early as 4 July 1870, the Honourable Mr Hector L. Langevin, minister of public works, recommended the appointment of a royal commission to review the adequacy of existing canals in Canada and the desirability of constructing any new ones.

It was a strong commission of eight members, including C.S. (later Sir Casimir) Gzowski, already a noted engineer, with Samuel Keefer, who knew the Ottawa River well, as secretary. The chairman was Hugh Allan of Montreal. Although the commission was appointed only on 16 November 1870, its majority report was dated 24 February 1871, an amazing feat considering that 2,400 copies of a circular letter of inquiry had been sent out and the returns considered. The printed report of 190 pages contains a useful and interesting historical section in which reference is made to the Toronto and Georgian Bay Canal (sometimes referred to as the Huron and Ontario Canal), yet another alternative to the Welland system, using Lake

Simcoe. Eighteen pages are used for a detailed discussion of commercial possibilities, in which shipment of wheat from the west is a prominent matter of concern even at this early date. Abstracts of the evidence received are carefully summarized; statistics are presented in convenient tabular form. And there is a minority report (thus starting yet another early tradition) by one member, Mr G. Laidlaw, a very conservative statement recommending the appointment of a board of engineers to advise the government on the matters discussed.

And the Georgian Bay Ship Canal? It is grudgingly mentioned, but any firm recommendation is avoided, because 'the wide discrepancy between different Engineer's Plans and Estimates, one being as high as $12,058,680, and the other $24,000,000, leaves them in doubt, both as to proper methods of improvement and their probable cost.' All that the commissioners would commit themselves to was to urge that 'further examination of the subject is necessary as early as possible,'[15] a statement with an all-too-familiar ring. On the other hand, they were in no doubt about the St Lawrence route, waxing almost poetic as they stated that

The first step, therefore, in the Improvement of the Inland Navigation of the Dominion is the enlargement of the Welland Canal, the great link of commercial intercourse, not only with the prosperous Western Country of the United States ... but with that vast territory belonging to the Dominion, which must ere long be peopled by thousands ... On improving the Welland we take the step pointed out to us by the unerring finger of Progress.

And in case there was any doubt about their findings, they went so far as to say that 'Our duty is to improve that [the St Lawrence route] navigation in the first place because it is the one which has been tried and found to answer all the purposes for which it was intended ... [adding that] ... all other routes are intended to be subsidiary to the St Lawrence route.' Thus was the way cleared for the construction of the third Welland Canal, with its depth over lock sills of twelve feet (by 1883) and fourteen feet (by 1887).

There were, even by that time, powerful voices urging the advantages of the St Lawrence and Welland route, since settlement in southern Ontario was already well developed. On the other hand, Ottawa, even though it was now the seat of the government of Canada, was still a small town, with a population of about 15,000. The Ottawa River was still an important waterway for lumber; the country through which the alternative route would penetrate was as yet wild country, little travelled and little known outside the Ottawa Valley. There were few voices raised, therefore, in support of this alternative to the St Lawrence route, an alternative that would then have had some validity had it been possible for it to have been studied carefully. But the railway era was at hand, and even those in the Ottawa Valley who might have been enthusiasts for the canal project probably had their attention diverted to all the changes that the railways were to bring to the valley. Even the first major railway projects were not unconnected with the advantages of inland water navigation. There was prepared, for example, at the request of Sanford Fleming when he was chief engineer of the first Canadian Pacific Railway, a report on the possible canalization of the French River (a vital part of the canal project) and on the suitability of the mouth of the French River for harbour purposes.

With the main railway lines in the valley built and being actively operated, settlement increased, as did also the prosperity and activity of Ottawa. The city was now joined by the other thriving smaller towns up and down the river in providing a public voice on matters of common concern. Canalization of the river was one such matter; for it had never been really forgotten. Towards the end of the century there developed renewed enthusiasm for the Georgian Bay Ship Canal project. A leader in this upsurge of interest was an Ottawa native. McLeod Stewart had been born in Bytown in 1847, educated at the Ottawa Grammar School and at the University of Toronto, where he took his BA and MA degrees. He became one of the capital's leading citizens, serving as mayor in 1887 and 1888 and also as president of the Canada Atlantic Railroad Company. But it seems certain that his chief concern was the development of the Georgian Bay route. He was definitely the prime mover in the establishment of the Montreal, Ottawa and Georgian Bay Canal Company, which was chartered in 1894. For the next thirty years, through various vicissitudes, this company was always near the centre of the continuing controversies that surrounded the proposed further development of inland water navigation in Canada.

Early efforts to win the support of the government of Sir Wilfrid Laurier for this private venture were unsuccessful. Eventually, however, the government agreed to establish a committee of the senate – yet another familiar procedure – to report upon 'the feasibility of a Waterway connecting Lake Huron with the St Lawrence via the Ottawa.' The committee was established on 18 February 1898; its final report is dated 1 June 1898.[16] (Parliamentary committees and commissions worked fast in those early days.) The report, which is entirely favourable to the canal scheme, is accompanied by some quite remarkable colour-printed maps and sections prepared by C.L. Bouchier, CE, illustrating vividly the geographical advantages of the proposed project. On one of these it is stated that since one mile of canal is equal to three miles of open navigation, the true saving in route mileage over the St Lawrence route is 530 miles, a piece of devious argument that is difficult to accept seriously. The committee heard eight witnesses and received written testimony (all that is quoted being favourable) from a considerable number of leading citizens, including Sir William Van Horne of the CPR, who joined in the general commendation of the scheme.

Hearings before the committee, chaired by Senator Clemow, were somewhat unusual, since McLeod Stewart, although not a member, not being a senator, conducted some of the questioning and had important statements entered in the record. The very first witness started his testimony by saying that 'I understand it to be the wish of Mr McLeod Stewart.' Later Mr Stewart introduced this statement from A.M. Wellington, a leading American civil engineer and expert in the economics of transportation: 'The finest place upon the globe for a deep ship canal is the Ottawa River.' This was typical of the eulogistic statements presented to the committee. Defence was brought in as a leading argument. Major-General Gascoigne, commanding officer of the Canadian Militia, was asked (naturally by Mr Stewart) if he shared the opinions regarding the defence value of the proposed ship canal of Admiral Hope and General Michel at a public meeting in Montreal, following their notable journey along its route. He affirmed that he was and added: 'I may state broadly, from a strategic point of view, I look upon this scheme as the most desirable possible ... If you make it 14 feet deep, I can only say that it will be of the utmost value, from a strategic point of view, to the country. I know the Imperial authorities look upon it in that light also ... I can not speak too highly of the value of the proposed canal.' This was the considered view of the senior military officer in Canada as the century neared its close.

Another remarkable witness was a civil engineer, Mr J. Meldrum, a senior member of the staff of S. Pearson and Company of London, England, said to be the largest civil engineering contractors in the world at that time. He testified that his firm 'had been approached by Mr McLeod Stewart as to whether we would undertake the construction of the Georgian Bay Canal,' adding that his firm was willing to make such an undertaking if suitable financial guarantees could be arranged. Another engineer, a Mr Wicksteed, volunteered that he was the father of the twenty-foot-deep canal proposition. Mr Clarke still regarded a depth of twenty feet as unnecessary.

In the face of all this favourable evidence, it was not surprising that the committee found that 'the construction of such a canal as that proposed by the Montreal, Ottawa and Georgian Bay Canal Company is, beyond a doubt, feasible and practicable ... [and that] ... its construction will be of a great commercial advantage to the trade of Canada' with some additional reference to the vast amount of power that could be generated from the falls in the river, clear indication that the potential of generating electrical power from falling water for long-distance transmission was already appreciated in the valley. The committee concluded that the project 'will be of inestimable benefit to the general prosperity of Canada ... and recommend [the] contemplated enterprise to the favourable consideration of the Government.' Even in the face of so favourable a report, the Laurier government took no action.

It could be that the fact that the chairman of the senate committee was one of the charter members of the company itself mitigated against any immediate acceptance of its findings. But there were also voices heard arguing against the prosecution of so great a public work by private enterprise, while the government, because of its vast expenditures on railway construction, was probably in no position to contemplate an early start on such an expensive undertaking. The publicity, however, continued. The *Saturday Globe*, published in Toronto on 29 October 1898, devoted most of the space in a four-page supplement to a glowing description of the project, even saying that since the governor-general, the Earl of Aberdeen, had been a member of the parliamentary committee on the Manchester Ship Canal, he was much interested. And Mr McLeod Stewart's portrait was naturally included. His enthusiasm, however, was running out. He turned to London, England, for financial support, arranging with a group of British financiers to buy the controlling shares of 'his' company. McLeod Stewart's keen interest and active support for the project continued to the day of his death (in October 1926), even though by that time the die was cast in favour of the St Lawrence-Welland Canal route as the seaway from the Great Lakes.

With the entry of the British syndicate into the picture, the character of the support for the project changed also. Little more was heard about its defence importance, even though in British military planning circles the need for the Georgian Bay Ship Canal still had high priority. In the printed repsort of the (British) Joint Naval and Military Committee of 2 April 1896, for example, reference is made to the fact that the command of Lake Huron, in case of armed conflict, was out of the question until the Georgian Bay Ship Canal was constructed. In an admiralty memorandum on the defence of Canada, dated February 1905, regret is again recorded that the canalization of the upper Ottawa had not yet been extended through to Lake Huron. Within a year the last British regular troops left Canada, only the dockyard facilities at Halifax and Esquimalt remaining under the British Navy until

1910. Fear of war with the United States however, remained, in the planning offices of British defence authorities. Even as late as 1920 the Plans Division of the British Admiralty was trying to advise the Canadian government on how best to defend the Great Lakes against the United States. Lest this caution seem almost too far-fetched to be true, it is worthy of record that one of the U.S. objections to the St Lawrence Seaway raised quite seriously in the middle of the present century was that it would permit British warships to sail into the Great Lakes; thus its construction would be a threat to the peaceful existence of the great republic.

The New Dominion Syndicate was the name of the British company that now took over promotion of the Georgian Bay Ship Canal. With a nominal capital of £5 million, its board of directors was headed by Sir Edward Thornton, and directors included representatives of great British shipping companies. Sir Benjamin Baker was listed as consulting engineer, and Lord Kelvin as consulting electrical engineer. Solicitors were Sir Henry Fowler and Robert (later Sir Robert) Perks, then a member of parliament. He became the very active leader of this new group. The syndicate apparently financed some surveys, especially of the possibilities for supplying the necessary water for the topmost locks on the route, since in May 1901 the company issued from its head office in Ottawa a beautifully printed thirty-five-page brochure on heavy-coated stock entitled *From the Great Lakes to the Atlantic*. Little is revealed about the company itself but a great deal about traffic possibilities. Well-executed colour maps and sections add to the favourable impression created by the brochure. It presents a new estimate of cost for the whole project, this one prepared by Henry MacLeod based on the original ideas of Clarke, the total cost being now given at $68 million. The publicity continued, now on both sides of the Atlantic. The *Times* of London published a long editorial on 11 December 1905 entitled 'Canadian Waterways' which contained the statement that 'Canada holds in reserve, however, a trump card in the proposed Georgian Bay Canal. She means and is prepared to play it ... The Canadian Government have been so impressed with the economic advantages and possibilities of this Georgian Bay and Ottawa canal route that it is an open secret that they will construct the works themselves and come to some arrangement with the present charter-holders.'[17] Surveys were said to be almost complete. In 1907 the company did present formal plans to the government for approval, but the government indicated neither approval nor disapproval, and so the company was left up in the air.

The first decade of the new century saw public interest in the proposed ship canal at its height and, correspondingly, the acrimony steadily mounting between supporters of the St Lawrence-Welland Canal route and those who wished to see an all-Canadian canal using the Ottawa Valley. Submissions were made to the government of the day, and delegations came to Ottawa urging their views. Once again, the device of a royal commission was used to defuse this public discussion, the government of Sir Wilfrid Laurier appointing three commissioners on 19 May 1903 – Sir William Van Horne as chairman, to be assisted by Harold Kennedy and John Bertram. The chequered career of this commission was initiated when, on 26 August of the same year the government had to appoint two new commissioners (Messrs Robert Reford of Montreal and E.C. Fry) to assist Mr Bertram as chairman, since Sir William and Mr Kennedy were unable to act. Mr Bertram died on 28 November 1904; Mr Fry retired early in 1905. The final report was therefore signed in Winnipeg on 11 December 1905 by Mr Reford as chairman and Mr Ashdown of Winnipeg, who had been appointed in January 1905. Even one of the two associate secretaries to the commission (J.X. Perrault of Montreal) also died, in April 1905. Despite these changes, the commission visited all parts of the dominion, since their mandate was for a report on every aspect of national transportation; they submitted a number of interim reports, their final report being a document of only sixty-one pages despite its wide coverage. The main burden of their recommendations was the development of the ports on Georgian Bay to which wheat could be shipped through Canadian waters and thence by Canadian railways to St Lawrence ports.

The two commissioners did include one paragraph headed 'Desirability of Through Waterway' most of which consists of the following single sentence, quite the most remarkable that I have ever read in an official document. It could well have been headed 'How To Handle a Hot Potato.' After a brief introductory sentence, the commissioners say:

But in view of the fact that the Government has undertaken the survey of a proposed route by way of the French River to Lake Nipissing and thence by way of the Ottawa River to Montreal, and as the feasibility of this route from a commercial as well as an engineering point of view, and if feasible, its cost, has not yet been ascertained, and further in view of the fact that the Government has also undertaken the survey of the Welland Canal and its vicinity, looking to its possible enlargement and diversion, your commissioners do not see their way clear to any recommendation as to route, but would commend that, in case the Ottawa scheme because of want of feasibility from a commercial or engineering point of view, or on account of its cost or for any other reason be not adopted, then the Welland canal be enlarged and deepened to the standard of the Sault Ste Marie canal, with a view to enabling vessels of the largest size to continue their voyage to Kingston or Prescott, thus bringing their cargo to within, say 180 miles or less of Montreal before discharging same.[18]

The survey mentioned in this magnificant example of circumlocution had indeed been authorized. In 1904 the Honourable Mr C.S. Hyman, then the minister of public works, with authority from parliament for the expenditure of $250,000, directed the chief engineer of his department, Mr Eugene D. Lafleur, to arrange for a completely new survey of the long-proposed ship canal route and the preparation of the necessary designs and estimates of cost. The resulting report, dated 20 January 1909, presented to the new minister of public works, the Honourable Mr William Pugsley, will long remain one of the great engineering reports in Canadian history.[19] It can be commended to all, and especially to young engineers who wish to see what an engineering assessment of such a vast project should be. There was some complaint that the total cost of the study was in excess of $500,000, more than double the original allotment, but when the contents of the final report are examined, the wonder is that it was done for anything like half a million dollars. Compared with some official reports of recent years that have cost many millions, it stands as one of the most efficient expenditures of public funds ever undertaken in Canada – even though it has not yet been put into effect.

The complete route was divided into three main sections, each being placed in charge of a divisional engineer who reported to Mr Arthur St Laurent, the eminent civil engineer who directed this notable work. One of the three divisional engineers left the public service before the project was complete, so his area was added to that of the Montreal engineer. The final report was therefore signed by the two senior engineers already mentioned and by C.R. Coutlee and S.J. Chapleau, the two divisional engineers. It was my happy privilege to count Mr Chapleau as a senior friend in my own early years in Canadian engineering. He was then a rather bent figure but still distinguished in appearance with his head of thick silver-white hair. My talks with him at his desk must have been my real introduction to the fascination of the great project; for he talked of the Georgian Bay survey, in his pithy way, as though he had only just finished his own report, even though more than twenty years had elapsed since the massive 600-page volume was released to parliament and then to the public. By coincidence I knew also H.M. Davy, the engineer who was placed in charge of the extensive test-boring program that was carried out along the entire route. For many years he was in charge of all such work for his department; he died as recently as 1965, still little changed in appearance since the busy days when he ranged

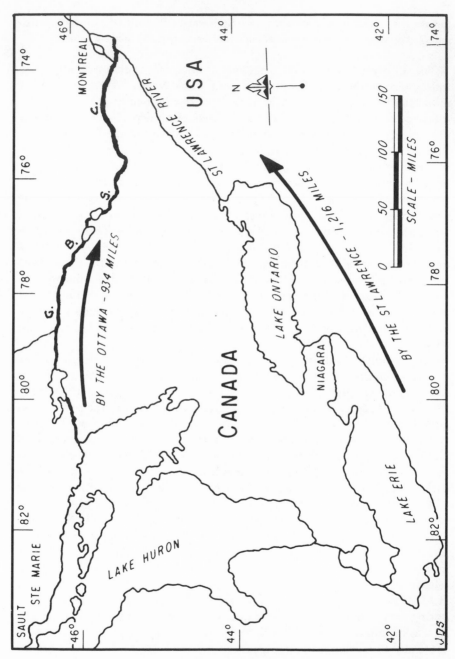

6 The two water routes from the west to Montreal, showing the Georgian Bay
Ship Canal as proposed, utilizing the Ottawa Waterway; mileages are from
Thunder Bay to Montreal.

the Ottawa Valley supervising his drilling crews, working at the lonely sites along the great river where dams would have to be built if the canal were to be a reality.

Among those who served as young assistants in Arthur St Laurent's enthusiastic team were some who would become famous in the annals of Canadian engineering. The more than twenty appendices give some indication of the wide-ranging studies that lay behind the main conclusions – notes on the history of the valley, on other canals, on electrical equipment, on hydraulic equipment, on times taken for ships to pass through locks, on trade statistics, on the history of the Canal Company. Of special significance to civil engineers is the account (by Mr Davy) of the 2,990 separate test borings put down to an average depth of ten feet, even though solid bedrock is exposed at almost every dam and lock site; the engineers responsible were leaving nothing to chance. I have not yet failed to find somewhere in this volume the answer to every engineering question that has arisen in my mind during my own studies of this immense project.

Typical of the approach taken in the report is the first paragraph. After the necessary introductory words it states: 'That a 22-foot waterway for the largest lake boats (600 ft. x 60 ft. x 20 ft. draft) can be established for one hundred million dollars ($100,000,000) in ten years, and that the annual maintenance will be approximately $900,000, including the operation of storage reservoirs for the better distribution of the flood waters of the Ottawa River.' After that come the more detailed conclusions, including estimates of the extra cost for increasing the canal depth to twenty-four or even twenty-five feet. And among the advice respectfully submitted by the four engineers was a firm recommendation as to the necessity for continuous and accurate records of river discharges not only for the Ottawa River but for all 'large river drainage valleys which are possible of development for navigation and power purposes.' (This task has now been done for all major Canadian rivers.) One hundred million dollars is still a vast sum of money. At the end of the first decade of the century, it was a figure that must have intimidated some of those most active in supporting the Georgian Bay Canal project. But it was still a manageable amount, as can be seen if it is compared with the money spent in succeeding years in developing the St Lawrence route and the Welland Canal. The report showed that what had been in some ways a visionary dream of an all-Canadian waterway linking Montreal and the St Lawrence with the Great Lakes was an eminently practical proposition. Its publication made all future discussion much more realistic than had previously been possible. And the discussion certainly did continue.

During the federal election campaign of 1908, even though the report had not yet been published, the Georgian Bay project loomed large in many speeches, especially those made in the Ottawa Valley. Sir Wilfrid Laurier himself, speaking at North Bay, had this to say:

There is no need to defend that Canal; its route has been a highway of commerce since the days of 1808 when flotillas of canoes carried supplies along it west from Montreal and brought back furs from the Western Provinces ... If people in our party look askance at the Georgian Bay Canal, I would say that they should have more faith in their country and realize that even with these canals and new railways being built, we shall hardly have enough transportation for our growing trade ... Let me say that this Canal is very much in my heart; it is not a monopoly for the people of Nipissing or Northern Ontario, it interests the people of Montreal ... We are not ready to build the Georgian Bay Canal because we have a falling revenue and heavy expenditures. But if Providence spares me and my colleagues in power, it will be our duty to take up the Georgian Bay Canal as soon as revenue permits.[20]

The Laurier government was returned to power. No sooner had the report been published than Sir Wilfrid was presented with a petition by 110 members of the House, urging the implementation of its findings.

Early in February 1910 Sir Wilfrid received yet another delegation, this one from the Canal Company led by the indefatigable London financier, Sir Robert Perks. According to the company, Sir Wilfrid 'stated that he was prepared to submit the whole scheme of Canal construction to Parliament at its next session – that is to say 1911–1912. He said that he was in favour of the construction of the Canal by a Company subject to proper reservations and controls, in preference to construction and administration by the Government.' Before that session, Sir Wilfrid and his government were to meet defeat, but it does seem to be as certain as can now be established that, had the Liberals continued in power after the 1911 election, the canal would have been built and the economy of Canada vastly changed.

Although reciprocity dominated almost all election oratory in the 1911 election, Sir Wilfrid had continued to refer in earlier speeches to the necessity of building the canal but without ever putting a date on when this could be. I have seen a letter written from the House of Commons prior to the 1911 election by Fred Cook, a member of parliament, to a Mr Elliot in Washington, in which he says with no qualifications that 'The waterway will be constructed – Sir Wilfrid Laurier has said so, and with a majority of 70 at his back he can carry his proposals ... Whether the Government will build the canal, or allow the company to do it under a Government guarantee of its bonds is a question of policy still undetermined.' (It is clear from his later speeches that Sir Wilfrid did not intend to have his government guarantee the company's bonds.) One of the most specific statements of all was that made by the Honourable Mr George Graham, speaking in Arnprior on 7 April 1912: 'We want both [the Welland and the Georgian Bay canals] and if the old Government had been returned both works would have been in progress today.' But the old Government was not returned, and the great 'IF' regarding the Georgian Bay Canal remains as one of the legacies from that crucial election.

Before we proceed to sketch briefly the concluding phases of this century-old proposal, however, it may be of interest to take an imaginary journey up the Ottawa River and over into Lake Huron, not looking at the river as it was but at the river as it might have been if the plans of the engineers of the Department of Public Works actually had been executed. The journey starts in Montreal Harbour, since the first lock of the 'Ottawa Seaway' (as it may be called) was quite naturally to be opposite the first lock of the St Lawrence Seaway of today, each designed to provide the first lift of vessels as they left the St Lawrence. The area between Nun's Island and the Island of Montreal would have been flooded to the higher level, created by a regulating dam in the harbour, the second lock being located at the west end of what was then the village of Verdun. This flooding would have raised the water level to that in Lake St Louis, so that a guiding embankment only was necessary to protect the south side of the dredged channel which was to run along the shoreline up to the existing lock at Ste Anne-de-Bellevue. Replacement of this lock by a new ship lock would have been a relatively simple operation, the water level above the lock being that of the Lake of Two Mountains just as it is today; very little dredging would have been required to give the necessary channel all the way to Pointe Fortune.

The big lifts are ahead, but the principle of design would always be the same – a dam to regulate the water level to that required above each lock; suitable provision for floodways to pass water over the dam; and dredging of channels when necessary to obtain the desired depth for navigation. The regulating dams could have had water-power stations designed as an integral part of each, but this was not done, because development of power was not part of the task assigned to the Department. As might be expected, however, one percipient appendix to the report deals with water-power, stressing its importance and pointing out how its development could so readily have been integrated with the plans as presented. One thinks of this aspect, in particular, as Pointe Fortune is approached; for here today is one of the great dams that does span the river, raising the water level above, that does have an integrated power house, and that is the only one of the Ottawa River dams with a ship lock as an integral part. The 1909 plans showed the regulating dam across the river almost exactly where the great Carillon hydroelectric dam stands today. The raised water level provided a good channel up to the next lock at Hawkesbury, at the head of the Long Sault. Here another single lock was designed to do just what the Carillon Dam does today: raise the water level to such an extent that it would be approximately level all the way up the sixty-mile stretch to Ottawa; relatively little excavation in the river bed was necessary because of the excellence of the existing channel. Five ship locks only, therefore, were necessary up to Ottawa, vessels being raised 120 feet in the 121 miles.

Two locks were to be built at Hull, located on a new channel following generally the route of Brewery Creek. The second lock would have operated at the water level in Lac Deschenes, the existing dams at the Chaudière rendering new dam construction a minor item. Little dredging would have been necessary in the lake in order to give deep water access to the entrance to the Chats Falls lock, which was located on the north shore so as to take advantage of the abortive rock excavation of the 1850s. A regulating dam close to the location of the new power dam would have been necessary, the water level thus raised extending up to the Chenaux Rapids twenty miles away. Once again the natural channel would have provided an excellent waterway. One dam with a lift of thirty-five feet would have sufficed at Chenaux Island with a dam and flood spillway across the river to the north shore.

Once again, the natural channel of the river would have afforded the navigation channel required with the removal of just a few rock peaks, since several sections of this narrow section of the original river were deeper than the soundings that were made in the survey. This particular stretch would have provided one of the most spectacular sails on any of the world's ship canals, had the waterway been built. High wooded banks, rocky crags, and a winding channel would have combined to give all travellers on large ships passing up beyond the Chenaux Lock a feeling of unreality. This would also have been one of the more difficult passages from the point of view of navigation. Two locks would have been necessary at Rocher Fondu, each with a lift of thirty-five feet, located three miles apart and still in the most picturesque section of the whole river. The next lock at Paquette Rapids, with its regulating dam at the narrows just below Marcotte Island, by providing a lift of only twenty feet would have backed up the water all the way to Des Joachims.

Above the Paquette Lock there would be a clear sail of fifty-six miles, past Pembroke, past Petawawa and old Fort William, and into the famed Deep River section, using the existing river channel with some dredging to give the necessary clear depth throughout. Beyond Des Joachims with its single lock, two locks were necessary at Rocher Capitaine (the first pair of locks on the canal, giving a total lift of sixty feet) with a further single lock at Deux Rivières to bring vessels up to the level of the famous junction of the Mattawa and Ottawa rivers. Here the route of the ship canal left the broad channel of the Ottawa to follow the winding Mattawa, no less than seven locks being necessary to raise vessels the 177 feet up to the level of Trout Lake, the summit of the route – single locks at Mattawa, Plain Chant, and Les Epines, with double locks (each pair with a total lift of sixty feet) at Upper and Lower Parasseaux Rapids. Much dredging would have been necessary in association with this flight of locks to give the requisite navigation channel in what is naturally a rather small river so that the major construction operations along the canal would have been in this most isolated section – isolated in only one way, since the main line of the CPR runs parallel to the Mattawa River. Transportation facilities for construction purposes, therefore, would have been easy and economical to provide.

For the operations of the locks at both ends of Trout Lake a supply of water would be essential to replenish the volume of water emptied from each lock when it was used. A feeder canal had been designed to convey water in sufficient quantity from the adjoining watershed of Amable du Fond into that of the Mattawa. A single lock at North Bay, just below the Twin Lakes, with a drop of twenty-nine feet, would bring vessels into Lake Nipissing for a pleasant thirty-mile sail across the deep waters of the Lake and into the French River, as far as the next lock at the Chaudière Rapids. A lock at Five Mile Rapid, with a drop of twenty-four feet, gave access almost to the mouth of the French River where, at the Dalles, the final lock was located, dropping 21.5 feet to the level of Georgian Bay, vessels having travelled 442.6 miles after entering the first lock at Montreal Harbour.

This, then, was the very practical plan developed by the team of engineers of the Department of Public Works under the direction of Arthur St Laurent and described so excellently in the splendid report of 1909. There is no doubt that the canal could then have been built as designed, if the government had so decided and if money could have been made available. But reciprocity interfered, with the result that Sir Robert Borden inherited the still unanswered question as to when the Georgian Bay Canal was to be built. He, too, was subjected to the intensive pleadings of those who wished to see the Welland Canal enlarged and the whole St Lawrence route further developed. He had also to deal with the Montreal, Ottawa and Georgian

Bay Canal Company, whose charter, with its singularly broad powers, was still in effect. Sir Robert Perks was in Canada in 1911 and again in 1912, urging strongly the claims of the company to be permitted to build the canal with suitable guarantees for their bonds from the government.

Public interest was still high. A large valley deputation saw the new prime minister on 14 March 1912; although cordially received, they were given a very non-commital reply. An even stronger delegation numbering 1,500, one of the largest ever to descend on Ottawa up to that time, led by Montreal's colourful mayor, Mederic Martin, travelled up from Montreal in 1914 and interviewed the minister of public works; it must have been an entertaining day for those who took part. Canada even had a taste of pamphleteering to add to the excitement that the Georgian Bay Canal created in those pre-war days. There had been formed in Ottawa at a meeting held in 1909, with the president of the Ottawa Board of Trade (Peter Whelan) in the chair, an organization with the resounding title of 'The Canadian Federation of Boards of Trade and Municipalities.' A delegation from the federation had been received by Sir Wilfrid Laurier with all that courtly statesman's usual charm, but with no commitment. By 1910 the federation had 125 boards of trade associated with it, but only $1,000 in cash had been received. It was centred in the Ottawa Valley, despite its name, and seems to have been organized mainly in support of the canal project. When, therefore, the Toronto Board of Trade published an attack on the canal scheme, the federation was moved to action.

It published an unusual but well-printed octavo pamphlet of sixty-four pages with no date and no identification on it other than the name and position of the secretary of the federation, Arthur J. Forward, at the end of the main text with an indication of his position. The only copy known to me is in the parliamentary library in Ottawa, in the catalogue to which it is suggested that the date of issue was possibly 1911. On the cover is this quotation: 'It is essential to the commercial independence of Canada, perhaps prerequisite to the preservation of the political union of the Provinces, that we shall have, WITHIN OUR OWN BORDERS, AND SUBJECT TO NO CONTROL BUT OUR OWN, the means of transporting the products of every part of our country to every other part, and also that we shall maintain all-Canadian routes by which the produce of the Provinces may reach the world's markets.'[21] No source is given, but one can easily imagine these words being voiced by Sir Wilfrid Laurier. The text of the pamphlet starts: 'When a public body of the dignity of the Toronto Board of Trade offers a contribution to the discussion of any important question, the public are entitled to expect at least accuracy and fairness of statement,' and thereafter the Toronto arguments (printed in small type) are answered one by one in no uncertain language, the answers in large bold-faced type. 'Inaccurate and misleading'; 'The misstatement would amount to deliberate untruth'; '—entire paragraph based on untruth and is misleading in the extreme' – these are just typical of the mounting frustration shown in the Ottawa pamphlet. One of the most devious of the Toronto arguments was that, because no coal would be shipped over the Georgian Bay route, it would actually be 1,300 miles longer than the Welland route rather than 282 miles shorter! The answer can best be imagined.

The Ottawa Valley was not alone in becoming exercised about the waterway question. There was organized on 11 June 1912 in Berlin (now Kitchener) the 'Grand Waterways Union of Canada,' and this group also produced a pamphlet. The organizer and chief writer was D.B. Detwiler, whose brief in the pamphlet is full of passion and fury. Feelings certainly ran high. The pamphlet appeared under a long title: *The inland Waterways of Canada: Ocean navigation via St Lawrence and Welland Route; Georgian Bay canal Route Impracticable.*[22] The inaugural meeting was attended by about seventy-five people. A 600-word resolution was passed unanimously 'protest(ing) against the apparent attempt to stampede the people in favour of the so-called Georgian Bay Canal,' suggesting that there was a lack of water to feed the proposed canal, and that this would make it a 'criminal' act on the part of the dominion government to embark on such an enterprise. Among the many objections raised to the Ottawa River project was that the government's own plans showed no less than seventy-seven curves of one-mile radius and thirty-nine of a half-mile radius that would make navigation dangerous! But enough has been said to show that the counter-claims of the Welland and proposed Georgian Bay canals were very much in the public eye. The government, however, had weightier problems to face in reaching a decision on the choice that had to be made.

The importance of generating power from falling water by this time was coming to be recognized as an important natural resource; the steady progress made in the high-tension transmission of electrical energy made the development of power at locations far removed from cities a practical possibility. Inevitably, this use of a natural resource brought in its train the keenly debated question of private versus public development of water power in Canada. Sir Adam Beck was already well launched with the development of the publicly owned Hydro Electric Power Commission of Ontario. He spoke against private development on the Ottawa River as early as 1912. This was an aspect of the use of the Ottawa River that had not been contemplated when the Canal Company's charter was granted, and so an unfortunate vagueness existed about what was to become quite the most important part of the river development; occasional references to 'the use of surplus power' indicated that it had not been a matter of great moment in the eyes of the company. Others saw it very differently. To add to these initial complications, the Laurier government had granted a lease in 1908 to the National Hydro-Electric Company for the development of power at the Carillon Rapids on the Ottawa; the president of this Montreal-based company was Herbert (later Sir Herbert) S. Holt, a man already well known for his interlocking financial connections. The charter was for the development of 250 hp only, but the charter had been granted, and the Canal Company was most annoyed. (This particular complication was still further enhanced when in 1926 the Meighen government through an untabled order in council increased the amount of horsepower that could be generated to 300,000; Mr Mackenzie King had to deal with this tangle.)

On the political level, two members – at least – of the Borden cabinet were supporters of the Georgian Bay project, one being the minister of public works, F.D. Monk. Other members were equally firm in support of the Welland Canal route, as was also much of Sir Robert Borden's strong backing in Toronto and southwestern Ontario. Mr Monk resigned in 1912 and was replaced in his key position by Robert Rogers. In March 1912 the government hastily decided to enlarge the Welland Canal. No reasons can be found for this decision, since apparently no detailed engineering or economic studies had then been made. It is possible that the fact that the great report of 1908 was made by engineers of the Department of Public Works, whereas all plans for the Welland and St Lawrence canals were made by staff of the Department of Railways and Canals, might have had something to do with the rivalry between the two projects. It can only be surmised that pressures from those who had been so strongly in favour of the Welland route could not be further resisted. About $2 million were voted for this work in 1912–13; work started in 1913 on the new Welland system but was retarded naturally during the war years and ceased entirely in 1918–19 after which it was resumed, to continue spasmodically until the completion of the great fourth Welland Canal in 1932.

This favouring of the Welland route did nothing to help matters on the Ottawa, and so the standing device of a royal commission was used yet again. In some ways this was the strangest of all the investigating bodies. Three commissioners were appointed in 1916 – W. Sanford Evans, an economic expert from Winnipeg, with F.S. Meighen and E. Gohier of Montreal. The terms of reference given to the commission – had they been implemented – would have kept it busy with a very large staff for a decade at least. Only two interim reports were issued, entirely statistical studies and no more, prepared and signed by Mr Sanford Evans only. The commission then faded out of existence – perhaps naturally under the pressure of the war years – and did not submit any final report. It therefore made no recommendations and contributed practically nothing to the difficult decision that had still to be made.

Once the war was over and the Canadian government could turn its attention to civilian matters, the Ottawa River again loomed large. Sir Robert Perks continued his visits to Ottawa and his interviews with Sir Robert Borden and any member of his cabinet when they visited London. The company's Ottawa representatives were assiduous in maintaining contact with the government through the appropriate ministers and officials and in keeping the British company advised of all developments. They had been given some encouragement by the knowledge that early in the war years the government had seriously considered taking over the charter from the company and compensating them for their expenses. A draft bill was actually prepared under the direction of Mr Arthur Meighen as solicitor-general; it is a short but interesting document, complete apart only from the amounts to be paid to the company. But it remained a draft and was never introduced into the House of Commons.

Yet another complication delayed the renewal of the company's charter in 1918, this being the beginning of a serious controversy between the provincial governments of Ontario and Quebec and the dominion government as to the ownership of water-power rights on the Ottawa River. Attention was diverted for a time from the Ottawa River to the St Lawrence because of the projected development of power at Beauharnois, but for the next ten years this constitutional question was to be in the background of all waterway discussions. For discussions still went on with a bewildering variety of alternative proposals brought forth from different quarters. It was seriously suggested at one time that the French River alone should be canalized to allow access of vessels from the Great Lakes to Lake Nipissing and the growing community of North Bay. Another idea was to develop only the section of the Ottawa River between Montreal and Ottawa. Indeed, it was reported that the dominion government itself might undertake this part of the waterway and incidentally develop 219,800 hp at the Carillon Rapids, although how it could have done so in view of the charter granted to the National Hydro-Electric Company is not clear. Nothing was done under the first administration of Mr Meighen (1918–21), and so, with the assumption of office by Mr Mackenzie King on 29 December 1921, the company had to start all over again. This it did with vigour but, as can be imagined, it received only inconclusive replies.

Water-power was now being actively discussed in many quarters; for this was an era of great activity throughout Canada in the construction of major water-power plants. Between 1920 and 1928, for example, the last critical years in the history of the Ottawa River negotiations, installed horsepower in Canadian water-power stations increased from 2.5 million to 5.5 million, more than doubling in a period of only eight years. It was but natural, therefore, that the undeveloped power available from the many and great rapids of the Ottawa River was the object of increasing interest, just as the idea of the ship canal correspondingly slowly faded into the background. The British company must have become greatly discouraged. There was apparently little difficulty experienced in the transfer of its interest in the river, through its charter, to a new Canadian group headed by two of the sons of Sir Clifford Sifton, Harry and Winfield. It is not clear from the records whether the Siftons first approached Sir Robert Perks or whether the British company made a definite attempt to get rid of its charter. The question is today of academic interest only, since the rights of the company were transferred to the Canadian group, organized as the Great Lakes Securities Corporation, for the consideration of $1 million in second-preference shares in the new organization. The Insull power interests of Chicago may have been involved.

This new development merely added fuel to the fires of controversy that already surrounded all public discussion of power development either by public bodies such as Ontario Hydro or through the medium of privately financed power companies such as the several large corporations then centred in Montreal. Even the International Joint Commission was involved – that really notable body responsible for dealing with all problems of boundary waters shared by Canada and the United States – since, in connection with its hearings on the development of the St Lawrence it held hearings at North Bay and was naturally given all the arguments in favour of developing the Ottawa River through the construction of the Georgian Bay Ship Canal with allied power developments. In its important report of 19 December 1921, the commission briefly discussed alternatives to the St Lawrence development, mentioning the proposed Georgian Bay Ship Canal as one, but concluding that 'none of them offers the advantages of the St Lawrence route, either as a means of relief from the acute transportation situation, or as a channel for the carriage of commodities between the region tributary to the Great Lakes and domestic and foreign seaboard points.'[23] The prestige of the International Joint Commission was such that this finding must have had considerable influence with the British company but the charter had been again renewed in 1923, prior to the sale to the new Canadian group. It was when the Sifton brothers had to arrange for the requisite private bill for the further renewal in 1927 that the final act in the long drama took place.

Debate on the private bill commenced on 25 February 1927, and it was soon evident that this was going to be a crucial debate instead of the more usual brief formal discussion. The debate lasted four full parliamentary days, the record of the emotionally charged speeches filling no less than 400 columns of *Hansard*. To those who would like to be reminded of the heated arguments of the late 1920s, a reading of this debate on Bill 78 can be recommended. It should be remembered that the bill was only for the renewal of the charter of the Montreal, Ottawa and Georgian Bay Canal Company. The proposed canal was mentioned, occasionally, almost always by members for constituencies in the valley. But it was private versus public power development that dominated the discussion, the 'power trust' of Montreal being one of the whipping boys. More than forty speakers took part in the fierce debate. The government demanded that the bill be given second reading, but when this was finally done it was with the understanding that, although the bill was a private member's motion, it would be treated as a government bill and referred to the Committee on Railways, Canals and Telegraphs. There the debate continued, with a remarkably forceful speech from Harry Sifton in favour of the bill in the course of which he said that the obvious hostility to the charter was not to the charter as such but to the implicit assumption of dominion control over water rights, that is, power rights on the Ottawa River. He averred that Ontario Hydro was hand in glove with the power trust but all to no avail. The committee voted against the bill. This was reported to the House of Commons on 7 April 1927, and the charter lapsed.

This was, in effect, the end of the great dream. The charter of the National Hydro-Electric Company was also allowed to lapse, and so the great river was free from any possibility of completely private control over its vast power resources when they were developed. With this safeguarding of the public interest went also all possibility of any attempt by private interests to improve navigation in any way on the river and also the possibility of a privately sponsored deep waterway from Montreal to Lake Huron, first proposed almost exactly a century before. The final stages of the prolonged debate were complicated by the prospect of power generation on a vast scale from falling water and its conversion to electrical energy for long-distance transmission to the industrial centres of eastern Canada. And this possibility on the Ottawa River highlighted the constitutional difficulties of a federal state in a particularly acute form. The premiers of both Ontario and Quebec strenuously opposed any renewal of the charters, even as they also contested the right of the dominion government to control the development of the water power of the Ottawa. This problem was not settled by the lapsing of the two charters but led to an appeal to the Supreme Court of

Canada. An immediate result, however, was the start in 1929 of construction of the Chats Falls hydroelectric station jointly by the Hydro Electric Power Commission of Ontario and the Chats Falls Power Company (of Montreal), a large-scale project that involved the building of a massive dam across the Ottawa at the site of the famous rapids – a dam that was designed without any navigation lock.

Despite this installation, and the later construction without locks of the great power dams at Chenaux Rapids and Des Joachims, the dream of the Ottawa Seaway refuses to die. In the late 1950s there was formed in Ottawa the Ottawa River Development Association with the avowed object of promoting the construction of a twenty-seven-foot-deep waterway from the St Lawrence at least as far as Ottawa. This was prior to the construction by Hydro-Québec of the great dam at Carillon in which a large navigation lock is an integral part. This activity naturally led to a revival of interest in the concept of the Georgian Bay route as a whole, but the interest could not be maintained, especially with the approaching completion of the St Lawrence Deep Waterway. Low water levels in the Great Lakes in the early 1960s gave further temporary impetus to thinking about the Georgian Bay route, now associated with rather fanciful ideas for bringing water to it from the north. The matter was debated with eloquence in the House of Commons in May 1964 but without result. As in years long past, a meeting of the mayors and reeves of municipalities along the valley was held in October 1968 in Pembroke, behind closed doors, to select a delegation to interview the Canadian government. The minister of transport assured this delegation in November 1969 that its proposal, now dignified with the appropriate name of 'The Champlain Canal,' would be studied by his department. But with the St Lawrence Seaway in difficulty over the financial aspects of its operation, any realistic assessment must come to the inevitable conclusion that, in the foreseeable future, the Georgian Bay Ship Canal must continue to remain a project on paper.

The Georgian Bay Ship Canal as a part of the defence works proposed for British North America does not appear in this last phase of the long and involved story of its initiation and development. If the overall view is taken, however, and the project is considered from the time of John By's letter of 1829 to the dramatic debate in the Canadian House of Commons in 1927, then it can be seen that, for most of this period of ninety-eight years, defence was indeed a major argument in favour of the project. By coincidence, perhaps, it was only when the development of the water power that would be made available by the building of the impounding dams for the canal locks came into the picture, well after the turn into the twentieth century, that defence requirements gradually faded out. Even navigation came to take second place to power development following the First World War. By that time, relations between Canada and the United States had become so close that any idea of warfare between the two was quite far-fetched. Few of those who have studied the recent history of the project even relate it to defence in any way at all. But throughout the nineteenth century, especially during that period in which Great Britain was responsible for the defence of British North America, the Georgian Bay Ship Canal remained a magnificent concept and one that could have played a crucial part in defence measures, had these ever been necessary.

Notes

CHAPTER 1: Prologue

Britain and the Balance of Power in North America 1815–1908 by Kenneth Bourne provides a full historical background to this volume; my indebtedness to it is indicated by the quotations from British sources to which it has led me. (Full details of all books mentioned are given in the bibliography which follows.) The brief summary of that part of British history relating to the canals is based on long-time reading on this subject, refreshed by a rereading of the *Short History of the English People* by J.R. Green, to which a few key references are given. The building of the Royal Military Canal in the south of England has been well described by P.A.L. Vine in his volume with that title.

1 Green *Short History* vol. 2, 757
2 Ibid. 767
3 Ibid. 769
4 Vine *Royal Military Canal* 37
5 Ibid. 65
6 Ibid. 71
7 Ibid. 82
8 Ibid. 99
9 Green *Short History* vol. 2, 770
10 Ibid. 771
11 Ibid. 777
12 Morison *Oxford History* 379
13 C.P. Stacey 'The War of 1812 in Canadian History' *Ontario History* 50 (1958) 153
14 Hitsman *Incredible War*
15 Bourne *Britain* 9
16 Dewey *Journey* 252
17 Morison *Oxford History* 398
18 Public Archives of Canada (hereafter PAC), C.38, 97, 104
19 Stacey 'War of 1812'
20 Bourne *Britain* 14
21 Ibid. 16
22 Ibid. 20
23 Ibid. 26
24 Ibid. 27

CHAPTER 2: Montreal to Kingston

A general account of the Ottawa River and its valley will be found in *Ottawa Waterway*. Early settlement in the lower part of the valley is described in Thomas's volume on Argenteuil and Prescott Counties. The building of the Rideau Canal, so closely linked with the Ottawa River canals, is given in *Rideau Waterway*.

1 Champlain (Biggar) *Voyages* 261
2 Bigsby *Shoe and Canoe* vol. 1, 134
3 PAC, C.38, 104
4 Ibid.
5 Ibid. 101
6 Ibid. 129
7 Ibid. 159
8 Ibid. 122
9 PAC, C.39, 7
10 Ibid. 13
11 Ibid. 11A

CHAPTER 3: The Grenville Canal: the start

There is little in the printed record about the contributions to Canada of the fourth Duke of Richmond, the paper by Brigadier Cruikshank being the only general record so far discovered. The brief summary given in the opening section of this chapter will indicate how important was his service as commander-in-chief and governor.

1 PAC, MG 22, CO 42, Q.149, Pt 1, 1
2 PAC, MG 11, CO 42, Q.149, Pt 1, 122–9
3 PAC, MG 11, CO 42, Q.152, Pt 1, 6; see also PAC, C.39, 53
4 MSS 19, Letters on the Duke of Richmond's death, 1819, University of Toronto, Thomas Fisher Rare Book Library
5 E.A. Cruikshank 'Charles Lennox; the Fourth Duke of Richmond' *Papers and Records of the Ontario Historical Society* vol. 26 (1928) 323–51
6 PAC, MG 11, CO 42, Q.167B, 52
7 PAC, C.39, 69
8 S. Woods, Jr *Molson Saga* 34
9 PAC, C.40, 23–9
10 PAC, C.39, 64–6
11 PAC, C.40, 19
12 PAC, C.39, 53–4
13 Duke of Wellington, Memorandum on the Defence of Canada, addressed to Bathurst, 1 March 1819, Wellington *Despatches* vol. 1, quoted by Bourne *Britain* 36–44
14 L.W. Gold and G.P. Williams 'An unusual ice formation in the Ottawa River' *Journal of Glaciology* 4 (June 1963) 569–73
15 PAC, C.40, 26
16 Ibid. 25
17 Ibid. 29
18 Ibid. 25

CHAPTER 4: The Grenville Canal: 1820 to 1827

1 PAC, C.40, 26
2 See appendix A.
3 Information from Major John Hancock, RE, Chatham
4 Information from Mrs G. Du Vernet, Ottawa
5 PAC, C.39, 72
6 Ibid. 75
7 Ibid. 78
8 PAC, C.40, 29
9 PAC, C.42, 38
10 PAC, C.40, 69
11 Ibid. 145
12 Ibid. 7
13 PAC, C.39, 163
14 PAC, C.40, 1
15 Ibid. 67
16 Ibid. 51
17 Ibid. 115
18 Ibid. 127
19 Ibid. 204
20 Ibid. 198
21 Ibid. 199
22 Ibid. 208
23 PAC, C.41, 31
24 PAC, C.40, 230
25 PAC, C.41, 28
26 Ibid. 7
27 Ibid. 30
28 Ibid. 41
29 Ibid. 38
30 PAC, C.40, 131
31 Ibid.
32 Ibid. 144
33 Ibid. 143
34 PAC, C.41, 13
35 Ibid. 37
36 Ibid. 73
37 Ibid. 86
38 See appendix A.
39 PAC, C.41, 103
40 Ibid. 106
41 Ibid. 93
42 Ibid. 214
43 Ibid. 113
44 Ibid. 89
45 Ibid. 126
46 Ibid. 146–7
47 Ibid. 137
48 Ibid. 143
49 Ibid. 133
50 Ibid. 185
51 Ibid. 162
52 Ibid. 166
53 Ibid. 171
54 Ibid. 195
55 Ibid. 206
56 Ibid. 206
57 PAC, C.43, 147
58 PAC, C.41, 210
59 Ibid. 214
60 Ibid. 220
61 Ibid. 221
62 Ibid. 235
63 PAC, C.42, 28
64 PAC, C.43, 227
65 W.H. Bradley 'The life of the Most Rev. Charles Hamilton' *Journal of the Canadian Church Historical Society* 4 (1961) 1–15
66 PAC, C.43, 244
67 PAC, C.44, 68
68 G.R. Rigby and R.F. Legget 'Riddle of the Treadwell Trenches' *Canadian Geographical Journal* 88 (1974) 38–42

69 F.N.A. Garry 'Diary of Nicholas Garry, Deputy Governor of the Hudson's Bay Company from 1822 to 1835' *Trans. of the Royal*

Society of Canada 2nd series VI (1900) 75–85
70 Bigsby *Shoe and Canoe* vol. 1, 65
71 Carmichael Smyth *Report* 68

CHAPTER 5: The Grenville Canal: 1827 to 1834

1 Carmichael Smyth *Report* 1
2 Wellington *Despatches* vol. 2, 573
3 PAC, C.44, 240
4 Ibid. 211
5 Ibid. 141
6 Ibid. 232
7 PAC, C.45, 15
8 PAC, C.44, 192
9 PAC, C.45, 57
10 PAC, C.49, 46, 48
11 Legget *Canals of Canada* 146
12 PAC, C.43, 54–63
13 PAC, C.45, 143
14 PAC, C.43, 42
15 See Legget *Rideau Waterway* 44.
16 PAC, C.45, 1
17 Ibid. 102–5
18 Ibid. 143
19 PAC, C.44, 229
20 PAC, C.45, 83
21 Ibid. 90
22 Ibid. 178
23 Ibid. 215
24 Ibid. 204
25 Ibid. 221
26 PAC, C.46, 147
27 Ibid. 145 ff
28 PAC, C.43, 35
29 Ibid. 37
30 PAC, C.47, 72
31 Ibid. 99
32 Ibid. 89

33 PAC, C.45, 69
34 Wellington *Despatches*, cited in Bourne *Britain* 42
35 PAC, C.48, 52
36 Ibid. 339
37 PAC, C.49, 29
38 PAC, C.48, 276
39 PAC, C.49, 58
40 PAC, C.46, 65
41 Ibid. 60
42 PAC, C.47, 40
43 PAC, C.48, 31
44 PAC, C.47, 245
45 Ibid. 247
46 Ibid. 81
47 Ibid. 111
48 PAC, C.49, 84
49 Ibid. 121
50 Ibid. 85
51 PAC, C.50, 145
52 Ibid. 206
53 PAC, C.51, 82
54 PAC, C.50, 223
55 Ibid. 224
56 PAC, C.51, 106
57 Ibid. 115
58 Ibid. 116
59 PAC, C.53, 42
60 Ibid.
61 PAC, C.55, 51
62 Ibid. 80
63 PAC, C.57, 11

64 PAC, C.55, 12
65 PAC, C.58, 69
66 PAC, C.55, 6
67 Ibid. 12
68 PAC, C.51, 128
69 PAC, C.52, 23
70 Ibid. 57
71 PAC, C.54, 178
72 PAC, C.55, 1
73 PAC, C.51, 78

74 PAC, C.54, 176
75 PAC, C.56, 90
76 PAC, C.47, 36
77 PAC, C.53, 47
78 PAC, C.54, 19
79 PAC, C.52, 210
80 PAC, C.54, 23
81 PAC, C.52, 29
82 PAC, C.53, 52

CHAPTER 6: Chute à Blondeau, Carillon, and Ste Anne-de-Bellevue

1 PAC, C.40, 135
2 PAC, C.44, 236
3 PAC, C.45, 20
4 PAC, C.44, 237
5 PAC, C.45, 12
6 PAC, C.47, 109
7 PAC, C.48, 294
8 PAC, C.49, 29
9 PAC, C.58, 221
10 PAC, C.48, 24
11 PAC, C.50, 145
12 PAC, C.51, 115
13 PAC, C.55, 51
14 Ibid. 75
15 PAC, C.58, 200
16 Ibid. 217
17 Ibid. 230
18 PAC, C.47, 202
19 Ibid. 261
20 PAC, C.52, 20
21 PAC, C.58, 22
22 PAC, C.52, 226
23 Ibid. 222
24 PAC, C.55, 113
25 PAC, C.56, 70
26 PAC, C.57, 24
27 PAC, C.58, 22

28 PAC, C.59, 69
29 PAC, C.47, 109
30 Ibid. 172
31 Ibid. 199
32 PAC, C.48, 24
33 Ibid. 294
34 Ibid. 296
35 Ibid. 321
36 PAC, C.49, 29
37 Ibid. 75
38 Ibid. 158
39 Ibid. 229
40 Ibid. 233
41 PAC, C.50, 35
42 Ibid.
43 Ibid. 38
44 Ibid. 99
45 Ibid.
46 Ibid. 105b
47 Ibid. 107
48 Ibid. 103
49 Ibid. 178
50 Ibid. 243
51 PAC, C.51, 19
52 Ibid. 9
53 Ibid. 11
54 Ibid. 75

55 Ibid. 77
56 Ibid. 96
57 Ibid. 109
58 Ibid. 92
59 Ibid. 104
60 Ibid. 109
61 Ibid. 112
62 Ibid.
63 Ibid. 127
64 Ibid. 132
65 Ibid. 96
66 Thomas *History* 167
67 PAC, C.50, 31
68 Ibid. 25
69 Ibid.
70 PAC, C.51, 120
71 Ibid. 168
72 PAC, C.47, 227
73 Ibid. 259
74 Ibid. 261
75 PAC, C.48, 252
76 Ibid. 316
77 Ibid. 325
78 Ibid. 308
79 Ibid. 308
80 PAC, C.59, 37
81 PAC, C.48, 329
82 PAC, C.49, 69
83 Ibid. 165
84 Ibid. 205
85 PAC, C.50, 174
86 Ibid. 201
87 PAC, C.51, 182
88 PAC, C.52, 61
89 PAC, C.56, 147

90 PAC, C.54, 123
91 Ibid. 176
92 PAC, C.55, 88
93 PAC, C.57, 16
94 PAC, C.56, 130
95 PAC, C.51, 96
96 Ibid. 94
97 PAC, C.53, 47
98 Ibid. 147
99 Ibid. 152
100 PAC, C.54, 91
101 PAC, C.55, 51
102 Ibid. 21
103 PAC, C.53, 141
104 PAC, C.59, 70
105 PAC, C.55, 21
106 PAC, C.57, 74
107 Ibid. 75
108 Ibid. 114
109 Ibid. 75
110 PAC, C.55. 21
111 Ibid. 26
112 PAC, C.57, 42
113 PAC, C.47, 173
114 Ibid. 274
115 PAC, C.50, 279
116 PAC, H1, 314/1831
117 PAC, C.52, 238
118 PAC, C.60, 240
119 PAC, C.59, 325
120 PAC, C.60, 102
121 Ibid. 103
122 Ibid. 107
123 Ibid. 96
124 Ibid. 284

CHAPTER 7: Under the British flag

1 Morison *Oxford History* 467

2 Lucas ed. *Durham's Report* vol. 1, 1

3 Ibid., vol. 2, 209
4 H. Phillpotts 'Report on the Canal Navigation of the Canals' *Papers ... (on the duties of the Royal Engineers)* vol. V, 140-93
5 Ibid., 157
6 Legget *Canals of Canada* 156
7 PAC, C.59, 362
8 Ibid. 246
9 PAC, C.61, 248
10 PRO (London) WO 33/11, 51
11 PAC, C.60, 142
12 Ibid. 164
13 PAC, C.61, 56
14 PAC, C.59, 381-4
15 Bonnycastle *The Canadas* vol. 2, 73
16 Private information from a family member
17 Thomas *History* 26
18 PAC, C.59, 11
19 Ibid. 360
20 Ibid. 330
21 PAC, C.60, 330
22 PAC, C.61, 106
23 Thomas *History* 308
24 Ibid. 62
25 Fraser *St Mungo's Centennial* 6
26 Information from the Rev. Mr W.E. Black (original records now in the archives of the United Church of Canada, Montreal). See appendix B.
27 PAC, C.59, 193
28 Ibid. 297
29 Ibid. 309
30 Ibid. 270
31 PAC, C.60, 144
32 Ibid. 146
33 Ibid. 304
34 PAC, C.61, 141
35 Ibid. 182
36 Ibid. 310
37 PAC, C.62, 85
38 Ibid. 93
39 Ibid. 41
40 Ibid. 22
41 Bourne *Britain* 166
42 Ibid. 167
43 PAC, C.61, 161
44 Ibid. 264
45 Ibid. 272
46 PAC, C.62, 97
47 Ibid. 20
48 Ibid. 126
49 Ibid. 143

CHAPTER 8: The Ottawa River canals under Canada

Since this chapter deals with the operation and use of the canals through more than a century, it can only be a succinct summary. Key references only are given. Until 1879, the canals were administered by the Department of Public Works, Canada (the oldest department in the government of Canada) and its predecessors; thereafter, under the Department of Railways and Canals and its successor, the Department of Transport. The annual (and other) reports of these agencies contain a wealth of additional information, for consultation by those with special interest.

1 W. Shanly in the *General Report of the Commissioners of Public Works* for 1867
2 Simpson vol. 2, 16
3 R.R. Brown 'The Last Broad Gauge' *Bulletin No. 18* Canadian Railroad Historical Association, Montreal, October 1954
4 Trollope *North America* vol. 1, 99
5 *The Gazette* (Montreal) 1 September 1860, 2
6 House of Commons *Debates*, First Parliament, First Session, 31 Vic., Queen's Printer, 1967

7 *Hansard*, First Parliament, second session (18 January 1869) 859
8 *Hansard*, First Parliament, Third session, (28 March 1870) 724–40
9 Ibid., 742
10 Ibid., Fourth Session (1872) 687
11 Graham *Water Highway*, 7
12 H.H. Lambart and G.R. Rigby 'Submerged history of the Long Sault' *Canadian Geographical Journal* 67 (November 1963) 147–57
13 Information on the Carillon plant from Hydro-Québec, courtesy Dr Pierre Crepeau

CHAPTER 9: Epilogue

1 For further information from the Historical Society of Argenteuil County (la Société Historique du Comté Argenteuil), write to P.O. Box 5, Lachute, Que., J8H 3X2.

2 R.F. Legget 'The Train That Never Came Back' *Canadian Rail* 294 (July 1976) 207–15
3 See Fraser *St Mungo's Centennial* 6
4 Lambart *St Matthews* 38

APPENDIX A: The Royal Staff Corps in Canada

1 J.T. Hancock 'The First British Combat Engineers' *Royal Engineers Journal* 88 (1974) 203–14
2 Vine *Royal Military Canal*
3 *Nova Scotian Royal Gazette* (Halifax) 3 May 1815
4 J.S. Martell 'Halifax during and after the War of 1812' *Dalhousie Review* 23, 289–304
5 J.J. Greenough 'The Halifax Citadel, 1825–1860: A narrative and structural history' *Canadian Historic Sites, Occasional Papers*

in *Archaeology and History* No. 17 (Ottawa 1977)
6 *Nova Scotian Royal Gazette* 6 September 1815
7 Ibid.
8 Ibid., 7 February 1816
9 Ibid., 8 May 1816
10 *Acadian Recorder* (Halifax) 11 May 1816
11 Information on Mrs Du Vernet from the Venerable A.E.L. Caulfield of Saint John, NB

12 J.C. Kendall 'The construction and maintenance of Coteau du Lac; the first lock canal in North America' *Journal of Transport History* 1 (February 1971) 39-50

13 By J.J. Greenough, to whom the writers are indebted for this reference

14 PRO, WO55, 870, 420

APPENDIX D: The Georgian Bay Ship Canal

1 PAC, C48, 1

2 PRO, WO78, 863, item 5

3 PRO, WO55, 864, item 14

4 PAC, C48, 2

5 Original seen in private collection of Mrs Judith Burns, Ottawa

6 A. Saunders *The Algoma Story* (Toronto 1963) 21-3

7 Originals seen in the Survey, Historical and Research Branch of the Ontario Department of Lands and Forests, Toronto (now Ministry of Natural Resources)

8 PRO, WO1, 553

9 R.W. Scott *Recollections of Bytown* (Ottawa 1911) 10

10 *Report on the Ottawa, French River navigation project to Legislative Assembly of Canada* (January 1858) 53 pp.

11 T.C. Clarke *Report to Legislative Assembly 1860* 58

12 W. Kingsford *The Early Bibliography of the Province of Ontario* (Toronto 1969) 90

13 Royal Archives, Windsor; RA Add. E1 / 4827 and 4839, 1865, by gracious permission of HM the Queen

14 Lt-Col. Millington Synge, RE 'The lakes and canals of Canada' *Journal of the Royal United Service Institute* 10 (1867) 183-208

15 Report of the Canal Commission; vol. VII of Sessional Papers of 4th session of the 1st Parliament of the Dominion of Canada 1870, 190 pp.

16 'Report of the Special Committee of the Senate of Canada upon the feasibility of a waterway ...' *Senate Journal* 33 (1898) Appendix No. 4

17 *The Times* (London) 11 December 1905

18 Report of Royal Commission on Transportation, Supplement to Report of Minister of Public Works, Sessional Paper No. 19A, 6 Edward VII, 1906

19 Georgian Bay Ship Canal, Report with Survey etc., Sessional Paper No. 19A, 8-9 Edward VII, 1909, 601 pp.

20 *Canadian Register* (1908) 42

21 *Canada's Canal Problem and its solution; a reply to the Toronto Board of Trade* (n.d. ? 1911?) 24 pp.

22 D.B. Detwiler *The Inland*

Waterways of Canada: Ocean Navigation via St Lawrence and Welland Route; Georgian Bay Ship Canal Route impracticable (n.d. ? 1912?) 24 pp.

23 International Joint Commission

'Report on the St Lawrence Navigation and Power Investigation' 67th Congress, 2nd Session, Senate Document 114 (1921)

Bibliography

Bigsby, J.J. *The Shoe and Canoe* 2 vols, London 1835

Bonnycastle, Sir R.H. *The Canadas in 1841* 2 vols, London 1842

Bourne K. *Britain and the Balance of Power in North America, 1815–1905* London 1967

Carmichael Smyth, Sir James *Report on the Defence of Canada* (MSS) Halifax 1825

Champlain, S. de (H.P. Biggar, ed.) *Voyages of Sieur de Champlain* Toronto 1925

Dewey, T.E. *Journey to the Far Pacific* New York 1952

Fraser, The Rev. J.M. *St Mungo's Centennial 1836–1936* Chatham, Quebec 1936

Graham, J. *The Water Highway of Argenteuil* Lachute, 1933

Green, J.R. *A Short History of the English People* 2 vols (Everyman ed.) London 1915

Heisler, J.P. *The Canals of Canada* Canadian Historic Sites: Occasional Papers in Archaeology and History, No. 8, Ottawa 1973*

Hitsman, J.M. *The Incredible War of 1812* Toronto 1965

Lafrenière, N. *The Ottawa River Canal System* Studies in Archaeology, Architecture and History, Ottawa 1984*

Lambart, H.H. *St. Matthews on the Ottawa 1832-1982* Grenville, Quebec 1982

Legget, R.F. *Ottawa Waterway* Toronto 1975

– *Canals of Canada* Vancouver 1976

– *Rideau Waterway* 2nd ed., Toronto 1986

Lucas, Sir C.P. *Lord Durham's Report on the affairs of British North America* 3 vols., Oxford 1912

Morison, S.E. *The Oxford History of the American People* New York 1965

* These two official publications contain much information of value, but unfortunately it is stated in each that the Royal Engineers were responsible for building the Ottawa River canals.

Thomas, C. *History of the Counties of Argenteuil, Quebec, and Prescott, Ontario* Montreal 1896

Trollope A. *North America* 2 vols, London 1862

Vine, P.A.L. *The Royal Military Canal* Newton Abbot, Devon 1972

Wellington, Duke of *The Despatches of ... during his various campaigns ... 1799 to 1818, compiled by Lt.Col. Gurwood*, twelve vols, London 1837

Woods, S.E. Jr *The Molson Saga* Toronto 1983

The brevity and character of this listing is indicative of the neglect of the Ottawa River canals in Canadian historical writing.

Acknowledgments

My interest in the Ottawa River Canals was aroused in the mid 1950s when I was working on *Rideau Waterway*. I then realized that the alternative water route between Montreal and Kingston would not be complete without some way round the Long Sault of the Ottawa River at Hawkesbury.

Exploring the small canals that then provided this by-pass, so fortunately before they were flooded in the early 1960s by the construction of the Carillon dam and power house, led me to visit the Museum at Carillon and this in turn drew me into membership of the Historical Society of Argenteuil County (la Société Historique du Comté Argenteuil). Members of the Society have helped and encouraged me in my study of part of their area, notably Dr G.H. Rigby (now resident in the United Kingdom) and Mrs Ethel McGibbon; but to all the members of this valiant Society I record my thanks.

This was the beginning of an ever-widening circle of friends, new and old, who have assisted me in a variety of ways since I started to piece together, in my spare time since 1975, the record of this fragment of Canadian history and of the history of engineering in this country. It is impracticable to mention all those to whom I am indebted, but for all this kindly assistance I am most grateful.

Some names, however, must be mentioned, notably those of two friends 'across the river' from Carillon. Mr Frank Nobbs of Hudson Heights has acted as my 'remembrancer,' never allowing me to forget that this book had to be finished despite all the odds against it. Dr W.F. Walford of Hudson (mentioned anonymously in the text) has helped similarly by his long-standing interest and encouragement but especially by his masterly and comprehensive critique of a first draft of the text circulated in 1980.

Copies of this first draft were then sent to twenty friends; all sent generous comments, some favouring me with helpful criticisms, notably Dr C.P. Stacey, who also did me the honour of sending me his own early notes for a paper on the canals which he had hoped to write, Dr Edwin Welch of Yellowknife, and Bill Byers of L'Orignal, and even two friends in the United Kingdom.

Charles Hadfield, justly renowned as the author of many books on canals climaxed by *World Canals* (1986) in which the Ottawa River canals appear, has helped with his critical comments and in many other ways. My special debt to Major John T. Hancock, RE, is well shown by our joint authorship of appendix A. Mr Stuart Harris introduced me, many years ago, to the Royal Military Canal; my nephew and niece (Clive and Freda Free) took us on a memorable tour of this direct predecessor of the Ottawa River canals.

Not only did the late Mrs Grace Du Vernet of Ottawa favour me with most useful comments on the draft but, together with her son John and daughter Diane, shared with me the private information they have about their widespread family. The late Miss Paige Pinneo, an artist whose last home was on the banks of the Carillon Canal, not only obliged me with comments and encouragement but also presented me with one of her paintings.

Friends in the Historical Society of Ottawa have been similarly supportive, the late Miss E. Taylor with valued comments based on her lifetime of memories, and Mrs Judith Burns offering me the privilege of examining her treasure trove of papers relative to the life and work of her ancestor, McLeod Stewart, who figures so prominently in appendix D.

Dr Larkin Kerwin, president of the National Research Council of Canada, and Dr B. Gingras, a vice-president, have been interested and practical supporters also, the project representing as it does my last contribution to the council in the field of building research, the preparation of the volume representing much study of the origins of building in Canada.

The list of references and captions to illustrations will show clearly how indebted I am to the splendid service given to Canadians by their Public Archives. Since all my use of this great facility for the purposes of this book was before 1986, the old name of Public Archives of Canada has been retained throughout for convenience, even though National Archives of Canada is now the official name, by legislation enacted in the year noted. I have been similarly helped by the staff of the National Library of Canada and of the National Gallery.

My friend and former colleague J. Douglas Scott has kindly transformed my rough sketch maps into the finished form in which they appear herein. Once again, Mrs Isabelle Noffke and Mrs Marie Jacques have, between them, typed the successive drafts of the text, with lively interest and skill.

It has been a pleasure and privilege to work with the University of Toronto Press as the publisher of this book. The press has kindly taken a long-standing interest in the project; Ian Montagnes, when general editor of the press, favoured me with valuable comments on the 1980 draft. All the delay in completing the volume has been due to me, unavoidably so, but once the text was finished and accepted, production has been expeditiously prosecuted under the expert and supportive direction of Gerald Hallowell (editor, history) and his associates. To all friends at the press I record my gratitude for their assistance and support, as also to their anonymous reviewer for reading the text so carefully and favouring me with some useful historical suggestions.

My dear wife shared in exploration of the canals and, until her death late in 1984, in all the work now represented by his book. It would have been a better book had she lived to help me with its final stages, but it is at least another small part of my tribute to her memory.

20 April 1988   Robert Legget

Index of names

Names listed in appendix B, and those given in the acknowledgments, are not included in this index.

Index of subjects